*Helping to Promote Social J*
promote social justice. It c
teaching and supervision,
and more. The focus on skill building make this text stand out among
peers. The exercises provided throughout the book engage the reader in
critical reflection and active learning. It is evident that the authors are deeply
committed to the practice of social justice and their reflections on their own
social identities, processes, and professional development are refreshing and
inspirational.

**Britney G Brinkman**, Ph.D., Associate Professor of
Psychology, Point Park University

The quest for social justice is a constant challenge in our society, and efforts
to both inform and guide us as practitioners and academics are always in
desperate need. *Helping to Promote Social Justice*, edited by Debra A. Harkins,
Kathryn J. Kozak, Lauren I. Grenier, and Lynne-Marie Shea, is a welcome
contribution to this field of study because of how it successfully bridges
the gaps between knowledge, theory, and practice. This bridge is critical
to helping us transform our society into a socially just one for significant
excluded portions of our country. Readers will be rewarded by reading this
book because of the tools it brings for seeking social justice!

**Melvin Delgado**, Ph.D., Professor of Social Work,
Boston University School of Social Work

While our desires to be of use to others may be simply and clearly felt,
the pathways to ethically embody these desires become clear only upon
sustained critical reflection. *Helping to Promote Social Justice* bears the task of
necessarily complicating the desire to help others, while offering ways to
navigate with accountability helping professionals' engagement with social
justice issues. Readers are guided to explore the effects of their positionality
on the work they do, carefully taking account of privilege and power. This
well-researched and clearly written volume is the fruit of the authors' decades
of experience in service-learning mentorship and is a needed complement
to service-learning curriculum.

**Mary Watkins**, Ph.D., Author of *Mutual Accompaniment
and the Creation of the Commons* and co-author
of *Towards Psychologies of Liberation*

# Helping to Promote Social Justice

*Helping to Promote Social Justice* is a richly informed and practical guide for advanced students and young professionals to become helpers capable of promoting social justice with whomever they collaborate with, mentor, serve and consult. Filled with insight and supplemental exercises, the book will direct readers to think critically and reflect on the broader social and political systems that create our current social injustices.

Beginning with a strong theoretical focus on power, social identity and intersectionality, the authors engage with readers' assumptions on helping, their value systems and their understandings of power and privilege when helping communities in need. The rest of the book focuses on the application of these critical concepts, guiding future helpers to consider how to intervene, assess need, lead, build a team, address conflict and work to promote change from a position of social justice.

Written by academic faculty with expertise in teaching, coaching and consulting, *Helping to Promote Social Justice* should be considered essential reading for students in social work, psychology and counselling.

**Debra A. Harkins** is a professor of education and psychology at Suffolk University. Her current research interests include using action-based research and process consultation models with multicultural, underserved and diverse communities.

**Kathryn J. Kozak** recently received her doctorate in applied developmental psychology at Suffolk University. Her research focuses on ways in which people come to and engage in social justice work.

**Lauren I. Grenier** is a doctoral candidate in clinical psychology at Suffolk University, where she works in the Community-Action Based Research lab under the mentorship of Dr. Debra A. Harkins. Lauren's research focuses on social justice and critical experiential pedagogy, particularly in the context of higher education through service-learning.

**Lynne-Marie Shea** is a fourth-year clinical doctoral student in psychology at Suffolk University. Under the mentorship of Dr. Debra Harkins, Lynne's clinical work revolves around community-based and systems-focused interventions for in-risk adolescents, and her research focuses on critical consciousness building, civic engagement, and holistic health and wellness.

# Helping to Promote Social Justice

Edited by Debra A. Harkins
Kathryn J. Kozak, Lauren I.
Grenier and Lynne-Marie Shea

Routledge
Taylor & Francis Group

NEW YORK AND LONDON

First published 2022
by Routledge
605 Third Avenue, New York, NY 10158

and by Routledge
2 Park Square, Milton Park, Abingdon, Oxon, OX14 4RN

*Routledge is an imprint of the Taylor & Francis Group, an informa business*

*Library of Congress Cataloging-in-Publication Data*
A catalog record for this book has been requested

ISBN: 978-0-367-51881-3 (hbk)
ISBN: 978-0-367-51880-6 (pbk)
ISBN: 978-1-003-05558-7 (ebk)

DOI: 10.4324/9781003055587

Typeset in Bembo
by Apex CoVantage, LLC

# Contents

# Foreword

This book comes at a time when we must transition from a Me Culture to a We Culture. These two cultures are driven by very different narratives. In a Me Culture, the dominant philosophy is "I have the right to feel valued so that I may be happy." In contrast, a We Culture is driven by a communitarian spirit: "We all have the right, and responsibility, to feel valued and add value, so that may all experience wellness and fairness" (Prilleltensky & Prilleltensky, 2021).

As amply documented by Robert Putnam (2020), the United States has been on a "Me" trajectory for the last 50 years or so. Michael Sandel (2020) and Amitai Etzioni (2018) also offer compelling evidence for the dominance of the Me Culture.

As can be seen in my definition of the Me Culture, social justice is conspicuous for its absence. As Putnam, Sandel, Etzioni and I have argued, the focus of the last half century has been on the power of the almighty self, an independent agent capable of overcoming adversity in the pursuit of the American dream. As these authors and others have argued, the American dream is a myth used to preserve structures of inequality, oppression and injustice. The myth consists of indoctrinating people in the belief that social structures are just and fair, and that the only barrier between you and happiness is your lack of motivation or skills. Paul Tough (2019) provides compelling evidence that higher education continues to propagate this mythology, while ignoring issues of fairness in access, retention and graduation. Anand Giridharadas (2018) dissects how the "Me" ideology dominates the business and consulting sectors. In earlier publications, I have exposed psychology's complicity in the veneration of individualism and the neglect of justice (Prilleltensky, 1994, 1997, 2012).

The consequences of blind adherence to the individualistic paradigm are dire for individuals and society at large. Inequality is exacerbated, injustice is preserved, and suffering is perpetuated, especially for those without power and privilege. The way to dismantle the Me Culture and build a We Culture is through an appreciation for the role of justice, or fairness, at all levels, from the personal to the planetary. This is why this book by Debra A. Harkins and colleagues is so important. Every chapter of the book supports the foundation of a We Culture. In line with my definition, the book offers a vision for a We Community, an outcome and a set of processes.

The book seeks to advance a vision in which all members of society are valued and have an opportunity to add value. These are the symbiotic requirements of mattering, feeling valued and adding value (Prilleltensky & Prilleltensky, 2021). The outcome the authors of this book seek is mattering for all. They envision a community in which we all have the right and responsibility to feel valued and add value. Unlike earlier incantations of unrestrained freedom, in which rights overshadow responsibilities, the contributors make it very clear that rights must be balanced with responsibility to act in solidarity. The authors and editors call on us to reflect on unearned privilege and its consequences (DiAngelo, 2018; Heumann, 2020; Kendi, 2019; Oluo, 2019; Wilkerson, 2020).

In line with the call to advance wellness with fairness, the contributors are sensitive to the processes and procedures required to maintain the well-being of our partners during the work of transformation. I commend the authors for balancing the need to confront privilege and injustice with the need to act as inclusive hosts. In many ways, the authors are engaged in what Mary Watkins (2019) calls mutual accompaniment, which is an ethical partnership, among equals, to foster caring and compassion while pursuing liberation and transformation.

In addition to clear outcomes and processes, the authors pay particular attention to the set of values required for emancipatory work. They balance carefully the need to promote personal values such as freedom and self-determination with collective values such as equality, justice and fairness. They do so by attending to bridging values such as empathy and solidarity.

While the treatment of vision and values is absolutely necessary, the authors are not naïve. They pay careful attention to the role of power in justice. The book elucidates various forms of power and how it gets enacted in relationships, organizations, communities and societies. Ideals must be supported by pragmatic approaches to become a reality. Whether it is the classroom, a community-based organization or a social movement, power is a ubiquitous dynamic that can be harnessed for oppression or liberation. Power is multifaceted and appears in subtle and blatant ways. This is why the book calls for processes of conscientization to acquaint ourselves with its many incarnations.

This book will become an essential part of our collective work to dismantle the Me Culture and create a We Culture in which wellness is enhanced by our efforts to foster fairness. The authors offer multiple avenues to contribute to the cause of justice. Readers will be able to find at least one way in which they can contribute. You may be a community organizer, a professor, a clinician or a policy maker. Regardless of your particular interests and inclinations, you will be able to expand your repertoire of skills by going through each chapter of this inspiring and engaging book. Like inclusive hosts, the authors draw you into a meaningful conversation about one of the important topics of the day. You will gain awareness, skills and knowledge from this volume. You can do this alone or with a group. In whichever form you choose to absorb it, its lessons will endure. Read the book and spread the message far and wide.

Isaac Prilleltensky,
Miami, Florida, January 2021

## References

DiAngelo, R. (2018). *White fragility: Why it's so hard for white people to talk about racism.* Beacon Press.

Etzioni, A. (2018). *Happiness is the wrong metric: A liberal communitarian response to populism.* Springer.

Giridharadas, A. (2018). *Winners take all: The elite charade of changing the world.* Knopf.

Heumann, J. (2020). *Being Heumann: An unrepentant memoir of a disability rights activist.* Beacon Press.

Kendi, I. X. (2019). *How to be an antiracist.* One World.

Oluo, I. (2019). *So, you want to talk about race.* Seal Press.

Prilleltensky, I. (1994). *The morals and politics of psychology: Psychological discourse and the status quo.* State University of New York Press.

Prilleltensky, I. (1997). Values, assumptions, and practices: Assessing the moral implications of psychological discourse and action. *American Psychologist, 52*(5), 517–535.

Prilleltensky, I. (2012). Wellness as fairness. *American Journal of Community Psychology, 49,* 1–21. https://doi.org/10.1007/s10464-011-9448-8

Prilleltensky, I., & Prilleltensky, O. (2021). *How people matter: Why it affects health, happiness, love, work, and society.* Cambridge University Press.

Putnam, R. (2020). *The upswing: How America came together a century ago and how we can do it again.* Simon & Schuster.

Sandel, M. (2020). *The tyranny of merit: What become of the common good?* Farrar, Straus and Giroux.

Tough, P. (2019). *The years that matter most: How college makes or breaks us.* Houghton Mifflin Harcourt.

Watkins, M. (2019). *Mutual accompaniment and the creation of the commons.* Yale University Press.

Wilkerson, I. (2020). *Caste: The origins of our discontents.* Random House.

# Contributor Bios

**Christina Athineos**

Christina Athineos is a therapist in New York, where she serves on a diversity, equity and inclusion council. As part of this team, Christina is involved in clinical work and research aimed at disseminating effective treatments in underserved community settings.

**Julia Catlin**

Julia Catlin is a licensed mental health counselor who works with underserved families who have experienced trauma. She works primarily with infants, children, adolescents and their parents to enhance attachment and well-being.

**Lauren I. Grenier**

Lauren I. Grenier is a doctoral candidate in clinical psychology at Suffolk University, where she works in the Community-Action Based Research lab under the mentorship of Dr. Debra A. Harkins. Lauren's research focuses on social justice and critical experiential pedagogy, particularly in the context of higher education through service-learning.

**Debra A. Harkins**

Debra A. Harkins is a full professor at Suffolk University in Boston, Massachusetts, where she holds joint appointments in education and psychology. Her research, writing, teaching and community service work focuses on issues of social class, poverty and homelessness with respect to youth, schools and community. This book represents the third in a series (*Beyond the Campus: Building a sustainable university-community partnership* (2013) and *Alongside Community: Learning in service (2017)* focused on community-based helping.

**Kathryn J. Kozak**

Kathryn J. Kozak is an applied developmental psychology doctoral candidate. Her research focuses on ways in which people come to and engage in social justice work.

## Sophia Anyela Joan Kozlowsky

Sophia Anyela Joan Kozlowsky is currently an undergraduate student at Suffolk University completing a double major in psychology and sociology with a concentration in crime and justice. She has a strong commitment towards social justice/community service and intends to continue her graduate studies in the future.

## Yanxi Liu

Yanxi Liu is currently a candidate in a master's of public health program at Tufts University. She supports community/environmental justice values and is an independent musician.

## Mary Beth Medvide

Mary Beth Medvide is an assistant professor of psychology at Suffolk University, where she teaches in the mental health counseling master's program. Her research interests include work-based learning and school-to-work transitions among marginalized youth.

## Lauren Mizock

Lauren Mizock is a core faculty member in the clinical psychology PhD program at Fielding Graduate University and in private practice in San Francisco, California. Clinical, teaching and research interests include culturally relevant pedagogy, culturally competent research methodology, serious mental illness, women's mental health, and transgender and gender-diverse populations.

## Sukanya Ray

Sukanya Ray is an associate professor in psychology at Suffolk University in Boston, Massachusetts. Her research interests include minority mental health risk, empowerment, health disparities, healthcare and well-being issues. She has been a community consultant, researcher and educator in multicultural issues and minority/immigrant health issues in the USA and abroad. She has supervised master's and doctoral dissertation projects. She has presented her work at national/international conferences and published her research in peer-reviewed journals and chapters in books. She has served as board member in many community service organizations.

## Hannah E. Robins

Hannah E. Robins is a graduate student working towards her PhD in clinical psychology at Suffolk University. Her research work focuses on health literacy, biopsychosocial perspectives and healthcare disparities.

## Elizabeth Robinson

Elizabeth Robinson has a master's degree in applied linguistics and a doctorate degree in education in language, literacy and culture. She has taught, learned and researched in public schools, overseas and in universities with her focus in all her work on using education as a tool for justice.

## Lynne-Marie Shea

Lynne-Marie Shea is a fourth-year clinical doctoral student in psychology at Suffolk University. Under the mentorship of Dr. Debra Harkins, Lynne's clinical work revolves around community-based and systems-focused interventions for in-risk adolescents, and her research focuses on critical consciousness building, civic engagement, and holistic health and wellness.

## Carmen N. Veloria

Carmen N. Veloria is an associate professor at Suffolk University in Boston, Massachusetts, where she holds joint appointments in education and sociology. She is the Chair of the Education Department, where she oversees both undergraduate and graduate programs in education. Her research, writing, teaching and community service work focuses on issues of race, ethnicity and language usage with respect to youth, schools and community. She speaks on these issues both nationally and internationally.

# Introduction

While there are many helpers in our society, most focus on trying to help individual people function within our current social and political system. Few of us have the training, education, or experience to address helping from a more socially just position. *Helping to Promote Social Justice* provides the knowledge and skills needed to prepare the advanced student and young professional to engage in helping that promotes social justice.

Our purpose is to provide you with a guide to become helpers who promote social justice with those you collaborate with, mentor, coach, supervise, and consult. This book is filled with ways for you and helpers to critically reflect on the broader social and political systems that create our current social injustices. We will guide you to examine your own assumptions about helping, the roots of your values, and your understanding of power and privilege when helping communities in need. You will be provided with the tools necessary to engage in helping that promotes social justice. This book offers a step-by-step guide to help you and the helpers you work with to consider how to intervene, assess need, lead, build a team, address conflict, and work to promote change from a position of social justice that restores community.

As helpers themselves, the authors of this book have had many experiences with the life-giving nature of the call to help. Given that this call to help, in and of itself, suggests a position of privilege, we have made many of the mistakes that, unfortunately, are often at the heart of our Western understanding of what it means to help. Having been socialized in a culture that promotes individualism, capitalism, white supremacy, and meritocracy, we have, at times, understood ourselves as "saviors" seeking to "improve" those we were taught to see as less capable than ourselves. We have sought to bandage wounds without stopping to consider the systems that created the hurt we want to mend. We have rushed to the aid of the vulnerable without reflecting on the ways in which our aid helps to maintain the systems that cause harm and to keep them largely unseen.

This book is the culmination of our desire to share the lessons we have learned and insights we have gained throughout our journeys as helpers. Each chapter is a reflection on ways in which we have worked to decolonize our thinking, our actions, and, most importantly, our helping. The various authors in this work represent different areas of the helping profession, and as such, the perspectives provided are often specific to the "helping lane" to which the author has chosen to commit their individual efforts. We understand our society as being interconnected and invite you, our reader, to apply the questions and reflections posed by each author to your own lane of helping. We hope that these narratives will support your personal reflection and insight building as we work together to dismantle the societal systems that allow profit for some at the expense of others. We look forward to having you join us, in your own helping lane, as we work to replace these systems with the kind of infrastructure needed for each of us to navigate society in ways that are meaningful and truly life-giving.

We structured this book as a field book, with reflective activities, exercises, space for journaling, and narratives from other helpers to assist you in thinking about how to engage others as socially just helpers. The information and exercises herein will allow you to guide others who wish to understand the dynamics of power differentials; addressing the challenges of working with the disempowered; building strong collaborations; and initiating social changes in yourself and in the communities that helpers serve. Finally, this field book provides effective strategies to continue on a lifelong journey of engaging in social justice.

*Helping to Promote Social Justice* exposes students and professionals to a wide range of topics including inclusivity, team building, leading with heart and mind, mentoring, teaching, research training, and supervising from a critical stance, advocating, grant writing, and sharing to expand social justice practices and initiatives. With the goal of increasing your knowledge and skill set to promote a more empowering helping, we hope you engage in the following:

- Explore values and skills that go beyond individual helping while you critically reflect on the role of your social identity, power dynamics that exist when helping others, and ways you can intervene that empower and encourage inclusivity
- Employ practical strategies to build your own socially just team building, leadership, mentoring, teaching, supervising, and training skills to help those on the margins of society
- Expand your social justice initiatives through research, advocacy, writing, and disseminating your work to spark further positive social change for communities in need

Our big goal for you is to bring together knowledge across academia, advocacy, and activism to explore how you might help others to make a positive social change in the world. We do this by examining some of the critical issues involved in social justice work (Part 1); exploring ways you can build your social justice skill set and help others do the same (Part 2); and sharing ways you can expand the impact of your and others' social justice actions (Part 3).

We begin Part 1 of this field book by discussing how to promote liberation when helping others. Chapter 1 explores the challenges of helping by examining the different types of helping, the underlying assumptions that exist within various forms of helping, and how to help others engage in more socially just helping. In Chapter 2, we ask you to deeply reflect on your own social identity and intersectionality through reflections and provide several activities you can do with others who could benefit from similar self-reflection. Chapter 3 examines how to educate helpers on the sources of their values; how to examine their values and privileges; and how those values may impact their work with a community partner. In Chapter 4, we explore how power impacts our work as helpers and our ability to engage in social justice work. Chapter 5 ends this section by describing best-practice community interventions that prioritize the values and expertise of the members of a community.

Part 2 of this book addresses how to build social justice skills in yourself and in others to empower underserved communities. We open this section by exploring the core elements of building a team discovered through our own dialoguing about what it means to be a team. In Chapter 7, we provide an example of leading through heart, hope, and hustle amidst conflict between institutional priorities and community needs. Chapter 8 describes a unique multi-tiered service-learning mentoring program created to promote social justice. In Chapter 9, we unpack approaches to teaching for critical research with a social justice lens. Chapter 10 ends this section by providing suggestions for training and supervising social justice–oriented clinicians.

Part 3 of this book addresses how to expand social justice by supporting others seeking to engage in social justice helping. We open this section by exploring the challenges and opportunities inherent to researching from a social justice position. In Chapter 12, we examine the ways helpers can advocate for public policy change through writing, petitioning, working with political leaders, and using social media. Chapter 13 provides a model for community-focused grant writing by exploring the role of funders and funding sources in influencing helping work and the mission of the helping agency. In Chapter 14, we provide considerations and strategies for sharing and disseminating your social justice work. Our final chapter revisits the complexity of helping, providing the helper with a toolkit for being a lifelong civically engaged citizen.

You may read through this book all at once, or you may bookmark certain chapters to reference in your work. You may give this book to your colleagues, students, or new hires to help them understand your approaches to socially just helping. No matter how you make use of *Helping to Promote Social Justice*, we hope you find the inspiration and resources to help you and your community pursue long-term, positive, social change.

# Part 1

# Helping Promote Liberation

# 1  Going Beyond Individual Helping

*Debra A. Harkins*

As recent civil unrest shakes the very foundation of United States society, basic assumptions of who we are, how we got here and how we should function are being questioned and challenged. Americans are **enculturated** to believe that America was founded based on the principles of "freedom and liberty for all"; yet, we often conveniently forget that we founded this country through the genocide of 4.7 million Indigenous peoples, that we enslaved African Americans for over 245 years, and that as recently as the 20th century, we interned Japanese Americans (1942–1946). Today, many Americans believe that we addressed most of our social injustices during the Civil Rights era, and while significant progress was made during the 1960s, those outside of middle-class America would beg to differ. Recent civil unrest related to the Black Lives Matter movement and the recent immigration concentration camps that have sprung up along our Southern border and have continued up until this writing remind us yet again that American citizens have a lot of unfinished business regarding social justice.

Why do we in the US struggle so hard to acknowledge the social injustice in our society? What makes it so difficult for us to see the injustices happening around us? Why can some of us see it and others cannot? What is needed for those who are mentally blind to the injustices happening around them to be able to see? This chapter explores many of these questions.

We hypothesize that the challenge many Americans have with seeing and believing that social injustice is occurring all around us relates to our strong individual-focused cultural mindset (Hofstede, 1985). This idea of US individualism impacting our ahistorical cultural norms was first proposed more than 35 years ago. After studying the effects of cultural values on human behavior in more than 90 countries, Dutch organizational anthropologist Geert Hofstede found that cultures varied significantly on whether they focused most heavily on the individual or the group. He found that some cultures focused heavily on the individual with loose ties to all except his or her immediate family. In these individually focused countries, the emphasis was on the "I" over the "we" (i.e., valuing individual needs over the group needs). Other cultures focused heavily on the group with strong ties to extended family and other in-groups, focusing more on the "we" over the

DOI: 10.4324/9781003055587-1

"I" (i.e., valuing group and community needs over individual needs). Hofstede found that all cultures can be found somewhere along this individualist-versus-collectivist continuum. While not surprising to many of us, Hofstede confirmed that the US has the most individualistically focused values of all the cultures that he studied. While globalization is changing this cultural landscape, more recent research continues to support his findings (Hofstede, 2001, 2011).

As Hofstede found, and most of us in the US can attest, a high value is placed on pursuing our own individual needs. This individual focus can be seen in how we as helpers help and is revealed in the primacy of individual-focused helping promoted by the American Counseling Association (2011), the American Psychological Association (2012), the field of social work (Cree, Jain, & Hillen, 2019), the National Institute on Drug Abuse (2018) and the World Health Report (2003). By *individually focused helping*, we mean helping practices that seek to help an individual develop, achieve or regain "normal" functioning. We know that psychiatry, psychology, social work, counseling and other helping professions provide important and meaningful help to millions of individuals suffering from mental disorders related to anxiety, mood, personality, eating, adjustment, dementia and psychosis, to name just a few. Millions of these individuals who seek professional help can attest to how it has helped them in relieving some or all of their suffering. Clinical, counseling and social work and other helping professions help.

Unfortunately, as the US Surgeon General's Report on Mental Health, Culture, Race and Ethnicity (2001) revealed, mental health professionals are not helping those outside of the **hegemony**. More recent research (Algería et al., 2008; Blair et al., 2013; Burkard & Knox, 2004; Shin, Smith, Welch, & Ezeofor, 2016) continues to find this differential impact of helpers not successfully helping those outside of middle-class white America.

> Hegemony: the social, cultural, ideological or economic influence exerted by a dominant group. In our case, the assumption of white, middle-class men as the normative experience reflects the perspective of those in power, not the makeup of the population.

In this chapter, we explore how helping is intimately tied to the US ideological systems of individualism and capitalism that promote our assumptions about development, intelligence, science, family, morality and economics. As we become more aware of our biased and faulty thinking, we can become overwhelmed and disheartened when we realize that our ways of helping might be contributing to social injustice. However, deconstructing our biases is the first step in critical thinking that allows us to reimagine how we can engage in more empowering forms of helping. We end this chapter on a positive note with ways that we can liberate ourselves from these ideological traps that prevent us from engaging in more socially just forms of helping that can benefit all segments of society.

## Capitalism and Helping

Most forms of helping in the US were formed under the economic umbrella of **capitalism**, the notion of private property, the Protestant focus on work and individualism, and the promise of science. While each of these movements led to the rapid rise of the US as a superpower with incredible innovations, scientific discoveries and life-saving medical treatments, we often ignore the darker side of our political, economic and moral framework. We explore how this darker side of our capitalist and ideological system impacts social justice later in this chapter.

Helping within the US often mirrors the economic, scientific and moral frameworks highly valued in the Western world (Parker, 2007). For example, most of us begin helping with the unexamined assumption that helping should mean helping someone with the emphasis on person (i.e., individual therapy, counseling and pastoring) and that helping the individual will reduce or relieve symptoms. This is true for many individuals, but we must examine if it is true for all. Who is helped and not helped by this unexamined Western notion of personal helping? What is unexamined for many helpers is how mental health may be a symptom of a social ill. This may be particularly true for those in oppressed communities (i.e., women, people of color (POC), LGBTQ+, low-income, disabled, non-Christian etc.) within our Western system. Helpers in this system often come to the field without the kind of education, training or resources needed to examine the ways in which social ills can create or maintain oppressive systems and without being provided with the time and tools necessary to consider how to address those social ills.

Given this socio-historical situation, it is not surprising to learn that the field of psychology and the helping disciplines in general are some of the most popular majors in every college and university in the US. This likely has a lot to do with the fact that for many, learning about helping from a Western lens feels "intuitively" right. That is, the notion that the individual is in control of their own thoughts and feelings and the sense of power and control this assumption provides to us as the helper feel just right to those learning how to help. This assumption about an individual's behavior gives us a tool that many already accept as truth to create behavioral changes in others. Unfortunately, many of us do not explore how this intuitive feeling may be a signal that something is amiss, that we are being co-opted into the Western framework of how one "should" help others. Ironically, these popular majors unintentionally train students to be the managers of the hegemony of our social system.

Unfortunately, individual helping is not enough for everyone. While traditional forms of helping work for some individuals, this framework does not consider whether it is helpful to those suffering from collective and historical oppression. Many physical and mental health issues that result from collective and historical oppression are bigger than any individual help can provide. Symptoms at an individual level may mask social ills that cannot be solved privately. For example, examination of the US COVID-19 death rates by race (see Figure 1.1) reveals stark differences related to racial injustice, the very argument being expressed through the Black Lives Matter movement. Without addressing racial injustice impacting this differential death rate, there is little we as individuals can do to help those experiencing "mental health" issues.

The symptoms that are addressed in traditional forms of helping may, inadvertently, keep people from attending to the impact that larger issues may be having on their physical and mental health. Sadly, little attention is paid to the reality that a capitalist ideology often creates physical and mental strain on those at the bottom of the social and economic ladder. Sonya Renee Taylor (2018) describes our societal structure as a kind of ladder— one that each of us climbs in an attempt to get to the rung that affords us happiness and wellbeing and validates our worth. This ladder, though, only exists because we climb it. Taylor explains that we all work to maintain the societal systems that relegate all those who fall outside of the (white, middle-class) default body identity to lower rungs. We do so through our ongoing work to climb to a higher rung on the ladder—one that our systems tell us we are inherently unworthy of reaching (Taylor, 2018).

But just because someone is oppressed does not necessarily mean that they understand how they are oppressed within the current social and economic system. In fact, the strength of the hegemony is that our system is hidden, in plain sight, from us.

Some people believe that the field of social work solves this problem. Despite standing out as a field that incorporates social issues in individual work, social workers do not typically engage in helping that creates transformational social change. While social work goes beyond other helping professions by working in clients' communities, focusing on the impact of race and diversity on mental health, and seeking social services to alleviate suffering, social workers, like other helping professionals, still focus on helping the individual.

---

As a social worker, we often work with clients to help with day-to-day activities. We work with a client to enhance their coping skills to address social injustices hoping that such changes improve their lives. As a field, we are dependent upon the ideologies of political institutions—liberal, moderate or conservative—that directly influence the scope of our role as a social worker. For example, I have found that a conservative ideology is less open to social change hence under such leadership, I realize my best bet is to simply help the client to cope.

—Mary William, MSW

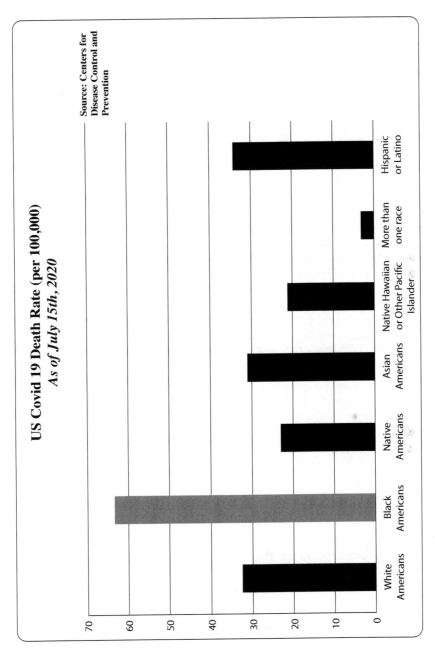

*Figure 1.1* US COVID-19 death rate (per 100,000)

When one learns to examine these unexamined approaches to helping to which we are all inoculated, we can begin to question these taken-for-granted assumptions. Once we do this work, we prepare ourselves to consider and then address the systemic factors that impact those help seekers oppressed by our society.

**Take a moment to examine how you have thought about helping in the past and what challenges to helping might exist within a broader social, economic and political perspective.**

_____

_____

_____

**How can you help others to examine some of these unexamined assumptions around helping?** How can we engage in helping that is more socially just? How can you help others approach helping from a place of trying to create freedom for those oppressed?

_____

_____

_____

**What have these questions raised for you? Have they made you feel uncomfortable or overwhelmed? In what ways might they make others uncomfortable or overwhelmed?**

_____

_____

_____

This book seeks to help you and those you mentor, coach, teach, consult and/or supervise. Leaning into the discomfort that results from examining helping from a more socio-political perspective will allow you to create more socially just helping practices.

The helping disciplines, especially psychology and psychiatry, historically focus heavily on identifying abnormalities of individual behavior that, unsurprisingly, align with traditional views of who society deems "mad" or "bad." Further, the field assumes that the "normal" individual is rational and able to make informed decisions with little influence from others. What is often ignored in this assumption is the years of enculturation into these models of helping that support our individualistic assumptions (Parker, 2007) about the world and how individuals should function. Problems arise when helpers assume they are neutral and objective and that those they work with are also neutral and objective. When the helper is faced with someone who stands up for moral positions, it can become a threat to the unexamined assumption that "healthy equals rational."

The only way out of this quagmire of faulty assumptions and avoidance of perpetual social injustice is to deeply reflect on how helping can be and often is co-opted by our current social and economic system; how helping can unintentionally create more alienation and despair in all of us who have been enculturated into believing that we are supposed to be able to do it all ourselves; and how our helping may be used to promote further oppression.

## Beyond Development

Many Western-focused helpers have been oriented towards individual development that aligns with the social and economic system. From this framework, development is viewed as a universal, stepwise or stage-focused process, and the vast majority of developmental theories contain these unexamined cultural assumptions about development (Kaplan, 1983). For example, the discourse of development often colludes with the language of "progress," "teleo" and "economic development." That is, development implies that those at the "higher" developmental stage are "better" than those at the "lower" stages of development and that the goal of individuals, communities and countries should be to strive towards higher developmental stages, in order to be "fully developed." This developmental rhetoric is particularly striking when used to discuss seemingly "neutral" topics such as:

- **Economic development**, which speaks of "developed," "underdeveloped" and third-world countries where "first world" implies better than second or third world
- **Social class**, which classifies society into upper, middle and lower class (note the language of upper and lower here)
- **Cognition** that views "rational" thinkers as more developed than emotionally focused people
- **Education** that speaks of "lower" or "elementary" versus "secondary" or "higher" education, with assessments such as SATs and GREs to determine success
- **Work environments** that use the language of "upper" versus "lower" management, with phrases like "rising through the ranks" and "climbing the corporate ladder" to describe moving from entry-level to executive positions, and bosses or managers considered more important or capable than entry-level or frontline employees

Although some developmental theories such as Bronfenbrenner's ecological theory (1974, 1977, 1995; Bronfenbrenner & Ceci, 1994; Bronfenbrenner & Evans, 2000) have expanded psychology's views to include social context, few psychology programs describe this theory in survey psychology courses. In addition, the very use of the term "development" reveals the strong hold that hierarchies of privilege have in fields of helping and why there continues to be so much civil and social unrest. Let's look more closely at some other preconceptions or beliefs we take for granted within the helping fields.

## Assumptions About Intelligence

Development is a preconception, an assumption held that culture, gender, race, social class and other social identities can be hierarchically organized from lower to higher in many dimensions of humanity—especially intellect. In practice, this assumption dictates that upper-class white males are at or near the top of the developmental ladder. Many psychological and psychiatric tests were historically adjusted when assessments failed to meet the preconception of white male superiority. For example, when the original IQ tests found that women scored higher than males, the tests were "adjusted" so males scored higher than females (Joseph, 2004). Similarly, when Black people scored higher on IQ tests than poor white people in South Africa, the tests were "adjusted" so that Black test takers scored lower than poor white test takers (Hook & Eagle, 2002). Based on these "adjustments," the South African apartheid prime minister, who happened to be a psychologist, argued that there were developmental differences based on race and hence justified the "need to differentiate" resources to each racial group (Parker, 2007).

A similar argument was made in the US with the book *The Bell Curve: Intelligence and Class Structure in American Life*, written by Harvard psychologist Richard Herrnstein and sociologist and political libertarian writer Charles Murray. Herrnstein and Murray used extensive and spurious statistics based on the statistical phenomenon of the bell curve to justify social inequalities based on race, gender and class. At the end of their 872-page tome, Herrnstein and Murray eventually got to one of their central and most politically divisive arguments:

> The technically precise description of American's fertility policy is that it subsidizes among poor women, who are also disproportionately at the low end of the intelligence distribution. **We urge generally that these policies represented by the extensive network of cash and services for low-income women who have babies, be ended**.

> (emphasis added)

This and other immigration-limiting arguments from their books were widely read and influenced US public policy, including serving as one of the core intellectual arguments for the Welfare Act of 1996—Providing Temporary Assistance to Those in Need. See Chapter 9 for more on how intelligence tests were used to categorize people based on race, gender and class.

## Assumptions in Scientific Methodology

We find similar racial injustice in how we practice science too. For example, Quinland et al. (2004) in a meta-analysis found that only 2% of a sample of 500 articles from five major psychology journals from 1990 to 2004 included people of color. Indeed, they found that more than 71% of the articles included a white sample as the group comparison while more than 72% of the research articles failed to break down minority subgroups (e.g., Latinx from Mexican). A personal discussion (DH) with the authors of this meta-analysis revealed that this phenomenon may be even more serious as research papers submitted, without a white comparison group, rarely make it through the review process.

To determine if this research bias was continuing, Jeff Arnett in 2008 analyzed more than 4,037 articles across six sub-disciplines within the top psychology journals of each sub-discipline (*Developmental* Psychology, Journal of *Personality* and Social Psychology, *Health* Psychology, Journal of *Educational* Psychology, Journal of *Abnormal* Psychology and the Journal of *Family* Psychology) over a 20-year period. Unsurprisingly, Arnett found that 96% of the participants and almost all the primary authors were from European countries. Given that the populations from Western countries represent only 12% of the world population and yet nearly all (96%) of the participants from this research were from the West, we can begin to get an inkling of the preconceptions within research methodology. Two years later, another study found similar results (Henrich, Heine, & Norenzayan, 2010).

Even more recently, the potential bias in scientific methodology was explored within the field of child development (NIDA, 2020; Nielsen, Haun, Kartner, & Legare, 2017). The authors of this meta-analysis surveyed every article in the top three high-impact developmental journals (*Child Development, Developmental Psychology* and *Developmental Science*) between 2006–2010 for a total of 1,582 articles. They found that less than 3% of the articles in these top three developmental journals included children from Africa, Asia, Israel, the Middle East or South America combined. This is quite astounding when we consider that these large areas of the world account for nearly 85% of the world population. Authorship outside of Western countries of these research papers was equally dismal, with only two articles published by authors from Central or South America and no authors from the Middle East or Africa.

> As a graduate student committed to social justice, I often find that I am working to learn and engage in research practices that address biases and the influence of systems designed to marginalize within organizations that, at best, know little about community based research and, at worst, deem this work to be of less value than "real" research. Interestingly, though, this lack of formal training

around participatory action and empowering interventions is what has given me the space to be humble enough to enter community spaces without a plan and instead with an intention to listen to the people who understand the problems and needs in a way that no research method, no matter how rigorous, could ever capture. The challenge, though, still lies in how to best honor this expertise in work being done to advance through and succeed in a program that is structured around western ideals of meritocracy and development.

Lynne-Marie Shea, MS

Many reasons are given for the scarcity of Global South (researchers from Africa, South America, and Middle East regions of the world) authors, including issues around language and translation, lack of funding for research, heavy teaching loads preventing professors from engaging in research, and the fact that members of editorial boards are overwhelmingly from the Global North (Williams, 2010). "Global North countries" usually refers to Australia, Canada, most Western European countries, Israel, Japan, New Zealand, Singapore, South Korea, Taiwan (ROC) and the United States. While Zimbabwean scientist Diane Jeater agrees that some of these issues just cited are impacting the lack of research from international authors, she points to potentially deeper issues related to knowledge and power that impact international authors' voices from entering US high-impact journals. Jeater (2018) interviewed senior researchers, faculty, deans and academic staff primarily from the social sciences and humanities in Zimbabwe. Jeater reminds her reader that Zimbabwe has well-funded and "high-quality research universities and research-active faculty" in her aptly titled paper, *Academic Standards or Academic Imperialism? Zimbabwean perceptions of hegemonic power in the global construction of knowledge* (2018). She argues that the lack of representation of authors outside of the Global North relates to who and what is defined as knowledge and "good research," who decides whether that knowledge is truth and that the review process is mostly controlled by researchers, editors and reviewers in the Global North. Keaton's paper is published in the journal *African Studies Review*, and likely will still not get the attention it deserves from Global North scientists, editors and reviewers.

**In what ways does this bias in scientific methodology perpetuate universalist notions of development?** How can you help others to understand this research bias?

_____

_____

_____

## Assumption About Family

We find the roots of gender injustice in how we make sense of who is family too. It is worth reflecting on how our view of family in Western countries is based on the **nuclear family**, "ideally" made up of a male husband, female wife and children with other family units historically viewed as residuary. Each family member serves a particular function in this "ideal" family, with the husband viewed as the "breadwinner" and the wife as the "caretaker." During World War II, when many men were sent off to fight in the war, women were needed to work in the factories, which led to a shift in social roles. After the war, John Bowlby's attachment theory (1952, 1953, 1956, 1957, 1969)—that infants needed to be with their mothers to thrive—was used to justify encouraging women to return to their homes so that men could return to the breadwinner role.

Some of these views of the ideal family have been challenged since the Civil Rights Movement continuing into today, with acknowledgement that families can take many different shapes and forms. Some families consist of one parent, two grandparents, and children; others may have two parents of the same gender with children; and some families do not have children at all! Despite this diversity in what a family may be, many of us still have this nuclear family model in our minds and use it as a baseline to compare all other family variants. We do this when we see two parents of the same gender and wonder who plays the role of "mom" and who plays that of "dad." We also do this when we see multigenerational families and think of them as a nuclear family plus grandparents. It is in this way, by assuming the nuclear family as the default and comparing other families to this model, that we subtly and unconsciously maintain ideological systems that benefit some at the expense of others.

---

When I was in college, I was a counselor at a summer camp for "disadvantaged" kids in an urban area—the program's language, not mine. I had been raised in an almost-entirely-White, fairly affluent suburb. I grew up with a mom, a dad, and two siblings. Most of my campers were Cape Verdean or Haitian, second generation immigrants, with a wide variety of family makeups. Some kids lived with cousins and aunts, or with grandparents, or in multi-family homes with lots of siblings, cousins, aunts, uncles, grandparents, and parents. Many of the kids had very young parents, some only a few years older than me. I had a few friends with young parents, but to me at age 20 it was unimaginable to have kids of my own.

One morning, one of the moms casually asked me if I had children. My gut response was to laugh—I was only 20! I realized later that day that I had been working off of my assumptions about family. It was unimaginable to me that I might have kids, because I was young, and unmarried, and in school. But many people are young, unmarried, in school, and have kids. That interaction prompted me to more carefully consider how I think about families and parents. Instead of being "careful" not to make assumptions, I've started using more open language, deconstructing my assumptions, and setting aside my own notions about who may or may not be a parent or who may or may not participate in raising a kid.

—Kathryn J. Kozak

**In what ways did or does this nuclear family model impact your sense of family?** In what ways does the language of balancing work and family maintain the nuclear family model?

_____

_____

_____

**In what ways does your understanding of family influence how you ask for and deliver help?**

_____

_____

_____

## Assumptions About Morality

We find gender injustice in how we make sense of morality too. In the area of morality, we can see how our bias of development plays out in the debate regarding whether moral development is based on reasoning versus care. Lawrence Kohlberg (1976, 1981) argued that the highest stage of moral development is based on an ethics of justice. His developmental theory posited that morality is based on universal abstract principles of justice. In contrast, Carol Gilligan argued that female morality is based on an ethics of care. Carol Gilligan's (1982) book, *In a Different Voice*, was the first book to challenge the male-centered view of moral development. Gilligan argued that Kohlberg's theory equated moral maturity with social problems that she argued were more the result of socialization than inherent morality. While Kohlberg never directly challenged his former student and colleague's theory, and considered Gilligan's theory complementary to his ideas, he never backed down from his theory that women are inferior to men when considered from a justice-oriented moral perspective. This debate still lingers within the field of developmental psychology and assumes that gender is binary. Note that the many layers of assumptions regarding morality point to how important it is to keep re-visiting our ideas.

**How does this debate about the highest stage of morality and its assumptions about gender reflect a preconception of development?** How can we disentangle from these assumptions about gender? How might one's own view of gender impact the moral framework they accept as truth?

---

---

---

## Assumptions About Culture

We can see how xenophobia hides and takes root in our thinking when we critically reflect on our ideas about culture and development too. Beginning in the 1700s, the term "development" was used in biology to describe the natural growth of plants or animals into their adult forms. Later, "development" began to be used to describe social and economic changes in terms of growth, maturation and evolution. That is, development became synonymous with evolution. At this point, cultures became ranked according to how they measured up to Euro-American ideals, providing the support and rationalization for colonialism. For example, Indigenous people were often described as "primitive" with the reasoning capacity of children. Early development became associated with "unsophisticated" thinking, while end-point development was associated with rationalization and individualism. The scientific rationalization of Euro-Americans was heavily admired in the West over the "primitive" thought processes of Indigenous people, which were often described by Euro-Americans as "pre-symbolic, concrete, emotion laden and superstitious" (Parker, 2007). This reflected the cultural priorities of Euro-Americans rather than an objective assessment of other peoples' or cultures' development.

## Assumptions About Capitalism

If we look closely at our language in how we intertwine capitalism, evolution and development when discussing various countries, we can begin to tap into our unexamined and toxic xenophobia. The language of "underdeveloped" at first appears innocuous, and likely was meant with good intentions, when President Harry Truman used the term in his inaugural address during the Cold War period. Truman described using the scientific and industrial advances of the West to help "undeveloped" areas of the world. However, separating the world into "advanced" versus those in need merely rationalized colonialism in the hearts and minds of all of us in Western society. The narrative frame used here also makes it difficult for those that are not part of the "ideal" to fight back against this ideological move as it appears on first glance that the Western world is truly helping people in need. Instead, the Western world was "helping" at an extreme sacrifice not fully understood by people on both sides of this ideological divide. From the West, while we provided help to those in need, we failed to consider how our "help" would impact the Indigenous culture. This framing is a double-edged sword as it is often used to rationalize Western exploitation and is an important tool for understanding and revealing the ways that Western exploitation has harmed peoples and cultures in other regions of the world. For those from Indigenous communities, there was no way to understand what would be the long-term effect of this type of Western "help."

---

Colonialism is the process of taking control over another community or country, usually by force or through policies and exploitation. Colonizers typically impose their religion and culture on the colonized, who are usually the Indigenous people. One of the largest colonizers was the British Empire, colonizing approximately 84% of the world by the early 19th century.

Examples of US colonization include Native American Indians during the "founding" of the US; Alaska, Cuba, Guantanamo Bay, Guam, Hawaii, Liberia, Nicaragua, the Philippines, Puerto Rico and Honduras.

---

**In what ways does the rhetoric of development contribute to colonization?**

_____

_____

_____

**How do you think those not part of the "idealized" developed world view themselves?** In what ways do Euro-American ideals of helping disempower those who do not identify as Euro-American? In what ways do we, as helpers, continue to disempower those we seek to help?

_____

_____

_____

**What are some steps you and other helpers can take to avoid perpetuating social injustice?** How can we avoid the inequality, dependency and oppression that can happen when we use an individual or developmental frame of helping?

_____

_____
_____

_____

Inherent in traditional and developmental frames of helping are evolutionary assumptions of winners (e.g., those who achieve more or align with the preferred ideology) and losers (e.g., those at the bottom of the societal ladder). From here, our traditional developmental ideology creates a situation where we, as helpers, search for and identify dysfunction and pathology. Often missing from this form of helping is a consideration of the historical, social and political forces that created the dysfunction in the first place. In fact, one could argue that those with dysfunction in an unjust society are healthier given that they are recognizing and responding to the structural dysfunction. Attempts to help marginalized people adjust to the systems that oppress them by those who have been afforded power and privilege by this same system implicate helpers in maintaining the status quo that benefits some at the expense of others.

We hope we have provided you with a beginning dip into the proverbial deep end of the need to critically reflect on the socio-political and -historical factors that impact helping. Given this kind of deep reflection rarely occurs within the helping disciplines, it is often disheartening to realize how socially unjust our helping work can be. In the rest of this chapter, we pivot toward ways we can liberate ourselves from these toxic assumptions and engage in helping that empowers and supports all people.

### Liberation Helping

The rest of this chapter will focus on ways that we can engage in helping that liberates, empowers and creates a more socially just world. Liberation helping requires flipping many of the assumptions that exist with an individual helping model and a development framework on their proverbial heads.

## Learn the History of the Oppressed

We need to become cognizant of how the current socio-political system maintains an unequal social structure and the ways helpers can unintentionally maintain and support unjust systems. We must recognize that our silence reinforces and sustains injustice, and that liberation is intimately tied to interdependence. This means that we, as helpers, need to learn and understand the social and political history that led to the initial social injustice. We can do this by reading about and discussing the history of marginalized

and Indigenous people. Unfortunately, we generally do not learn these topics in our formal training and education, so this knowledge must be sought
outside of our formal training framework. As you learn about this history,
examine how different the story is from the hegemonic narrative learned
during formal education and training.

One example of how narratives from the hegemony may differ from
those on the margins is described in Howard Zinn's seminal book, *A
People's History of the United States*. Zinn describes the hegemonic narrative most of us learned in elementary school that Christopher Columbus
*discovered* America and was very kind to the Indians when he arrived. Zinn
also provides the original diary notes by Christopher Columbus that reveal
how he saw the Indians as savages that would make great slaves back in
Spain. Why we tell ourselves that Columbus *discovered* America—when
there were at least 2.1 million Indians living here before he arrived—when
the truth is quite different is the type of critical reflective work we all need
to do to understand why some of us are on top of this social and political
ladder and why others are on the bottom and how that impacts mental
health disparities. This will lead to many deeper questions like: Why did
I not know this truth? Why was I not taught this truth in school? What
is the purpose of telling me the hegemonic story? Further resources for
exploring the socio-political history of the US can be found at the back
of this book.

**What communities do you feel you know the least about?** Which
communities do you know the most about? Where will you start to broaden
your knowledge of the non-hegemonic narrative?

_____

_____

_____


## Build Critical Consciousness

We need to engage with our newfound knowledge of socio-political history through a process of deep critical consciousness including reflection,
inclusion, dialogue, shared decision-making and shared responsibility. Paulo
Freire describes this process as conscientization (Freire, 1968). This critical
consciousness-raising work requires discussions with a community of people
ready to explore the roots and structural maintenance of social injustice.
Not everyone is ready or willing to engage in this work, even those who
are oppressed. Remember, we all swim in an ocean of social injustice, and
it is often too much work and too painful for many to explore. Exploring
these systems can be incredibly difficult for those they oppress and can strip
those oppressed of the defenses they may have built up to deal with the
oppression. Our privilege as helpers allows us the opportunity, if we choose
to accept it, to more deeply explore this process and the roots of our ideological system.

**Do you have a community of people where you can explore these issues?** If not, how could you create a critical consciousness-raising community for yourself and others? What identities will you include in your critical consciousness-raising community to help challenge yourself and others?

_____

_____

_____


### Balance Looking Backwards and Forward

We need to use a liberation method of balancing between looking back and looking forward (Watkins & Shulman, 2008). We look backwards to deconstruct the socio-political history that created "dysfunction." And, we look forward to open space to create, celebrate, give voice, provide empathy and promote connection. This requires us to address the power relations that have informed and currently maintain social injustice. It requires us to shift and reframe our focus from "pathology" and "dysfunction" of individuals to how culture, history and politics has created and masked an unjust and dysfunctional society. We need to work towards uniting people with similar "pathology" so that they can work together to deconstruct the social injustice that they experience and engage in collective action.


## Engage in Transformative Helping

While traditional Euro-American helpers focus on the individual, transformative helpers focus on how individuals are interconnected through a complex web of relationships. In this way, your liberation is truly my liberation, and the goal for individuals and communities is peace, love, equality and freedom. These relational goals cannot be achieved individually as they are obtainable only through collaboration. Creating liberation at the personal, relational, communal and ecological level requires a village of people committed to transformative change.

Creating social change requires a psychological shift in thinking about helping from a view of fatalism, disempowerment and dysfunction to one of strength, empathy, hope, critical consciousness and solidarity with others (Watkins & Shulman, 2008). This psychological shift requires deep reflection on how we, as helpers, often function from a mindset that is stuck in traditional ways of thinking and helping that promote and maintain the dominant societal framework, a mindset that benefits the privileged at the expense of the oppressed. For example, the disability movement has been able to shift the conversation from a focus on a disabled individual to how disabling environments need to be adjusted for all individuals. Subtitles and closed captioning, for example, can make movies and internet videos accessible to deaf and hard-of-hearing individuals. Universal design ensures that buildings are accessible to all people with minimal need for additional adjustment or accommodation.

International development provides another powerful example of how our mindset can block us from seeing how we are not helping in the ways we believe we are. Large-scale development projects often ignore local community voices, community needs and cultural norms. This leads to more local poverty, more social dysfunction and a rise of international leaders into the community who intentionally or unintentionally block protest and dissent of these projects. Sadly, European countries began many such projects in Africa. Despite the best of international intentions, local farmers abandoned the Food and Agricultural Organization and the World Summit even though there were plenty of funds, technology and Western help (United Nations Development Group, 2001).

**Why do you think these development projects failed?** How can we educate others on the challenges of economic development?

_____

_____

_____

What was missing in many of these failed development projects was a lack of local planning and participation. Ensuring that the voices of the local populations are respected and followed is often challenging for those of us who believe we know best how to help. Culturally sensitive helping requires us to put the people living in a local community at the center of all program initiatives. In this way, we become partners with the community, rather than imposing our understanding of how help should occur. In some cases, we, as helpers from dominant groups, must protect communities from groups like ourselves who are bringing "development and progress" to the community. Instead, we may need to help local communities resist and defend their cultural identity to create safe spaces for them to experiment with new ways of being. The UN's CDG is beginning to recognize that development projects will fail without local planning and participation. Transformational and sustained change is only possible if there is full participation by the local community (Rockefeller Foundation, 2001).

At this point, the Food and Agricultural Organization now focuses on local participation and knowledge as the starting point of a development project, including communication that is participatory and collaborative; engagement in indigenous practices; expecting long-term projects of 10–15 years at minimum; paying attention to gender roles; ensuring positive and productive ways to evaluate program success; and sharing responsibilities across all stakeholders. This important shift in helping is based on a model that starts with what a local community has, wants and needs.

## Helping From a Counter-Development Position

What is often hard for us as helpers to acknowledge is that not everyone wants our "progress." Instead, communities may want more liberation, more peace, more humility, more equality and more freedom. They may view "development" from their communal experience as a system that simply creates more inequity, scarcity and greed. Most of us are unaware of the impact that the development projects have on local populations. We are often unaware that when we buy products from other countries, we may simply be supporting an economic model that sustains oppression. Products bought from other countries may be made by local people but are produced through transnational conglomerates run by Western companies who benefit from making their products in unregulated and low-wage countries. We do not see the impact of this "progress" on the local community in the form of industrial and chemical pollution, decreased air and water quality, and social changes such as worsened traffic, unemployment and violence. Using the language of "development and progress" shields us from acknowledging the "developmental hoax" (Norberg-Hodge, 2016) that may be happening right under our helpful noses.

> Ladakhis represent one of the last subsistence economies in the world, yet "the messengers of development—tourists, advertisements, and film images—have implicitly been telling the Ladakhis that their traditional practices are backward, and that modern science will help them stretch natural resources to produce ever more. Development is stimulating dissatisfaction and greed; in so doing, it is destroying an economy that had served people's needs for more than a thousand years. Traditionally, the Ladakhis had used the resources in their immediate vicinity with remarkable ingenuity and skill, and worked out how to live in relative comfort and enviable security. They were satisfied with what they had. But now, whatever they have isn't enough."
>
> —Norberg-Hodge

The primary goal of a counter-development form of helping should be to promote community self-reliance and sustainability, thereby creating more global diversity and sustainable development throughout the world. Helping should be addressing and dismantling unjust systems: rather than just helping those in the system. Similarly, helping should not mean trying to make people "happy and well adjusted" in an unjust world. Instead, we need to become even more aware of the uncomfortable feelings that signal doubts about the direction in which our community, country and world are headed. This is true when we realize that when 10% of the world consumes 85% of the goods, when 1% own more than 50% of the wealth and when the wealthy earn more than 100 times what the poorest earned, we are suffering as a global society. People who are anxious, worried and depressed may actually be the empathetic and compassionate ones that are having a healthy response to an unhealthy global crisis.

Globalization is a fairly new phenomenon brought about by the ease of communication and mobility and often viewed in a positive light. By "globalization," we mean how people and businesses interact through trade, products, investment and information technology that creates more global influence and global economy. That is, cultures, governments and economies are interacting more throughout the world, leading to further global economic, cultural and political interaction and integration. When explored deeply, globalization is actually a two-edged sword for many countries. How can countries with less economic or political power compete or negotiate with countries with massive power? How do we "help" without destroying countries attempting to recover from centuries of colonization?

**What do you think are some of the advantages and disadvantages of globalization for countries that are viewed as "developed" and "underdeveloped"?**

---

---

---

Dismantling the language of "development" will help us see the connections between economic, social, spiritual, psychological, political and ecological liberation. Individual liberation without economic or political liberation, intentionally and unintentionally, prevents freedom for others. Indeed, personal liberation without other forms of liberation blocks social liberation and perpetuates inequality under the guise of capitalism.

We need to explore how and why some voices are silenced and others are centered, and in what ways this process maintains our current unjust systems. We need to use our power as helpers to provide space for the "other" to be heard, to be able to imagine and to create new ways of being. Engaging in liberation helping requires that we go beyond development, that we seek to renew communities, that we use our power to be in solidarity with the oppressed, and that we attempt to break up hierarchical frameworks that oppress and colonize to achieve a more socially just world.

In what ways can you use your power to create a more socially just world? How can you help others use their power to renew communities and engage in solidarity?

_____

_____

_____

_____

## References

Alegría, M., Chatterji, P., Wells, K., Cao, Z., Chen, C.-N., Takeuchi, D., & Meng, X.-L. (2008). Disparity in depression treatment among racial and ethnic minority populations in the United States. *Psychiatric Services*, *59*, 1264–1272. https://doi.org/10.1176/ps.2008.59.11.1264

American Counseling Association. (2011). *American Counseling public policy and legislative agenda*. www.counseling.org/PublicPolicy/2011_ACA_PPL_Agenda.pdf

American Psychological Association. (2012). *American Psychology Association policy*. www.apa.org/about/policy

Arnett, J. J. (2008). The neglected 95%: Why American psychology needs to become less American. *American Psychology*, *63*, 602–614. https://doi:10.1037/0003-066X.63.7.602

Blair, I. V., Steiner, J. F., Fairclough, D. L., Hanratty, R., Price, D. W., Hirsh, H. K., Wright, L. A., Bronsert, M., Karimkhani, E., Magid, D. J., & Havranek, E. P. (2013). Clinicians' implicit ethnic/racial bias and perceptions of care among Black and Latino patients. *Annals of Family Medicine*, *11*, 43–52. https://doi.org/10.1370/afm.1442

Bowlby, J. (1952). Maternal care and mental health. *Journal of Consulting Psychology*, *16*, 232. https://doi.org/10.1037/h0050582

Bowlby, J. (1953). *Childcare and the growth of love*. London: Penguin Books.

Bowlby, J. (1956). Mother-child separation. *Mental Health and Infant Development*, *1*, 117–122.

Bowlby, J. (1957). Symposium on the contribution of current theories to an understanding of child development. *British Journal of Medical Psychology*, *30*, 230–240. https://doi.org/10.1111/j.2044-8341.1957.tb01202.x

Bowlby, J. (1969). *Attachment: Attachment and loss: Vol. 1. Loss*. Basic Books.

Bronfenbrenner, U. (1974). Developmental research, public policy, and the ecology of childhood. *Child Development*, *45*, 1–5. https://doi.org/10.2307/1127743

Bronfenbrenner, U. (1977). Toward an experimental ecology of human development. *American Psychologist*, *32*, 513–531. https://doi.org/10.1037/0003-066X.32.7.513

Bronfenbrenner, U. (1995). Developmental ecology through space and time: A future perspective. In P. Moen, G. H. Elder, Jr., & K. Lüscher (Eds.), *Examining lives in context: Perspectives on the ecology of human development* (pp. 619–647). American Psychological Association. https://doi.org/10.1037/10176-018

Bronfenbrenner, U., & Ceci, S. J. (1994). Nature-nurture reconceptualised: A bio-ecological model. *Psychological Review*, *10*, 568–586. https://doi.org/10.1037/0033-295X.101.4.568

Bronfenbrenner, U., & Evans, G. W. (2000). Developmental science in the 21st century: Emerging questions, theoretical models, research designs and empirical findings. *Social Development*, *9*, 115–125. https://doi.org/10.1111/1467-9507.00114

Burkard, A. W., & Knox, S. (2004). Effect of therapist color-blindness on empathy and attributions in cross-cultural counseling. *Journal of Counseling Psychology*, *51*, 387–397. https://doi.org/10.1037/0022-0167.51.4.387

Cree, V., Jain, S., & Hillen, D. P. (2019). Evaluating effectiveness in social work: Sharing dilemmas in practice. *European Journal of Social Work, 22*, 599–610. https://doi.org/1 0.1080/13691457.2018.1441136

Freire, P. (1968). *Pedagogy of the oppressed.* Bloomsbury Publishing.

Gilligan, C. (1982). *In a different voice: Psychological theory and women's development.* Harvard University Press.

Henrich, J., Heine, S. J., & Norenzayan, A. (2010). The weirdest people in the world? *Behavioral and Brain Sciences, 33*, 61–135. https://doi.org/10.1017/S0140525X0999152X

Hofstede, G. (1985). The interaction between national organizational value systems. *Journal of Management Studies, 22*(4), 347–357.

Hofstede, G. (2001). *Culture's consequences: Comparing values, behaviors, institutions, and organizations across nations* (2nd ed.). Thousand Oaks, CA: Sage.

Hofstede, G. (2011). Dimensionalizing cultures: The Hofstede Model in context. *Online Readings in Psychology and Culture, 2.* https://doi.org/10.9707/2307-0919.1014

Hook, D., & Eagle, G. (2002). *Psychopathology and social prejudice.* University of Cape Town Press.

Jeater, D. (2018). Academic standards or academic imperialism? Zimbabwean perceptions of hegemonic power in the global construction of knowledge. *African Studies Review, 61*, 8–21. https://doi.org/10.1017/asr.2017.132

Joseph, J. (2004). *The gene illusion: Genetic research in psychiatry and psychology under the microscope.* Algora Publishing.

Kaplan, B. (1983). A trio of trials. In R. M. Lerner (Ed.), *Developmental psychology: Historical and philosophical perspectives* (pp. 185–228). Routledge Press.

Kohlberg, L. (1976). Moral stages and moralization: The cognitive-developmental approach. In T. Lickona (Ed.), *Moral development and behavior: Theory, research and social issues.* Holt, Rienhart, and Winston.

Kohlberg, L. (1981). *The philosophy of moral development: Moral stages and the idea of justice.* Harper and Row.

National Institute on Drug Abuse (2018). https://mnprc.org/2018/10/22/national-i nstitute-on-drug-abuse-nida/

NIDA. (2020). *How effective is drug addiction treatment?* Bethesda, MD: NIDA. www. drugabuse.gov/publications/principles-drug-addiction-treatment-research-based-guide-third-edition/frequently-asked-questions/how-effective-drug-addiction-treatment

Nielsen, M., Haun, D., Kartner, J., & Legare, C. H. (2017). The persistent sampling bias in developmental psychology: A call to action. *Journal of Experimental Child Psychology, 162*, 31–38. https://doi.org/10.1016/j.jecp.2017.04.017

Norberg-Hodge, H. (2016). *Ancient futures: Lessons from Ladakh for a globalizing world.* Local Futures.

Parker, I. (2007). *Revolution in psychology: Alienation to emancipation.* Pluto Press.

Quinland, D., Jackson, L., Alvarez-Jimenez, A., Obasaju, M., Gorham, K. B., & Wasim, F. (2005). Ethnic focus or ethnic convenience: An examination of APA clinical journals from 1990–2004. *Paper presented at Diversity Challenge Conference*, Boston College, Boston, MA.

Rockefeller Foundation. (2001). https://assets.rockefellerfoundation Health-Well-being.pdf

Shin, R. Q., Smith, L. C., Welch, J. C., & Ezeofor, I. (2016). Is Allison more likely than Lakisha to receive a callback from counseling professionals? A racism audit study. *The Counseling Psychologist, 44*(8), 1187–1211. https://doi.org/10.1177/001100001666881

Taylor, S.R. (2018). *The body is not an apology: The power of radical self-love.* Berrett-Koehler Publishers.

United Nations Development Group. (2001). *A glimpse of UNDP's practice*. Communication for Development.

U.S. Department of Health and Human Services. (2001). Mental health: Culture, race, and ethnicity: A supplement to mental health: A report of the surgeon general.

Watkins, M., & Shulman, H. (2008). *Toward psychologies of liberation*. Palgrave Macmillan.

Williams, E. (2010). *The translation gap: Why more foreign writers aren't published in America*. Publishing Perspectives. https://publishingperspectives.com/2010/01/the-translation-gap-why-more-foreign-writers-arent-published-in-america/

World Health Report. (2003). *Adherence to long-term therapies: Evidence for action*. World Health Organization. www.who.int/chp/knowledge/publications/adherence_report/en/

# 2 Social Identity and Social Justice Helping

*Kathryn J. Kozak and Debra A. Harkins*

## Exploring the Role of Social Identity in Community Service

We are all made up of many **social identities**, or a sense of who you are with respect to perceived membership in a particular social group. Some social groups or social identities face **structural** and **systemic oppression**, while others are afforded some level of **privilege**. This framework—social identity, privilege, and oppression—is often used to understand the role of **power** in society, and to ground discussion around justice, equality, and liberation. Understanding social identities can be a helpful first step towards recognizing the role of power in one's own experiences, and can contextualize other theories and perspectives about the white supremacist, heteropatriarchal society in which we live.

When we're in a position as helpers, it's important for us to understand our own social identities and how they interact with the people or organizations with whom we work. But as we move into positions as authority figures, teachers, and scholars, we need to build a deeper understanding of how and why social identities emerge from and interact with systems of power. This chapter provides an overview of social identity; introduces intersectionality and other key concepts and theories that ground our understanding of social identity and power; and builds a framework for educating others on intersectionality, social identity, and systems of power.

Often chapters like this, college courses, or workshops for young professionals start with the assumption that our audience has a basic or minimal understanding of power, oppression, and social identity. In this chapter, however, we want to be open to a wide range of readers—some who have never heard of these frameworks, some who are looking to learn a little more, and some who live this every day. We aren't making assumptions about your gender, class, race, ethnic identity, religion, or country of origin. Rather, we hope to provide a framework for anyone who wants to guide others through reflection of their social identities to move towards critical, ethical, social justice helping. In this chapter, we will explore dimensions of social identity; briefly outline the history of intersectionality as a concept and connect it to contemporary understandings of social identity; and provide an in-depth

DOI: 10.4324/9781003055587-2

discussion of strategies, approaches, and considerations for helping yourself and others to acknowledge and account for social identity in your work.

## Reflection on Power, Privilege, and Social Identity

As a middle-class, educated, straight, white woman with a desire to help in underserved communities, I (DH) am constantly needing to check my privilege. Most recently, with COVID-19, I am realizing just how much privilege I have, and it is making me quite uncomfortable. Here are just a few of the ways that my power and privilege manifests during a global pandemic:

- As a professor, I am able to continue to work in the safety of my home.
- As a paid employee, I am able to continue to purchase most everything I need from the comforts of my home through online services.
- Living in a high-income community, younger adults have the need, time, and resources to shop and deliver my groceries for me.
- As I sit here writing, I am able to stay in my home while packages get delivered that I ordered online, that others with far less privilege will make, package, and deliver to me.
- As a middle-class person, I am able to purchase online resources to begin another business just in case I am unable to continue my job as a professor.
- As an educated person, I am able to read scientific and policy papers regarding the epidemiological patterns of COVID-19 and similar viruses to make informed choices to keep me safe and be less likely to contract the virus.

While I have extreme privilege, I (DH) have some social identities that land more on the oppressed side of the power spectrum and some of these identities have manifested during this global pandemic:

- As a 60+ person, I must be more careful socially interacting with others given my high-risk status.
- As a woman, I make on average 20% less than my male colleagues, which forces me to continue working when it would be economically easier to retire.

Note, my privileges are far more than my oppressions, which allows me greater advantages to survive this pandemic. Data is indicating that communities of color and economically disadvantaged communities have significantly higher incidence of COVID-19, and this is likely due to the lack of privilege of being able to stay home and the inability to avoid being in spaces (e.g., buses and trains) where the probability of being exposed to the virus increases. This is further related to having to work in settings where interaction with unknown people increases and living in smaller spaces.

## Reflection Activity

How have your power and privileges affected your experiences during the coronavirus pandemic?

_____

_____

_____

How has your relation to oppression affected your experiences?

_____

_____

_____

Explore your answers with people whose backgrounds or identities differ from yours. What do you notice?

_____

_____

_____

## Tracing Intersectionality and Contemporary Approaches to Social Identity

Before we dive into a framework for exploring our own social identities (and even helping others explore theirs), we will begin by making connections to the concepts, perspectives, and theoretical models built by activists and academics. *Intersectionality* is a buzzword that you will see many times in this book (well, it's a buzzword when it's used by white people like us). It's a powerful, paradigm-shifting concept that has totally changed the game for activism, scholarly research, and practice around helping and social justice. At the same time, people have gone rogue with the concept of intersectionality—the term often gets misdefined, misapplied, and taken out of context (again, usually by white people) in a way that can actually cause harm.

## Intersectionality

Intersectionality was coined by Kimberlé Crenshaw (1990) to describe the impact of unique combinations of social identities on a person's experiences in the world. Crenshaw had noticed that Black women's experiences with the legal system were impacted by both their race and their gender—their treatment was fundamentally different from that of Black men or of white women. The *intersection* between their race and their gender dictated the obstacles they faced in a way that couldn't be boiled down to only race or only gender, but instead a combination of the two. **Intersectionality** refers to the ways that race and gender (and other dimensions of social identity) interact to produce fundamentally different experiences of oppression than those based only on other marginalized identities.

Crenshaw's (1990) paper *Mapping the Margins: Intersectionality, Identity Politics, and Violence Against Women of Color* explores the problems that prevent alignment between identity politics and social justice. In this paper, Crenshaw uses concrete examples to illustrate what she calls *structural and political intersectionality*, or situations in which intersections of factors such as race, gender, class, and immigration status contribute to instances of oppression that marginalize women of color beyond experiences of just racism or sexism independently. For example, Crenshaw explains that immigrant women experiencing domestic violence may be uniquely vulnerable above and beyond other women because they may rely on their husbands for information about their legal status. These women may thus not be able to access necessary support given their fears of deportation, and this experience of domestic violence is fundamentally different from, for instance, that of white women who are United States citizens. It is critical to remember that intersectionality was coined and developed in the context of understanding Black women's experiences of structural oppression, though the concept has utility in understanding other manifestations of oppression among other people experiencing multiple marginalizations.

Unsurprisingly, at some point *intersectionality* became a buzzword. Kathy Davis (2008) explores why intersectionality became so popular in the late 2000s, noting that as a concept intersectionality makes space for integrating race and class into feminist discussions. At the same time, Davis argues, intersectionality is open to enough interpretation to allow its widespread adoption across theoretical and empirical literature—while also, unfortunately, contributing to conceptual confusion and ambiguity of application. As diversity and inclusion became a focal point outside of academia, intersectionality provided a natural fit for exploring, explaining, and acting on diversity in mainstream contexts.

Similarly, Jennifer C. Nash (2008) explores the ways in which intersectionality both contributes to and detracts from efforts towards liberation. Nash points to a common question about what "counts" as "intersectional" because technically speaking, *everyone* has multiple, intersecting identities. Is the utility of intersectionality in helping us better understand that we all have multiple, intersecting identities? Or is it a tool specifically designed to explicate the compounded marginalization that results from particular intersections of identities? According to Nash's review, we as progressive scholars and practitioners need an advanced, nuanced model of social identity that accurately and meaningfully captures the ways in which social identities, and processes associated with these identities, are both distinct and related in the ways they contribute to oppression and marginalization.

Importantly, as Crenshaw herself acknowledges in *Mapping the Margins*, Crenshaw wasn't the first or only person to describe this phenomenon. The **Combahee River Collective Statement** was a 1977 paper borne out of a collective of Black feminists that outlined the genesis and politics of Black feminism, explaining that a major obstacle to organizing for Black women lies in their exclusion from both Black men's struggle against racism as well as white women's fight against sexism. The Combahee River Collective describes interlocking systems of oppression that contribute to the conditions under which Black women live. In this way, oppression is understood not just as intersections between dimensions of an individual's experience, but as the result of interactions between oppressive systems.

The Combahee River Collective also explicitly identified white feminism as an area of concern and a barrier to liberation, calling for accountability among white feminists to eliminate racism in the movement. As a white person contributing to this chapter, I (KJK) am aware of my own position in writing up a history and commentary on intersectionality in order to help helpers engage in social justice—oriented work. Part of my job here as a white person is to bring in other white folks to do the work of dismantling anti-Black racism and creating space for Black people to imagine and build a better future. That work also includes acknowledging that my own race, ethnic identity, and class inform the pieces of theory and applied research that I draw out and explain to teach about social identity. The frameworks and concepts that are salient to me were first taught to me while briefly studying gender studies in Central Europe, geographically outside the context of the United States. These concepts have since been re-introduced and deconstructed with and for me as a graduate student by peers, colleagues, and community partners in Boston, Massachusetts, a city that likes to conceal its deeply racist and segregationist history through romanticizing, rewriting historical narratives, and ignoring or concealing racist practices like redlining (see Lukas, 1986). Along these lines, in Chapter 4 we revisit this issue as we explore ways in which class analysis can be used to hide or dismiss the impact of structural racism.

In the context of social identity and feminism, Mikki Kendall's 2020 book *Hood Feminism* provides contemporary examples to illustrate the ways in which social identity and factors like race, class, and gender influence a person's lived experiences of privilege and oppression. Through personal anecdote and social and cultural analysis, Kendall expands feminism beyond issues that can be directly and specifically related to women. In some cases, this is because issues like gun control and hunger or food insecurity disproportionately impact women and lead to economic, social, and political injustice. In other cases, this is because women are excluded from the conversation about feminism due to manifestations of racism, classism, and other oppressions. For instance, Kendall explains that Black women are community and activist leaders in part because of the system of structural racism that has led to the systematic mass incarceration and murder of Black men. In this sense, the challenges and successes of Black women must be understood in the context of sociopolitical history.

So, why has this whole section of a chapter on social identity focused so much on feminism? Well, in part, because that's the scholarship one of the authors is most familiar with. But really, it's because intersectionality is both a buzzword and a gateway. It's a relatable heuristic by which social justice can become accessible, and by which activists and scholars can begin to illustrate the ways in which experiences of oppression differ based on social identity. It allows us to explain to our students or peers or colleagues why their experiences as a white, cisgender gay man are different from those of their Black, queer client. It helps us understand why our position as educated or employed or well read or networked gives us some relative privilege compared to those who do not have formal education, who have not had access to scholarship or activist literature, or who do not have connections to non-profit organizations. It gets our grant or research proposals accepted or at least read over, because people recognize the term and know it means something meaningful or important.

Intersectionality allows us to consider and explore the impact of social identity on experiences with power and privilege. It explains why it's problematic to compare the experiences of white women to those of Black women. It clarifies why we must be careful to acknowledge the role of race, class, and gender while fighting for LGBTQ+ justice and equality. And it serves as a building block to start to understand the ways in which instances of oppression are often perpetrated by individual people, but are also embedded within a sociocultural infrastructure.

**Reflection:** How does the concept of *interlocking systems of oppression* affect the way we think about social justice work? How does helping get easier when we consider intersectionality? What becomes complicated when we account for intersectionality?

_____

_____

_____

## Helping Others Explore the Role of Social Identity

We've spent most of this chapter so far addressing some of the theory and concepts related to social identity. You've perhaps considered the role of your own identities and how they have brought you to your work (or this book), and you've read through a history of intersectionality and theories of interlocking systems of oppression that illustrate why we must understand

(and deconstruct) social identity in social justice helping. But this isn't just a book for thinking and reflection and applying to yourself, so the third section of this chapter explores some common strategies, approaches, and exercises to help others explore and apply to their own social identities. You might find yourself leading a group of peers, or suggesting to a professor, boss, or supervisor that you dig a little deeper into your own identities to better serve your communities. Or you might find yourself trying to mitigate harm from an inexperienced or poorly trained consultant trying to "teach diversity" to your class or workplace.

Exercises to identify and explore social identity are a common part of courses or workshops that seek to teach about diversity or cultural competence. For anyone interested in empowerment- or liberation-focused helping, identity exercises can be important for situating yourself in the work or exploring how your own experiences affect your participation in helping. Those of us working as leaders, educators, or trainers should also understand why we use social identity exercises as well as how to implement them effectively and ethically.

Teaching these concepts and skills within a social justice framework requires grappling with the role of anti-Blackness in our own lives and work. For any white or non-Black person of color reading this book, you should also do your own, personal anti-racism work to interrogate how anti-Black racism has impacted your own thoughts, feelings, attitudes, and behaviors before you try working with others. If you're in academia, we highly recommend looking into the workshops and resources from *Academics 4 Black Survival and Wellness.* A list of additional resources is at the end of this chapter, and we include some thoughts within the activity descriptions on how to integrate anti-racist intentions into these activities and approaches.

Social identity exploration can be conducted as individual exercises (and even one-on-one conversations) or as group activities. Major considerations for choosing and conducting your exploration include the context, goals, and group makeup. Think carefully about why you want your group members to explore and consider their social identities.

- Are you trying to illustrate your group members' relative privilege, and get them thinking about the role of race, class, education, or other dimensions?
- Are you using this type of exercise as a building block to understanding other concepts such as intersectionality or social determinants of health?
- Are you opening up a broader conversation about identity, and simply trying to get participants to think critically about their own identity, personal history, and lived experience?

You also need to account for some important considerations that can affect your ability to safely, effectively, and ethically guide your group through an identity exercise:

- Does your activity encourage or require participants to share personal details?

  - Are you asking participants to disclose marginalized identities?
  - Are you in a setting where this information could potentially be used against participants if disclosed (e.g., do you live somewhere with weak or no protections against discrimination for LGBTQ+ people who could lose their job, housing, or healthcare based on their identity)?

- By your estimation, is your group new to this type of exercise?

  - Do you expect that group members have similar experiences with/ exposure to considering social identities, or are some members more familiar than others?

- How well do group members know each other?

  - Is this a group that interacts regularly or has a pre-existing relationship?
  - Can this group handle a "high-trust" activity?

- What is your capacity for debriefing, processing, or continuing education?

  - If conflict or difficulty arises as part of this exercise, do you have the time and resources to address it?
  - What other resources or support structures do you need in place in case participants find this emotionally or psychologically difficult?

Activities can be low- or medium-risk, and require about the same trust and disclosure as you would have in any other group environment. These activities require only a little personal information if any, leave participants lots of space to choose what to share, and typically minimize the risk of conflict. Medium- to high-risk activities require a lot of trust and connection between participants. They might require participants to share personal information and trust that others will respect that information. These activities may also leave less space for participants to "opt out" or moderate how much they share. High-risk activities should be conducted by experienced facilitators or with help from a trained peer mentor or supervisor, and only among groups of people with pre-existing relationships. Make sure everyone is fully informed about the nature of the activity and has given consent to participate—never spring a high-risk activity on a group without plenty of preparation and explanation!

If you find yourself in a position where participants (including yourself!) might need access to social supports or mental healthcare as a result of identity work, or where leading an activity could cause unintentional harm of violence or abuse, do not attempt to lead an activity on your own. If you're in academia, reach out to your institution's diversity offices, wellness centers, peer mentoring programs or student affairs departments for appropriate resources and support. If you do not have access to these resources, look for a trained consultant, advocate, or community organization to help you.

## The Identity Wheel

The "Personal Identity Wheel" is a visual tool that helps participants conceptualize the many dimensions of their personal identity. Several versions of this tool exist, but the common components are a circle or wheel with spaces to "fill in" how the participant identifies according to common social groups or categories. For example, the LSA Inclusive Teaching Initiative at the University of Michigan has a version of the wheel with spaces for ethnicity; socioeconomic status; gender; sex; sexual orientation; national origin; first language; physical, emotional, developmental (dis)ability; age; religious or spiritual affiliation; and race. The center of this wheel includes five brief prompts to consider the salience of each of these identities in the participant's life.

This activity can be modified to be low-, medium-, or high-risk. When leading this activity, be sure to clarify expectations up front about whether participants should be prepared to share or disclose what they write on their sheet. Some participants may have privacy concerns if they hold invisible marginalized identities, and may alter responses if the sheet will be collected or shared. Consider the following prior to leading your group through an identity wheel exercise:

- What happens when only your "privileged" participants feel comfortable sharing/disclosing?
- How do you make sure your "marginalized" participants don't have to engage in the emotional work/education without speaking over them?
- What reflective questions can help illustrate salience of identities/different experiences?

In my (KJK) personal and professional experience, an identity wheel is a helpful tool that some people will hang onto far beyond the scope of the formal activity. Some people may feel violated by the expectation to fill out an identity wheel, especially if they then feel forced to share their responses during class. In this case, they might feel evaluated or judged based on who they are, what privileges they had, and what marginalized experiences might be associated with their identity "responses." Others may value this exercise greatly, referring back to it multiple times to help advocate for institutional change for example, as new procedures that acknowledge their supervisor's privilege at work. The point here is that if you are in a facilitator role with an identity wheel, get as much of a sense of your participants, students, or group members as possible, and make the activity voluntary.

We further recommend using an identity wheel or similar tool to help explore personal values, which you can learn more about in Chapter 3.

## Case Studies, Scenarios, and Role Playing

One low- to medium-risk way to help participants reflect on social identity is through the use of scenarios, case studies, or role plays. These approaches have a few advantages: They can allow some distance between the participants and the subject matter, since you aren't requiring people to share their own experiences or stories. They also can allow you to explore issues outside the experiences of your participants, which can be helpful if your group is fairly similar demographically. Finally, they can help provide a model or example for what participants might consider or explore within their own experiences.

### Case Study

A case study is a description of a real event or situation. Sometimes it has been **deidentified**, or had the details modified so that you can't figure out the identity of the person, people, or places involved. A case study can allow a person or group to explore the contextual and historical factors that led to a particular experience or response. Rather than making inferences about what you might do in that situation, a case study allows you to consider why the people responded the way they did, or what allowed a particular outcome. For example, I (DH) use case studies and personal anecdotes in a community psychology course and textbook (Harkins, 2017) to help illustrate safety and boundaries issues in service-oriented work. Having a former student explain what happened to her while at a service site allows current students in the course to think not only about what they like to think they'd do in that situation; but students can also think about what they might *actually* feel pressured to do and how they can avoid finding themselves in situations. Case studies and personal anecdotes about helping reveal how an innocent situation (e.g., sitting with someone experiencing homelessness at night) can quickly escalate into unexpected and dangerous scenarios (e.g., feeling like that person is invading your personal space and worrying about your own safety). See Harkins (2017) Chapter 3, "Serving as Change Agents," for more on this case example.

### Scenarios + Role Play

Reflecting on and discussing fictional or hypothetical scenarios can give the facilitator some control over the direction of conversation that might be more difficult or less comfortable when participants are using their own experiences as the subject material. This can be particularly helpful if you're training a group to respond to certain cultural needs or exploring a specific dimension of identity or community. For example, I (KJK) facilitated activities with undergraduate student leaders who were going to be leading teams of their peers on community service trips. We would use specific scenarios about potentially difficult conversations that might come up on the trips based on past experiences. One such scenario: How might you respond to a site supervisor who instructs everyone to hold hands, bow their heads, and join in a Christian prayer before the day's work? How might this request affect the other students on your trip? How might your response affect the relationship with the supervisor? How does this scenario make *you* feel based on your experiences with Christianity?

Sometimes it can be helpful to have participants act out the situation in order to practice how they might respond. It can be helpful to try dealing with a situation in a relatively safe environment where you can get feedback from a group. However, it's important to create clear guidelines and group norms for engaging in role play activities. Sometimes students go very far to "act the part," and may feel it's appropriate to use offensive language or their perceptions of stereotypical behavior in order to "be realistic." Others may find themselves in a position where they are role playing their own experiences, even if it seems like a situation that's not relevant to your group.

There are some steps you can take to use these activities safely and ethically. Avoid assigning roles, and let participants volunteer or take turns. Avoid creating scenarios where you may ask participants to engage in racist or bigoted behavior for the sake of role play. Leave plenty of time for your group to debrief the experience: What was it like to participate in the role play? What was it like for the participants watching? What feelings or emotions came up for you? What other resources or information would be helpful moving forward?

## Critical Reflection

Critical reflection is more of an approach than an activity. *Critical* in this sense mostly means that there's an awareness of power, or that there's an intentional, systematic, and careful analysis involved. *Reflection* refers to exercises in which someone is prompted to consider their personal experiences, values, attitudes, and behaviors related to a given topic or situation.

### Critical Reflection in Service-Oriented Courses

For meaningful critical reflection to occur, students need a strong foundation of the sociopolitical context that has impacted the hegemonic practices that surround them. Initially, many students will engage in helping practices that mimic traditional forms of helping, often with the mindset that the way they should help is to do something for someone else without consideration of how the act of helping recreates the power dynamics that led to the social inequalities. Chapter 5 of this book offers an in-depth exploration of how these dynamics can play out.

---

**Service-oriented courses** are often defined as a pedagogy that integrates service, academic content, and critical reflection.

---

## *Suggestions for Designing Critical Reflection Journals and Discussions*

Based on empirical research into best practices as well as our own experience using critical reflection, there are a few options for smoothly and effectively integrating reflection into coursework, mentorship, or leadership activities.

First, requiring readings and then reflective journaling and discussions on the *social, political, and historical* factors that contributed to the current social inequities is one of the best ways to get critical reflection started. This activity often requires assigning readings that are "outside" of the standard helping curriculum (see resources for some suggested readings). Reading deeply, journaling, and critical discussion often lead to a realization that there are significant gaps in one's education regarding certain communities and events. Exploring with students why these gaps exist in their knowledge is where deep critical reflection happens. It is through this process that we build an understanding of how we are all knowingly or unknowingly implicated in maintaining social injustice through our lack of knowledge and awareness.

Another strategy involves engaging in journaling and discussions on how *contemporary* social issues (e.g., Black Lives Matter, LGBTQ+, women's issues, disability justice, etc.) relate to social justice helping. This can include bringing in a current event or prompt and encouraging students, peers, or colleagues to write down or discuss their reactions, connections, and reflections. Effective prompts will encourage participants to make connections between their own beliefs, experiences, or attitudes and the issues raised by the topic in question.

Finally, starting with the self can be a powerful way to begin engaging in critical reflection. This can involve exploring one's own *social identity*, including the sociopolitical forces that led one's ancestors to live where they lived, work in the occupations they did, and engage in the religious and social practices that they did. This allows for consideration of how one's ancestral history impacts oneself today.

In this chapter, we reviewed the concept of social identity and explored why understanding social identity is crucial to effective social justice helping. We examined connections between social identity and the theory of intersectionality, and discussed the importance of considering *systems of interlocking oppression* when understanding the impact of social identity on lived experiences of power, oppression, and helping work. We also introduced common strategies for exploring social identity as well as ethical considerations related to social identity.

The next steps for the social justice helper require looking even more deeply inward. It's not enough to just think about who we are and how our identity affects our experiences. To be social justice helpers, we need to deconstruct the values, beliefs, and attitudes that influence our approaches to social justice, helping, and liberation. In this section of the book, we'll also introduce theories for understanding, interrogating, and dismantling systems of power and conclude with an applied example of how to integrate social identity, personal and cultural values, and social justice work.

As you continue through this book, think about how your social identities have brought you to where you are. How do dimensions like your age, gender identity, racial and ethnic identity, religion, and education level influence your goals related to social justice? What further exploration would you like to engage in to better understand how your social identity influences the work you do or the people you want to work with and for? What do you wish those around you knew about their own social identities, and how might you ethically, safely, and compassionately help them engage in their own exploration?

# References

Crenshaw, K. (1990). Mapping the margins: Intersectionality, identity politics, and violence against women of color. *Stanford Law Review*, *43*(2–3), 7–20. https://doi.org/10.7146/KKF.V0I2-3.28090

Davis, K. (2008). Intersectionality as buzzword: A sociology of science perspective on what makes a feminist theory successful. *Feminist Theory*, *9*, 67–85. https://doi.org/10.1177/1464700108086364

Harkins, D. A. (Ed.). (2017). *Alongside community: Learning in service*. Routledge Press.

Kendall, M. (2020). *Hood feminism: Notes from the women that a movement forgot*. Penguin.

Lukas, J. A. (1986). *Common ground: A turbulent decade in the lives of three American families*. New York: Vintage Books.

Nash, J. C. (2008). Re-thinking intersectionality. *Feminist Review*, *89*(1), 1–15. https://doi.org/10.1057/fr.2008.4

## Resources

Personal Identity Wheel: https://sites.lsa.umich.edu/inclusive-teaching/sample-activities/personal-identity-wheel/

Redlining Exhibit at Boston Architectural College: www.wbur.org/artery/2019/04/25/redlining-exhibit

# 3 Learning the Role of Values in Social Justice–Focused Helping

*Sukanya Ray, Hannah E. Robins, Sophia Anyela Joan Kozlowsky, and Yanxi Liu*

## Exploring the Role of Values in Social Justice Helping

Rokeach (1973) defines a value as "an enduring belief that a specific mode of conduct or end-state of existence is personally or socially preferable to an opposite or converse mode of conduct or end-state of existence." This enduring belief can help guide evaluations of different people, as well as choices and subsequent actions. The realization of values, and the importance of values in decision making, can be activated in certain contexts (e.g., valuing equality and making the choice to stand up against racial injustice). Not surprisingly, these personal values can often be linked to professional values. This includes how we provide professional services. A key component for creating effective leadership is having a strong foundation of both personal values and principles. Specifically, within healthcare settings, personal and professional values seem to be inextricably linked for effective leaders.

When it comes to clinical decision making, healthcare providers rely on both their personal and professional values. As a result of the link between these values, researchers have advocated for a greater emphasis on incorporating personal values in clinical training and in the recruitment of individuals interested in clinical training. For example, within the nursing profession, professional identity is most commonly defined as the "values and beliefs . . . that guide . . . thinking, actions, and interactions with [a] patient" (Fagermoen, 1997, p. 435).

Our personal values are closely connected with our work ethics, values such as beneficence, autonomy, empathy, and justice. Moreover, authors in the medical ethics area emphasize the cultural responsiveness and ethical challenges in healthcare systems, which certainly resonates with essential values such as patience, respect, compassion, and sensitivity among providers towards diverse and underserved populations. This practice of cultural responsiveness has an underlying moral drive and is fundamentally rooted in the principles of acknowledging the importance of an individual's culture, while respecting cultural differences and minimizing the negative consequences that may come as a result of these differences. Therefore,

DOI: 10.4324/9781003055587-3

the relationship between ethics and cultural responsiveness is inherently bidirectional—to truly engage in one is to practice the other (Betancourt, Corbett, & Bondaryk, 2014).

Healthcare leaders in particular are ethically obligated to provide a safe environment for patients as well as other providers. Additionally, it is important that they maintain a connection to the community served. This obligation starts first with the organizational subculture (i.e., social interactions, shared values and norms, common affiliations, mutual supports) amongst providers and employees, which in turn influences the culture that is experienced by patients and the outside community. Additionally, the extent to which organizations, and by direct extension the leadership of such an organization, engage in ethical practices is often linked with patient-reported quality of care and provider-reported job satisfaction. Therefore, healthcare leaders perhaps bear some of the greatest burdens in ensuring that ethical practices are maintained (Morrison, 2008).

Training approaches can guide helpers to navigate the unique challenges of maintaining ethical practices and ensuring quality as well as satisfactory services. This aligns with transformational leadership wherein healthcare leaders prioritize the needs of cultural responsiveness within their organization. Research suggests that transformational leadership qualities are prominent among healthcare leaders and are additionally linked to job satisfaction. Value-based leadership also applies to educators of professional training programs. It is essential that helpers reflect on their personal values, which can ultimately shape perspectives on community service. A value-based leader working in organizations can initiate new policies and procedures that address personal values. Important to this work includes developing systems that reward employees actively engaged in values-based work. Thus, an environment that reinforces the connection between personal values and broader organizational culture ensures that leaders can promote a work environment that is linked to greater job satisfaction and improved performance (Graber & Kilpatrick, 2008; Hemingway & Maclagan, 2004; Spinelli, 2006).

Moreover, these values are closely connected with one's lived experiences. For example, members of marginalized backgrounds often have better insight into their community's needs. The development of a professional identity commences alongside formal training and is influenced not only by work experience and professional knowledge, but also by less formal self-identified gender and cognitive flexibility (Adams, Hean, Sturgis, & Clark, 2006). Thus, it is important to engage in dialogue concerning one's insight into personal values that influence helpers' engagement in community services both directly and indirectly. Training programs must emphasize the facilitation of helpers' insight into their values while building other skills. Some reflective questions are listed in the following for this purpose.

**What are some of your own personal values? What experiences in your life have made these values important to you?**

_____

_____

_____

> The first (SR) and third author (SK) underscore the value of education and one's right to access it through their own personal experiences in public schools. These exposures and experiences have truly strengthened their passion towards advocacy for equitable access to quality education.

**How do your personal values interact with your privilege in the work you do?**

_____

_____

_____

**Reflect on your personal values and the ones that are most important to you. Which values come to mind first, and in what ways do you believe they impact the way you act and the interactions you have while working with people? How do they affect the people you work with?**

_____

_____

_____

> The second author (HR) values integrity and growth. They make an effort to act with honesty and respect for other people, which they believe encompasses the value of integrity. They also strive to be open to change, receiving constructive criticism, and learning from mistakes, which they believe is part of valuing growth. It's their hope that these values guide them in being a positive team player and a supportive member of the community.

Thinking about the same values from the previous question, do you believe you have always had these values, or do you believe they were formed, strengthened, or nurtured throughout your life? If they were formed throughout your life, what people, events, or experiences helped form them? Are there ways in which you believe these values could have been better fostered by others or yourself? If so, how?

_____

_____

_____

The values of integrity and growth are ones that have been strengthened and nurtured over the course of the second author's (HR) lifetime. Their family has been most influential in these values, along with their mentors in their education and career. They still have work to do to live in line with these values, and enhancing their cultural humility as a therapist is one way in which they hope to do so.

Identify your top three personal values. Then identify your top three professional values. Do these values intersect? How could the intersection of values help you be an advocate for social justice?

_____

_____

_____

The second author's (HR) top three personal values are integrity, growth, and compassion. Their top three professional values are in alignment with these. Leaning further into this alignment would lend itself to advocacy work in their field.

## Exploring the Role of Social Identity in Social Justice Helping

The scope of training in community service must highlight understanding one's social identity as part of their learning objectives. It is essential to dialogue around how one's social identity across domains such as race, gender, socioeconomic status, sexual orientation, and others is the key component of one's lived experience, and how it shapes one's worldview. It is essential for trainers to focus on specific attributes of helpers. This includes social justice interests, beliefs, and accountability domains. Thus, it is useful to understand relevant theoretical and empirical literature to expand on this point. Many authors have informed this work through their personal narratives, which could guide us in our professional journey as trainers and trainees in community service areas. Examples of values described by some of our (authors) role models are in text boxes here.

---

I would like to be known as a person who is concerned about freedom and equality and justice and prosperity for all people.
—Rosa Parks

You must be the change you wish to see in the world.
—Mahatma Gandhi

---

As introduced in Chapter 2, social identities are multidimensional and include things like race, ethnicity, socioeconomic status, gender, sex, sexuality, and religion, among others. It's possible and in fact common for one aspect of a social identity to afford privilege, while another may be marginalized in society (e.g. a white female may experience sexism but also benefit from the pervasive white supremacy in society). Intersectionality, a term coined by Kimberlé Crenshaw and explained in more depth in Chapter 2, refers to this intersection between different aspects of social identities that creates layers of advantage or disadvantage (Crenshaw, 1989). Examining how intersectionality plays a role in community work is not only important, but necessary. Without it, we miss key elements in the processes of discrimination, power, or oppression that we are working to challenge. As such, intersectionality has emerged as a framework to understanding how these multiple dimensions rely on each other for meaning and significance. Inherently linked with awareness of one's intersectional identities are individual reflections of experiencing power, privilege, and oppression.

Important to consider is how varying demographic identities associate with changing levels of both privilege and oppression and are even further influenced by the other identities carried by an individual. The recognition of a privileged identity can influence the recognition of an oppressed identity, and vice versa (e.g. being a minority but also a straight cisgender male). For example, a recent meta-analysis of studies examined implicit racial/ethnic biases in healthcare providers and found mixed findings affecting patient care. Alternatively, by examining the role in which their own identities play in their professional life, healthcare providers are better able to understand the impact of identity on their patients, and consequently the care that their patients receive. At this time, there is limited research available on the intersectional relationship of power, privilege, and oppression in a leadership context. Given that a leadership role automatically involves power over others, the extent to which healthcare leaders understand the impact of their own privilege and oppression and the privilege and oppression of their patients warrants further exploration (Croteau, Talbot, Lance, & Evans, 2002; Maina, Belton, Ginzberg, Singh, & Johnson, 2018; Van Herk, Smith, & Andrew, 2010).

Another important area to consider is the role of one's awareness about equity as well as privileges in community service work. Privilege is not about guilt; it's about acknowledging the ways in which our society is built to advantage some people and disadvantage others. Acknowledging privilege as a helping professional also does not mean you yourself haven't faced difficulties and challenges in life, overcome obstacles, or worked hard to get where you are. It simply means that certain components of your social identity (i.e., race, gender) have not been a part of the challenge for you. As Tim Wise importantly states about white privilege, it's not about guilt, it's about responsibility (Wise, 2005). This responsibility may in fact play into the work you do, and examining it provides context for your role in these efforts.

Do aspects of your social identity play a role in why you chose to go into a helping profession (e.g. does your belonging to the LGBTQ+ community play a role in your healthcare advocacy efforts)? How does this intersect with your personal values? Is the work you do in line with your personal values? Considering these values can be helpful in staying on track or redirecting efforts towards what's important. Skitka and Mullen (2002) present the "Value Protection Model" to explain how individuals' values shape the way in which they perceive justice or injustice in their work and the world around them (i.e. outcomes are perceived as fair if they are consistent with an individual's moral values). Schwartz (1999) defined values as desirable goals that serve as guiding principles in a person's life. He specifies that values can serve the interests of social entities, motivate action, and function as standards for judging or justifying action, and that values are developed through both socialization and individual experience. In reflecting on your personal values, it can be helpful to examine where these values came from. Did your personal experience facing oppression or discrimination fuel your pursuit for equity in your community? Did witnessing others facing injustices contribute to your valuing of justice? In what ways do these values serve as "guiding principles" in your life?

### *"Using" Your Privilege in Social Justice Work*

What does it mean to be a "privileged ally" (Giannaki, 2016)? As written by Stephanie Nixon, "allyship is not an identity, but an ongoing practice"

(Nixon, 2019). Beyond reflecting on your personal values and their interaction with your community work, it is also prudent to examine how "privileged" aspects of your social identity may impact your work. For example, one might identify the value of autonomy as having personal importance. By engaging in social justice work, you are exercising your own autonomy to create change in the world around you. However, it's possible for the actions of privileged "allies" to impede on the autonomy of the oppressed group (i.e. when privileged helpers act as "saviors" to an oppressed people's movement). It should be noted that the value of "autonomy" is often a value of individualist cultures that helpers from these places often project onto people from collectivist cultures. Allyship from those with privileged social identities is most productive when it functions as a partnership, and when those with privilege are aware and cognizant of the ways in which their personal privilege may be utilized to magnify the work at hand and the voices of the oppressed instead of co-opting a movement to which they cannot claim ownership.

Patel (2011) highlights the importance of challenging the binary understanding of allyship, and argues that a more inclusive model would account for individuals who both benefit and suffer from a system of oppression; Patel points to her own identity as an Asian American. Understanding how systems of oppression may affect different people in unique and often multiple ways may aid in developing a pluralistic fight for justice.

Using privilege in productive and meaningful ways may mean making appeals to and gathering support around the movement from others in your social standing; taking action that specifically calls out the privilege you have in contrast to the injustices experienced by the oppressed; and holding others with privilege accountable for the ways in which they may enable oppression. For example, in recent and ongoing protests to end the police brutality against Black people in the United States, white allies have supported Black-owned businesses, amplified Black voices (e.g. drawing attention to the work of Black authors), and provided financial support to Black organizations fighting against racism. These are all ways in which privileged allies can contribute meaningfully to being anti-racist. There are also ways in which individuals can use their privilege to uplift others within their existing communities and workplaces. For example, a man may be an ally to a woman at their workplace by ensuring her voice is heard at meetings (e.g. "Excuse me, I think she was still talking and had more to say").

When considering how your social identity and the privileges within it may impact the work you do, it's important to acknowledge the population of people you are working with. How are these people similar or different? How has their experience of navigating society been different than yours? If you were to be in a similar situation to them, would you have more options? More resources? These are all aspects that make up privilege. Author and scholar Ibram X. Kendi writes the following about white privilege: "To be white is to be afforded one's individuality. Afforded the presumption of innocence. Afforded the assumption of intelligence" (Kendi, 2019). Acknowledging privilege you hold as a helping professional, whether that be white privilege, male privilege, able-bodied privilege, or any number of other privileges in your social identity, is crucial. Moreover, it's important to assess how your social identity may impact your ability to be culturally responsive in your work. As a helping professional, do you have shared lived experiences with those you are helping? If not, what are you doing to ensure your services are culturally sensitive and relevant? It's important to recognize that intellectual knowledge is not equivalent to lived experience, and sometimes it is helpful to think about what made you decide to work as a social justice professional. In the next section of this chapter, we explore how we can deepen knowledge of helpers while undertaking their roles as professionals to empower our communities.

### The Connections Between Social and Institutional Values

How does your social identity connect with and influence how you approach institutional values? By institutional values in this context, we mean the attitudes, ideas, and encouraged behaviors that are held by an organization. These values typically influence how those within the organization behave. For example, an institutional value held by a manufacturing company may be efficiency, as they want to produce their products as fast as possible in order to make a larger profit. This value of efficiency will most likely influence how the company encourages behaviors they deem as efficient or punish those behaviors they deem inefficient. This will in turn encourage employees to work in an efficient manner and further promote the value of efficiency. What we want to do now is dissect how this plays out in helping institutions and how it affects individual helpers.

There is no universal consensus as to what occupations fall into the helping profession at large, who qualifies as a helper, or what helpers do. This makes it difficult to define institutional values for the whole of helping. There is, however, more consensus of institutional values on the level of individual helping occupations such as social work. A considerable sample of the literature on social work has identified the "core" values of this profession as "social justice, human dignity and worth, respect for people, integrity and competence" (Bisman, 2004). As stated earlier in this chapter, many within helping professions hold personal values that align with the values of the institutions for which they work. In their study of social workers, MacKay and Zufferey found that their subjects' personal values were "inextricably linked" with their professional institutions' values (2015). That is, those who highly value equality, for instance, and who wish to go into a helping profession, are likely to connect that personal value with the institutional value of equality in social justice work. Additionally, as discussed in Chapter 2 and earlier in this chapter, one's social identity strongly influences their personal values. So, if your social identity shapes your personal values, and your personal values influence the institutional values that you identify with and/or seek out, your social identity is therefore connected to institutional values.

Another aspect of one's social identity that plays into personal values and accountability, which will be discussed in the next section, is cultural values. Schwartz (1999), a pioneer in value research, defines cultural values as "the bases for the specific norms that tell people what is appropriate in various situations" according to their cultural identity. In their cross-national comparative study, Zotzmann, Van der Linden, and Wrywa (2019) found that cultural values differed across countries and these cultural values influenced how employees viewed and acted upon errors, i.e., how accountable they were. As elaborated on later in this chapter, part of accountability is how you respond to and deal with errors.

When working with people in helping professions, errors can have serious consequences for clients, and accountability is a vital way to avoid negative outcomes resulting from an error. Errors are often associated with negative outcomes; however, Zotzmann et. al. explain that errors can also have positive outcomes such as learning from an error, improvements in future performance, and greater attention to detail. They found that one's cultural values factored into whether one viewed an error as entirely negative or saw some positive in the error and whether or not one would act to correct and learn from the error, i.e., whether or not they were accountable. They also found that personal and institutional values come together with cultural values to decide how one views an error and whether or not they are accountable for it. Accountability will be discussed further later in this chapter.

**What are the key components of your social identity?** Use what you've learned from the value section to picture your ultimate goals in social justice work.

_____

_____

_____

As a white, cisgender, straight, Jewish woman the second author (HR) has privilege in her race, gender, and sexual orientation but also may experience oppression due to patriarchal systems and anti-Semitism.

**Why is it important to understand intersectionality while working with marginalized populations?** How can we, as developing scholars, better understand where power comes from and where it collides through the lens of intersectionality?

_____

_____

_____

The second author (HR) notes that she must understand the ways in which her experience is similar and different from those that she works with as a therapist. A better understanding of this allows for cultural humility and respect.

**What would happen if we ignored the role intersectionality plays in social justice work?**

Give an example of the consequences of overlooking the intersections between social problems and to people who are subject to many societal injustices.

_____

_____

_____

The first (SR) and last (YL) authors suggest that white feminism is an example of overlooking intersectionality since it assumes all women face the same problems and ignores the harm that white women have contributed to in the realm of systematic racism.

**Would you be able to identify some of your privileges?** How would you utilize your own privileges in order to become a privileged ally to people you work with?

_____

_____

_____

The second author (HR) holds privilege in her race, gender, sexual orientation, and able body. She can use her privilege as a cisgender person to call for more inclusive language which includes those of all genders, and also by identifying her pronouns as a way of normalizing this practice.

**As a helping professional, do you have shared lived experience with those you are helping?** If not, what are you doing to ensure your services are culturally sensitive and relevant? It's important to recognize that intellectual knowledge is not equivalent to lived experience, and sometimes it is helpful to think about what made you decide to work as a social justice professional.

_____

_____

_____

Although the second author (HR) has family and close friends with varied sexual orientations and gender identities, she herself does not have the personal experience of being marginalized due to these identities. It's important for her to understand that although she may be familiar with these challenges, they are not ones she has personally lived. Therefore she cannot speak on behalf of this marginalized population.

## Exploring the Role of Commitment and Accountability in Social Justice Helping

While values are the driving force behind helping actions, lasting change often comes about when people maintain commitment to their values and are held accountable. Specific attributes such as commitment and accountability in this sense are imperative in helping professions. Our leaders who have championed social justice in their commitment and accountability have truly enabled changes and growth in our communities at large.

Tim Wise, racial activist, speaker, and scholar describes accountability in his line of work as "taking constructive criticism seriously, integrating insights provided by others and incorporating these insights into your own work, and following the 'lead, direction, and advice of those who have the most to lose from'" your work (Wise, 2005, 2010). He goes on to elaborate that accountability does not necessarily mean one needs to have every action approved by a panel of coworkers, but that it means accepting when you make a mistake, apologizing for it, and working to avoid making the same mistake in the future. In his profession as a social justice helper, Wise first holds himself accountable to the needs and concerns raised by the population that he works with and then holds himself accountable by making those needs and concerns not only known but also clearly laid out to those that can assist in alleviating them.

In recent years, there has been some theoretical and empirical literature exploring the values of **accountability** and **commitment** among students and professionals engaging in social justice and community work. In one study, researchers found that community-based counseling psychologists were able to work and advocate for social justice goals because of their work with marginalized groups of people. Accountability and commitment relates to the social-cognitive career theory (Miller & Sendrowitz, 2009) that indicates individuals' self-efficacy beliefs and outcome expectations influence their career interests and goals (i.e., long-term involvement). Miller and Sendrowitz describe the "nonlinear developmental model of social justice engagement," in which one:

1. has contact with the reality of oppression,
2. becomes increasingly aware of social injustice,
3. develops a sense of efficacy,
4. begins to understand their own role in relation to creating change,
5. gains a greater understanding of the sociopolitical context of social injustice, and finally
6. engages in social justice.

The domain-specific social justice self-efficacy beliefs facilitate both direct and indirect effects on students' development of social justice. Social justice commitment is also determined, to an extent, by proximal social justice supports and by barriers to social justice. For example, the higher levels of social supports (i.e., value of interests, groups and individuals with similar missions, etc.), and lower social barriers (i.e., hostile environments, a community's lack of willingness to understand or learn) will result in a higher likelihood of an individual committing to future social justice efforts. Lastly, these social supports and barriers might also demonstrate an indirect effect on social justice commitment by either increasing or decreasing an individual's feeling of self-efficacy (Miller & Sendrowitz, 2009). Additionally, self-efficacy had an indirect effect through outcome expectations on social justice interest. In other words, the higher an individual's social justice related sense of self-efficacy, the more positive their outcome expectations (specific to social justice–related activities), the higher the likelihood to commit to prolonged interest in social justice–specific activities. Social justice supports also tend to increase one's commitment to social justice. So engaging in social justice work increases your commitment to social justice work.

Our educational training programs need to examine these areas in depth to facilitate the process of engaging in social justice for our trainees. The role of mentoring and opportunities for community empowerment projects are crucial to foster social justice framework in training programs for helpers (Harkins et al., 2020; Robinson & Harkins, 2018). O'Brien, Townsend, and Ebden (2010) suggest that "young adults may benefit from intentional and structured mechanisms including informal community service or more formal service-learning experiences such as a social issues course." These experiences would likely facilitate the introduction and consequential development of social justice self-efficacy beliefs and increase positive outcome expectations. Similarly, establishing a mentor program that may, for example, allow younger or less experienced students to learn from older or more experienced students (i.e., graduate students and professor-student relationships) might help to increase college student's self-efficacy by way of vicarious learning, performance accomplishments, and social persuasion (cf. Bandura, 1986). Ultimately, these mentoring relationships have the potential to facilitate college students' commitment to advocacy on campus and in the community (see Chapter 8 on mentoring).

Moreover, social justice–specific career-oriented guidance for new trainees will strengthen their professional interests as well as a commitment to social justice. Finally, assisting college students and young adults in the community in identifying and building social support systems might foster and bolster social justice interest and commitment. For example, in person or online, social justice advocacy groups might be an effective and efficient mechanism for facilitating social justice interest and commitment and for developing plausible strategies for dealing with social barriers to advocacy. Connections with social justice advocacy groups could provide a realistic model for accountability, commitment, and support for trainees. In addition, this will be an ideal structured platform to share information and resources regarding local, national, and international social justice advocacy actions. In essence, educators must invest time and efforts to cultivate interests and offer opportunities and guidance to integrate knowledge, values, and strategies to engage in ethical and intentionally collaborative services with community partners. This approach will foster inclusive mindsets for helpers, strengthen connection and sense of belongingness among community partners, and consequently promote health and well-being of our underserved communities. The following reflective questions could be useful to address the critical role of these attributes in your social justice service work.

**How can you as a helper be accountable for your actions without getting down on yourself so much that you feel afraid to help the populations that you serve?**

_____

_____

_____

_____

> The first author (SR) highlights the importance of acknowledgement of mistakes made by professionals to plan for their future steps towards corrective action by repairing ruptures in relationships in consultation with clients and coworkers. This insight will help us perceive our mistakes as a learning experience rather than a complete failure.

Think of a story you have heard in which someone in your current or future profession was not held rightfully accountable for mistakes they made that harmed others. **In what ways were they not held accountable, and how, in your opinion, should they have been held accountable?** In your everyday professional actions, do you hold yourself to the same standards of accountability to which you hold the person in that story?

_____

_____

_____

_____

_____

> The first author (SR) shares a story in which a helping professional's negligence led to a client who was unable to access resources needed for that time period. As a result, the supervisor terminated that professional's service. This decision by the supervisor reflected the organization's commitment towards maintaining higher standards of professional ethics, accountability, and service across all employees irrespective of their position.

Consistent reflection upon both professional and personal structures of accountability can help you individually as well as the organization that you will or do work for. The following reflection questions help explore alignment between personal and organizational values.

**How do I/my organization prioritize the needs and/or concerns of the people with whom I/we work? How do we hold ourselves accountable?**

_____

_____

_____

Are there additional ways outside of the code of conduct for your profession in which you personally hold yourself accountable for your actions?

_____

_____

_____

Both the first (SR) and third author (SK) emphasize the need to inquire about clients' needs and concerns during initial appointments. Moreover, during follow-up meetings with clients, we must explore the nature of changes to their needs and concerns to offer adequate support to them according to their priorities. This will also encourage and empower clients to expect accountability of professionals working with them.

## References

Adams, K., Hean, S., Sturgis, P., & Clark, J. M. (2006). Investigating the factors influencing professional identity of first-year health and social care students. *Learning in Health and Social Care.* https://doi.org/10.1111/j.1473-6861.2006.00119.x

Bandura, A., (1986). *Prentice-Hall series in social learning theory: Social foundations of thought and action: A social cognitive theory.* Prentice-Hall, Inc.

Betancourt, J. R., Corbett, J., & Bondaryk, M. R. (2014). Addressing disparities and achieving equity: Cultural competence, ethics, and health-care transformation. *Medical Ethics, 145,* 143–148. https://doi.org/10.1378/chest.13-0634

Bisman, C. (2004). Social work values: The moral core of the profession. *The British Journal of Social Work, 34*(1), 109–123. https://doi.org/10.1093/bjsw/bch008

Crenshaw, K. (1989). Demarginalizing the intersection of race and sex: A Black feminist critique of antidiscrimination doctrine, feminist theory and antiracist politics. *University of Chicago Legal Forum, 1989,* 139–167. http://chicagounbound.uchicago.edu/uclf

Croteau, J. M., Talbot, D. M., Lance, T. S., & Evans, N. J. (2002). A qualitative study of the interplay between privilege and oppression. *Journal of Multicultural Counseling and Development, 30*(4), 239–258. https://doi.org/10.1002/j.2161-1912.2002.tb00522.x

Fagermoen, M. S. (1997). Professional identity: Values embedded in meaningful nursing practice. *Journal of Applied Nursing.* https://doi.org/10.1046/j.1365-2648.1997.1997025434.x

Giannaki, A. F. (2016). The role of 'privileged' allies in the struggle for social justice. *Humanity in Action.* John Lewis Fellowship. www.humanityinaction.org/knowledge_detail/jlf-16-the-role-of-privileged-allies-in-the-struggle-for-social-justice/

Graber, D. R., & Kilpatrick, A. O. (2008). Establishing values-based leadership and value systems in healthcare organizations. *Journal of Health and Human Service Administration, 31*(2), 179–197.

Harkins, D. A., Grenier, L. I., Irizarry, C., Robinson, E., Ray, S., & Shea, L. M. (2020). Building relationships for critical service-learning. *Michigan Journal of Community Service Learning, 26*(2), 1–17. https://doi.org/10.3998/mjcsloa.3239521.0026.202

Hemingway, C. A., & Maclagan, P. W. (2004). Managers' personal values as drivers of corporate social responsibility. *Journal of Business Ethics, 50,* 33–44. https://doi.org/10.1023/B:BUSI.0000020964.80208.c9

Kendi, I. X. (2019). The greatest white privilege is life itself. *The Atlantic.* www.theatlantic.com/ideas/archive/2019/10/too-short-lives-black-men/600628

Mackay, T., & Zufferey, C. (2015). A who doing a what?: Identity, practice and social work education. *Journal of Social Work, 15*(6), 644–661.

Maina, I. W., Belton, T. D., Ginzberg, S., Singh, A., & Johnson, T. J. (2018). A decade of studying implicit racial/ethnic bias in healthcare providers using the implicit association test. *Social Science Medicine, 199,* 219–229. doi: 10.1016/j.socscimed.2017.05.009

Miller, M. J., & Sendrowitz, K. (2009). Counseling psychology trainees' social justice interest and commitment. *Journal Counseling Psychology, 58*(2), 159–169. doi: 10.1037/a0022663

Morrison, I. (2008). *The future of the healthcare marketplace: What's next?* http://www.coloradonursingcenter.org/wp-content/uploads/2019/06/Plenary-Morrison-Ian-Future-of-Healthcare-Marketplace-Whats-Next.pdf

Nixon, S. A. (2019). The coin model of privilege and critical allyship: Implications for health. *BMC Public Health, 19*(1). https://doi.org/10.1186/S12889-019-7884-9

O'Brien, L., Townsend, M., & Ebden, M. (2010). 'Doing something positive': Volunteers' experiences of the well-being benefits derived from practical conservation activities in nature. *Voluntas: International Journal of Voluntary and Nonprofit Organizations, 21*(4), 525–545. www.jstor.org/stable/27928238 (accessed January 3, 2021).

Patel, V. S. (2011). Moving toward an inclusive model of allyship for racial justice. *The Vermont Connection, 32.* https://scholarworks.uvm.edu/tvc/vol32/iss1/9

Robinson, E., & Harkins, D. A. (2018). Lessons learned from faculty service-learning mentoring. *Journal of Community Engagement and Higher Education, 10*(9).

Rokeach, M. (1973). *The nature of human values.* Free Press.

Schwartz, S. H. (1999). Are there universal aspects in the structure and contents of human values? *Journal of Social Issues, 50*(4), 19–45. https://doi.org/10.1111/j.1540-4560.1994.tb01196.x

Skitka, L. J., & Mullen, E. (2002). Understanding judgments of fairness in a real-world political context: A test of the value protection model of justice reasoning. *Personality and Social Psychology Bulletin, 28,* 1419–1429. https://doi.org/10.1177/014616702236873

Spinelli, R. J. (2006). The applicability of Bass's Model of transformational, transactional, and laissez-faire leadership in the hospital administrative environment. *Hospital Topics, 84*(2), 11–18.

Van Herk, K. A., Smith, D., & Andrew, C. (2010). Examining our privileges and oppressions: Incorporating an intersectionality paradigm into nursing. *Nursing Inquiry, 18*(1), 29–39. doi: 10.1111/j.1440-1800.2011.00539.x

Wise, T. J. (2005). *White like me.* Soft Skull Press.

Wise, T. J. (2010). *Appreciation and accountability.* Nashville, Tennessee: Timwise. Timwise.org. http://www.timwise.org/appreciation-and-accountability/

Zotzmann, Y., Van der Linden, D., & Wrywa, K. (2019). The relation between country differences, cultural values, personality dimensions, and error orientation: An approach across three continents: Asia, Europe, and North America. *Safety Science, 120,* 185–193.

# 4 Theorizing on Social Justice and Power

*Kathryn J. Kozak*

## Reflexivity and Theory

Most books that you read as part of a course will start out broad and narrow down to more specific topics, or will start by introducing major theories and then dive into concepts. For example, you might have read a psychology textbook that starts with a section on the major psychologists and their theories, learning about William James and Sigmund Freud and Carl Jung before you explore concepts like personality, intelligence, and attachment. You may have noticed that in this section of the book, we started quite broad in Chapter 1 by offering a survey of concepts, history, and theory to explain why we look beyond individual helping models. We narrowed back down to discuss identity and values, but now we're going to offer a review of theory to help make connections between the broad and the narrow before you get to the roadmaps for action in Parts 2 and 3 of this book.

We didn't start out with theory for two reasons: First, because this book's goal is to help you build an understanding of social justice in the context of helping. If you sit down with someone to explain why they should care about others, it might not work too well if you start by describing Paolo Freire's *Pedagogy of the Oppressed* or trying to explain Isaac Prilleltensky's theoretical model of praxis. Instead, we want to use the same structure that you might use: starting by looking inward, at how your own identity and values shape your experiences, and then building up to the more complex models of understanding justice.

Second, we take a *reflexive* approach to understanding theory in order to use theory more accurately and relevantly. **Reflexivity** refers to the practice of reflecting on your own values, goals, and attitudes, and then using this reflection to inform behavior. That is, thinking about things informs what we do. Theory doesn't exist in a vacuum. Instead, we interact with the concepts and context, and make judgments and decisions based on our evaluations. Just as we interact with concepts and contexts to make judgments and decisions, so were these theories created as the theorists, activists, and scholars who developed them processed their own context and understanding of the world. This is similar to some of the strategies introduced in Chapter 2,

DOI: 10.4324/9781003055587-4

where we explore how to use the concept of social identity to better understand our own positionality as helpers, mentors, or helper-educators.

**Reflect:** Have you ever reflected on your own values and beliefs? What did it look like? Why did you do this? Did you learn anything about yourself?

_____

_____

_____

So, what is theory? **Theory**, generally speaking, refers to a set of ideas or beliefs used to explain something. Importantly, the precise definition and usage of "theory" depends on the context, academic discipline, and specific use case.

For example, in the context of research using the scientific method, theory refers specifically to an explanation about the natural world that can be repeatedly tested. In casual conversation, theory usually refers to a hunch or assumption. And in other academic research, theory refers to attempts to explain or understand a particular phenomenon (and isn't quite as strict or specific a concept as a "theory" within the scientific method) (see Table 4.1).

These distinctions can help address confusion about whether your ideas are "legitimate," because many discussions about theory in the social sciences try to fit inside the box of the scientific method. However, it's helpful—and often critically important—to have a **theoretical framework** when considering goals, drafting visions or missions for an organization, and creating a curriculum or syllabus for students, volunteers, or employees. A **theoretical framework** is a set of concepts and arguments about a particular topic or domain. Choosing and working within a theoretical framework allows you to clearly organize and communicate your arguments, goals, and concepts.

There are a number of foundational theories and frameworks for understanding power, justice, and liberation. Understanding these theories and

*Table 4.1* Contextual Uses of Theory

| Context | Definition | Example |
|---------|-----------|---------|
| Scientific method | A set of observations or facts that can be repeated or tested that support an explanation about the natural world | The *theory of evolution* is a set of testable hypotheses and observations about how genetic information is passed to offspring among living things. |
| Casual conversation | A hunch or assumption about something | You might have a *theory* about why some coworkers feel comfortable speaking in meetings while others do not. |
| Academic research | An analytical tool, lens, or perspective for explaining or understanding a particular phenomenon | *Critical theory* looks beyond individual factors to explore the role of society and culture in social problems. |

feeling comfortable discussing or teaching about related concepts allows us to challenge our own assumptions; develop more meaningful goals and projects; and bring others on board with us as we work towards common visions of a more just world. It's helpful to know how to understand and process theory in general, because it helps us digest and communicate complicated ideas about how the world works. In the realm of social justice–informed helping, using theory is important for understanding why the world is unjust, how we can address this injustice, and what a more just or liberated world might look like.

Researchers almost always have a theoretical framework in mind based on their training, discipline, and personal philosophy towards their work. But theoretical frameworks can be useful and informative in applied work as well. They help us align our goals and values with clearly defined concepts, provide a roadmap for how to achieve those goals or work towards those values, and allow us to communicate our work with others while understanding the work that others are doing.

For example, a community organization might use Bronfenbrenner's bio-ecological systems theory to inform their family offerings. Bronfenbrenner's theory, developed by psychologist Urie Bronfenbrenner in the 1970s and updated until his death in the early 2000s, generally argues that human development occurs as a series of interactions between the individual and their context (Tudge et al., 2016). This theory provides concepts such as **microsystem, mesosystem**, and **macrosystem** and also offers an explanation as to how a person's broader culture and more immediate context (like family or school) influence wellbeing.

Rather than just being academic jargon, those concepts can help an organization focused on child literacy identify challenges within their community; evaluate appropriate services to develop and offer; apply for relevant grants, funding, and research support; and communicate their approach towards improving literacy outcomes. The organization might train their volunteers about how **microsystems** such as family or school affect a child's relationship to books and language. In the same training, they might explain how the macrosystem, or cultural context, might influence the messages that children hear about reading, literacy, and school. By learning about the relationships between these systems, volunteers may be better suited to understand the organization's approach to literacy. They might also be more aware of potential strengths of or challenges faced by the children and parents with whom they work.

In another example, school-teachers often think carefully about their approach to education. When learning how to be teachers, they read about philosophies of education and study **pedagogy**, or the study of teaching and learning. When my sister, an elementary school teacher, put together her teaching portfolio, she included her own mission statement of what she believes about children and education. But she also included key quotes and concepts from relevant prominent theorists including Russian psychologist

Lev Vygotsky and French developmental psychologist Jean Piaget. By including references to these theoretical frameworks, her portfolio demonstrates a few things:

- That she has learned about key theories and figures in education
- That she has given thought to the kind of teacher she wants to be
- That her approach to teaching aligns with particular best practices in education

**Reflect:** Where in your life might it be helpful to use a theoretical framework? Do you have a theory or similar framework for making sense of your work? How did you find it? How might a theoretical framework help you in your work?

_____

_____

_____

## Theories for Social Justice

There are many theories and models that provide useful concepts, frameworks, and tools for understanding and working towards social justice. Disciplines and fields like critical race studies, gender studies, community psychology, sociology, anthropology, and education have produced a lot of academic work deconstructing, dissecting, and analyzing the historical, political, and social structures or patterns that create an unequal society.

It's important to note that some strains of thought have emerged because of structural barriers and oppression in other fields. For example, as we discussed in Chapter 2, Black woman thinkers and feminists pioneered concepts like intersectionality and made crucial contributions to our understanding of power and identity, but these theories are often considered separate from "mainstream" frameworks. Queer theory emerged to account for the role of queerness, LGBTQ+ experiences, and minority sexual and gender identities in power structures. Oftentimes, if a concept or explanation emerges within a mainstream academic discipline, odds are that this concept was introduced decades earlier by someone who was systematically excluded from that field due to racism, classism, or other bias. Intersectionality (see Chapter 2) is a key example—while many white feminists may think the idea of intersectionality emerged in the 1990s and became popular in the 2000s, it can actually be traced all the way back to ideas shared by Sojourner Truth in the mid-1800s (Brah & Phoenix, 2004).

We should also note that when we talk about power, this often also requires talking about politics and political power. That's because **politics** isn't just about government, but refers more broadly to the activities and relational power dynamics involved in group decision-making. When we talk about political power, we don't just mean who's in an elected governmental position. We are also referring to who in a society or community gets to decide how to allocate resources, or how people in that society should be treated.

Think about climate justice and environmentalism. We might think of this issue as "apolitical," because it affects everyone regardless of their political views or opinions. But in reality, it's a hugely political issue—how did the land become contaminated or polluted? Which people or neighborhoods are protected from pollution, and which (e.g., Flint, Michigan) are vulnerable without any significant consequences to the polluters? Who has the power to create regulations that protect the environment, and who has used their power to avoid or dismantle these regulations? In these ways, you may begin to see how almost every aspect of our lives is, in fact, political. And from there, we can start to see how volunteer work or activism that focuses on alleviating *outcomes*, like pollution, might not go as deep as work that gets at *root causes*, which often requires dismantling systems of oppression.

This section reviews a few foundational theories and concepts that explain or explore social and political power. The goal is to introduce a few of the "major players" used to frame research and practice related to social and political power; explore accessible ways of discussing theory; and provide a roadmap for using common or useful theoretical concepts in your own work. I'll also note that this is not comprehensive—these are a handful of theorists, philosophers, and thinkers that are often cited in conversations around social justice, or whose writings and teachings have informed current approaches to justice and liberation.

And because this chapter is *reflexive*, I'll include a few of my own thoughts and reflections about why I'm grounding our discussion in these particular traditions, philosophers, and discourses. It is important to recognize that as a white person, my exposure to and cultural understanding of philosophy is very much rooted in a white, US American system of values and traditions. Think about how your family, education, socioeconomic status or class, racial and ethnic identity, and community have influenced the ideas to which you have been exposed. I grew up in a mostly white, middle-class suburb of Boston to fairly liberal parents. There were many opportunities to learn about and critically explore issues of gender, sexuality, race, and power. At the same time, the perspectives of people teaching and discussing these issues were limited by their own privileges of race, class, and education.

## Class Struggles | Marxism

You've probably heard of Karl Marx, the infamous father of communism whose manifesto laid out key concepts and ideas that revolutionized (literally) the way we think about power and class. Marx was a 19th-century philosopher, political theorist, and economist born in the Kingdom of Prussia (now Germany) who believed that through revolution, capitalism would give way to socialism as the dominant system of social relations. I first learned about Marx during a high school history class, where we had to memorize terms like "proletariat" and "means of production" in the context of the Industrial Revolution of the 19th century. Marx came up for me again in college and graduate school as I learned more about theories of power, and I actually printed out and read the Manifesto of the Communist Party while working on a research project related to feminist identity. If that seems random or weird to you, read on—the connection might make more sense later on in this chapter!

It is almost impossible to find a contemporary framework for understanding social justice that doesn't in some way relate to Marx or Marxism—either because the framework uses Marxist concepts, or because the framework specifically diverges from a Marxist framework in some way. In this section, we'll give a general overview of the Marxist basics to remind you which one is the proletariat and which one is the bourgeoisie. We'll identify some places where Marx's ideas and Marxism more broadly have been integrated into other strains of thought, and explore why it's such a commonly used framework for understanding power. And finally we'll introduce some Marxist thought that demonstrates why you need to use an intersectional approach that incorporates race, gender, and other identities to understand class struggle.

The Manifesto of the Communist Party was published in February of 1848 by Karl Marx and his collaborator, German socialist thinker and writer Frederick Engels. Marx and Engels were writing and organizing during a period of social upheaval as the abhorrent conditions of the European working class under capitalism were coming to light. Marx and Engels contributed to numerous books, papers, and other writings, including the Manifesto. The whole thing including prefaces and endnotes is only about 70 printed pages long, and is available for free download through the Marxists Internet Archive (Marx & Engels, 1967). This document outlines some key concepts and history in order to build an understanding among the proletariat, rather than offering a comprehensive theoretical framework.

Now, if you're having a strong reaction to the words "communist," "socialist," or "Marxist" and are worried about authoritarianism or fascism, this is a good time to unpack some of our assumptions and major narratives.

**Reflect:** What is your initial response to the topics of Marxism and socialism? What do you know about Marxism and the Communist Manifesto?

_____

_____

_____


Where did you first hear the terms "communism" and "socialism"? How were these terms framed when you learned about them?

_____

_____

_____

Let's take a look at what Marx and Engels actually wrote about and believed.

In the preface to the 1883 German edition, following Marx's death, Engels writes:

> The basic thought running through the Manifesto—that economic production, and the structure of society of every historical epoch necessarily arising therefrom, constitute the foundation for the political and intellectual history of that epoch; that consequently (ever since the dissolution of the primaeval communal ownership of land) all history has been a history of class struggles, of struggles between exploited and exploiting, between dominated and dominating classes at various stages of social evolution; that this struggle, however, has now reached a stage where the exploited and oppressed class (the proletariat) can no longer emancipate itself from the class which exploits and oppresses it (the bourgeoisie), without at the same time forever freeing the whole of society from exploitation, oppression, class struggles—this basic thought belongs solely and exclusively to Marx.

So . . . what does this mean?

According to Marx (Marx & Engels, 1967), we can understand history as a series of **class struggles** or fights between groups with different types and amounts of power. He explains that society is always rearranged based on social ranks, and that the contemporary social rank consisted of just two major classes: the **bourgeoisie**, who control the means of production, and the **proletariat**, or the laboring class. Marx and Engels clarify that the **bourgeoisie** is the class of modern capitalists who employ wage laborers, and the **proletariat** is the class of people who must sell their labor to survive. The Manifesto is written to try and help members of the proletariat understand the ways in which the bourgeoisie controls society through control of capital.

When Engels talks about the way in which economic production *constitute[s] the foundation for the political and intellectual history of that epoch*, he's referring to the ways in which our historical and political reality is shaped by capitalism. There are lots of things people in the United States might take for granted because they grew up within a capitalist society.

---

For example, you might think about how it feels "normal" for one person to work three jobs and barely make ends meet, while at the same time the CEO of one of their workplaces makes millions of dollars a year. Or how it feels "normal" that:

- If someone loses their job, they also lose their health insurance and coverage.

- A freelancer, whose invoice wasn't paid so they don't have any money in the bank, gets evicted from their apartment because they weren't able to pay rent.
- A shift-worker without a salaried position can only take time off for illness or emergencies *if* they can find someone to cover their shift.

If you aren't from the United States, or if you have been part of a different type of social system, these examples may seem confusing or counterintuitive! What might these scenarios look like under a different system?

Given this, Marx argues, the goal of communism is to overturn the system by which workers live only to work, and where one's welfare and livelihood depends on those who employ them or want their goods or services. The goal is to get rid of this class struggle by ensuring that the means of production is owned by society as a whole, not a subset of people who benefit while others are exploited. These concepts and central tenets provide a powerful way for understanding why a capitalist system cannot facilitate social justice.

To summarize, Marx's basic argument was that capitalism has created a society of two major classes: one that owns and benefits from all the resources and property, and one that must work to survive and has no claim to resources or property. Society will be unequal until the workers unite to overthrow the ruling class, and a more just society is one in which all people have access to all property.

You might not like to think about it, but you don't have to be a "one-percenter" to be part of the bourgeoisie. If you own a business that employs other people; if you rely on passive income from investment property; or if you have access to a trust fund or inherited wealth to maintain your livelihood, you may not be a proletarian. Our society relies on a system by which people have to "sell" their labor to survive. This includes the people who have to work white-collar 9-to-5 jobs in order to afford food, a house, and healthcare. It also includes people working multiple minimum-wage jobs, migrant workers, and people working "under the table." At the same time, you may have access to particular resources or privileges, but your trust fund or rental property may not allow you to live indefinitely without selling your labor. Marxism has grown and adapted to changing social contexts, and has been heavily critiqued and revised to fit contemporary social conditions.

Decades (and over a century later), Marx's ideas still resonate with activists and theorists trying to understand and fight against our current power structures. For example, materialist feminism emerged in the 1970s as feminist critiques explored the ways in which previous models of Marxism failed to account for the role of gender and sexual divisions of labor. Rosemary Hennessy's *Materialist Feminism and the Politics of Discourse* explores how different theories about and approaches to Marxism and feminism have emerged from and relate to different ways of understanding social categories like gender and society (Hennessy, 2012).

One major critique of many iterations of Marxist theory is its neglect of race and gender and inability to neatly account for systems of white supremacy and patriarchy (Bohrer, 2018). Indeed, some folks use Marxism to argue that classism is the only manifestation of oppression we need to focus on. However, this ignores many valid critiques that seek to update Marxism or modify its arguments to better account for racism, sexism, and other forms of oppression. Instead of trying to boil down oppression to class struggle, effective contemporary frameworks use Marxism as a foundation for understanding the many interlocking forms of oppression that exist in our world.

Walter Rodney, a Guyanese historian and activist who was assassinated in 1980, also used Marxism in *How Europe Underdeveloped Africa* to build the argument that "developed" countries exist in relation to "underdeveloped" countries whose resources or people have been exploited (Rodney, 2006). Rodney extends Marx's arguments about the historical, political, and economic shifts of social relations to explain how and why Europe systematically exploited African cultures, contributing to a significant gap in "development" at the time of writing in the 1970s. Without interrogating and deconstructing this power dynamic, generations of (particularly white) US Americans have attempted to "fix" or "save" people in countries that have been systematically exploited by the United States and European countries. Chapter 3 discusses this "saviorism" in more detail, because it often presents an obstacle to effective helping work when we fail to clarify the values that lead us to want to help. Even today, organizations such as the Gates Foundation attempt to intervene in African communities without acknowledging the ways in which exploitation of people and resources has contributed to US American economic development and success (Birn, 2014).

As the world changes, and the role of capitalism changes, theorists and scholars continue to update and challenge Marxist theory or find new ways of fitting Marx's writings into contemporary contexts. Marxism as it currently exists has evolved and diverged from the original writings of Marx and Engels. Thus while we can learn a lot from the Communist Manifesto— and acknowledge that there is a lot about it that is still relevant today—it is also important to look to the ways in which Marxism has been critiqued and expanded. A few key examples can be found in this chapter's resources section.

## Power | Foucault

In some academic circles, it's tough to have a conversation about power or discourse without bringing up Michel Foucault. Foucault was a French philosopher in the 20th century whose work made connections between power, knowledge, and social structures. He had a particular focus on sexuality, and provided key concepts and ideas that laid the groundwork for gender studies and other analyses of power in the 20th and 21st centuries. Foucault's understanding of power differs significantly from that of Marx, and offers another perspective for considering oppression.

According to Foucault, power is "the name that one attributes to a complex strategic situation in a particular society" (Foucault, History of Sexuality, 1990). In other words, power isn't a *thing* you can have but an *arrangement* of society or a way in which society is structured. This has important implications for research, activism, and practice that focuses on redistributing power or dismantling systems of inequity and injustice.

Some key concepts from Foucault that can help us make sense of power in society:

- **Discourse** is the system of thought, assumption, and messages in culture that makes up how we determine what makes sense in society. Discourse, or the sharing of messages and thought, is one of the primary ways in which societies control themselves.
- **Normalizing judgment** refers to the system of values and norms by which people monitor and police each other, and is one of the primary control techniques that Foucault proposes and describes.
- The **repressive hypothesis** is the idea that Western, post-Victorian societies silence sexuality in order to regulate reproduction for capitalist purposes.

Foucault's overarching arguments build a model in which societies police or control themselves through judgments, norms, observation, and repression. According to Foucault, part of this process also includes a process of *medicalization* or *pathologizing* through which society began to assign medical diagnoses or pathological value to human behavior. That is, before the 19th century, it was not necessarily considered a medical problem to have beliefs, attitudes, or behaviors that didn't "fit in" with society. But around the 19th century, doctors and philosophers began describing issues of sexuality and power within medical terms. This is how we arrived at a system in which things like depression, gender dysphoria, and hygiene are understood on an individual level in relation to medical problems or illness, rather than as conditions related to social structure.

This can be seen through approaches to social justice that start with deconstructing pathologization of experiences of inequality and injustice. That is, we need to stop considering experiences of oppression as an individual person's medical problems. Experiencing racial trauma isn't a *medical* problem (though we recognize that racial trauma can cause or manifest in biological, physiological, and psychological symptoms and syndromes), but rather a result of living in a community, society, or nation that encourages racism and violence. Depression and anxiety aren't always *medical* problems resulting solely from biological dysfunction on an individual level (though we do not discount the role of biochemistry and physiology!), but rather the product of interactions between individual factors and the expectations or pressures of a capitalist society.

When people are talking about power through a *Foucauldian* lens, they are often tracing the relationships between what is known in a society, what is valued in a society, and the structures in that society for maintaining control.

## Psychopolitical Validity | Prilleltensky

The work of Isaac Prilleltensky builds a helpful and widely used framework for recognizing and deconstructing the role of power in the field of psychology. Prilleltensky, a community psychologist and humor writer born in Argentina and currently serving as Associate Provost at the University of Miami, explores the ways in which power influences the work of psychologists, pointing out that psychology is never neutral even when psychologists attempt to set aside bias or engage in "apolitical" or "nonpolitical" work. Because we are using power when we engage in research and practice, and because the findings of our research are applied for political purposes, psychology is thus political. At the same time, Prilleltensky argues, psychologists can engage in work that pursues wellness and liberation.

Prilleltensky offers a valuable framework for understanding *wellness* that can inform successful social justice work—*Academics 4 Black Survival and Wellness* uses Prilleltensky's levels of wellness to illustrate how specific instances of anti-Black racism prevent wellness for individuals and communities. According to Prilleltensky, **wellness** is a state of being in which three types of needs are achieved at the same time: personal needs, such as health and opportunities for growth; collective needs like healthcare and economic equality; and relational needs, which are satisfied when we have healthy relationships between people and groups (Prilleltensky, 2008).

Prilleltensky calls for us to make space in our work to pursue the balance between individual, collective, and relational needs. He introduces the concept of **psychopolitical validity** as a tool for understanding how power impacts wellness, oppression, and liberation at these three levels. Psychopolitical validity as outlined in his 2008 paper exists in two forms: Epistemic validity requires systematically understanding and accounting for how power affects levels of wellness in your work. Transformational validity, on the other hand, is when we act on inequalities in order to address wellness. So the first arises when we are understanding and accounting for the role of power, and the second when we are actually acting on it.

If this sounds a little familiar, that might be because this framework builds from Paulo Freire's concept of **critical consciousness**, or "conscientization." Freire was a Brazilian educator and philosopher concerned with the ways in which oppression is maintained through restricting education, and his 1968 book *Pedagogy of the Oppressed* is an oft-cited contribution to critical pedagogy (which you will learn more about in Chapter 5). When people have access to education, Freire explains, they are able to learn about themselves, their conditions, and the power systems that maintain those conditions. Freire argued that political change and empowerment comes through **critical consciousness**, or an awareness of the role of power and oppression in one's life in order to begin to change one's conditions (Freire, 1972). Once a person or community has the tools to understand their oppression, they can begin to fight it. This concept underlies Prilleltensky's psychopolitical validity—as practitioners or helpers, our work must account for the role of power and then go the step further to undo the harm caused by power inequalities and injustice.

## Connecting Theory to Practice

As you may have noticed, these theories don't exist in a vacuum. They were created by educators, activists, and scholars attempting to make sense of their lived experiences. It is important to use theories and concepts not only to better understand the world around us, but also to inform the action we choose to take towards making the world a better place.

## Case Example: Movements to Abolish the Police in the United States

In March of 2020, at the beginning of lockdowns related to COVID-19 in the United States, a young Black woman named Breonna Taylor was murdered in her bed by police executing a search warrant completely unrelated to Breonna or the boyfriend she lived with. In late May, a Black man named George Floyd was murdered by police in Minneapolis who claimed he had attempted to use a counterfeit 20-dollar bill (Altman, 2020; Murphy, 2020). Protests erupted around the world by early June (with some continuing on at the writing of this book in November), with renewed public attention to the role of police brutality and the violent history of policing in the United States. In particular, a new collective understanding (among white people) emerged, with many white Americans finally beginning to see how these attempts to maintain social order are connected to patrols developed to intercept slaves.

In my own experience, I went from seeing policing as something revered and respected without question in the predominantly white social media circles of my hometown to something to be rightly criticized, condemned, and even "defunded." Calls to "Defund the Police" circulated widely among the US American public, pointing not only to the extreme incidences of racial violence by police, but also to the failures of policing to address social challenges like homelessness and mental illness that require public support.

The idea, then, has been to reallocate resources to other offices and personnel who can better address these concerns.

In some cases, these movements have been connected with the Black Lives Matter movement; in other cases, I see white folks in my network considering this to be something "separate." Without a broader understanding of how systems of power contribute to systems of oppression, it may feel to some like the history of anti-Black racism in the United States can and should be disentangled from current police brutality (Waxman, 2017). In context, however, it becomes clear that contemporary manifestations of police violence and experiences of anti-Black racism are both related to broader systems of oppression and dehumanization.

Mariame Kaba (2020) writes about the ways in which police and policing are deeply entrenched within our cultural and social understandings of safety and society. Instead of asking why police continue to murder Black people and others in the United States, Kaba argues that we should begin asking what we need to do to stop police from murdering Black people and others with impunity.

With much of the United States facing a reckoning with a long, violent history of police brutality, the work of activist and scholar Angela Davis has become more common in conversations about reform (typically in the form of defunding police budgets and departments) versus an abolitionist approach of dismantling systems of policing altogether. Davis wrote *Are Prisons Obsolete* in 2003, a book which interrogates the role of prisons in society. The book ultimately argues that we need to re-examine our definition of crime, as well as our treatment of the social structures that give rise to inequality and disparity that we attempt to address or ignore through imprisonment. Defunding police departments, then, may only address small parts of a much larger problem without acknowledging the history of mass incarceration in the United States.

#8toAbolition provides a concrete roadmap for moving towards a world where we can all be safe. Rather than an organization, #8toAbolition is an abolitionist platform with resources for educating others and transforming the system. The resources and infographics on their website can be a helpful first step for imagining a world with no prisons, no police, and therefore no police murders.

Using this model of abolition, those of us who are white can try to understand the perspective of Black US Americans and other people of color fighting for their safety and survival. We might consider whether defunding police departments goes far enough to challenge the prison-industrial complex. We can explore interviews with Angela Davis or read her book and recommend it to people in our lives so that they, too, can build a deeper understanding of the prison abolition movement and how it intersects with current experiences of oppression. We can read books like *The New Jim Crow* by Michelle Alexander (2012), and critically reflect on how racial supremacy can be found within our legal, educational, economic, and healthcare infrastructure in the United States. We can dig even deeper and find other activists and theorists connected to prison abolition, and see how we can support their efforts towards liberation and justice. The best way to gain an understanding if this issue has not directly touched your life might be to get involved in an abolitionist project that challenges the prison-industrial complex, or to volunteer for organizations that directly support incarcerated people and their families.

## Figuring It Out for Yourself

There are no clear answers about the "right" framework or approach to take in your own pursuit of social justice and liberation. Scholars, activists, and people who just really like reading will get in heated debates about the "right" approach to class analysis, or exactly how to incorporate inter-sectionality into an emerging theory of power. The important part lies in using your own experiences and values, your critical thinking skills, and an openness to hearing about and considering the experiences of the people you want to help.

Not everyone has access to a gender studies class or a critical theory seminar, which is okay—because academic study is only one path to under-standing theories of power and social justice. Don't feel shy about asking your supervisors, professors, managers, site leaders, or friends about their approach to social justice. Is there a particular framework, tradition, or the-ory they use to inform their work? What are their goals—what is their vision of justice or liberation, and how do they hope to get there?

It's also helpful to recognize that different people conceptualize the "end goal" or future of social justice movements in different ways. Shawn Gin-wright has a brief video in which he explains the difference between equal-ity, equity, and liberation—and then points out that oppression poses a threat to our imagination, and makes it difficult to think about what "comes next" after liberation. Instead of considering ways of deeper or freer participation in society, Ginwright narrates, what would our goals look like if we were striving for joy, love, or flourishing? Ginwright has also written extensively on social justice and activism among African American youth, describing a framework of **radical healing** that facilitates a better understanding of what activism, political participation, and civic life looks like for Black youth in the United States (Ginwright, 2010a, 2010b).

Consider the manifestations of oppression in your own life and experi-ences, and the driving forces behind your decision to be a helper or pursue social justice. What are you working towards? Do you envision a more col-lective society, where the people, rather than a capitalist class or bourgeoisie, control goods and resources? Are you pursuing a community led by a strong, representative government designed to protect its most vulnerable? Is your work motivated by a desire to remove barriers to education and literacy for disenfranchised people so that they have the skills, knowledge, and capacity to take action and change their conditions? Each of these goals aligns with a different theory of power, framework of social justice, or model of liberation, and your work gets stronger when you can use the tools and concepts designed to reach the community or society you envision.

For myself, my work is steeped in Freire's critical pedagogy. My research has explored ways to help people engage in transformative civic and community work, to build the skills and knowledge and confidence to pursue social change. At the same time, knowing about Marx and Foucault and Davis and Rodney and a whole host of others has allowed me to critically examine my own conditions, my own goals, and my own approaches.

This foundation also helps me better understand what motivates and inspires others. My leftist-anarchist friends, who seek a society without government that is instead organized according to community need and support, have taught me about how dual power structures and mutual aid can be used to fight the forms of oppression which leave people vulnerable to food and housing insecurity as well as other forms of violence. My Marxist friends provide me with excellent memes as well as new ideas about how we can dismantle systems that perpetuate injustice based on race, gender, class, and other dimensions. And friends of mine who are scholars in critical studies help me to digest the rich and dense literature exploring how our perceptions of time, culture, and epistemology influence the way we understand and interact with the world.

Theory isn't just about stuffy old white men coming up with ideas, and it isn't just about academia. It's about finding new and innovative ways of understanding our world. It's about grounding our work in common ideas, concepts, and tools. It's about explaining the connections between phenomena and relationships between lived experiences. And now that you have some basic exposure to theories of power, I hope that you continue exploring for yourself what you understand and believe about power, oppression, justice, and liberation.

**Reflect:** What is your understanding of power and oppression? Where do you believe power comes from? What maintains oppression? What other information might help you with this understanding?

---------------------------------------------------

---------------------------------------------------

---------------------------------------------------

## References

Alexander, M. (2012). *The New Jim Crow: Mass incarceration in the age of color blindness*. The New Press.

Altman, A. (2020). Why the killing of George Floyd sparked an American uprising. *Time*. http://time.com/5847967/george-floyd-protests-trump/

Birn, A. E. (2014). Philanthrocapitalism, past and present: The Rockefeller Foundation, the Gates Foundation, and the setting(s) of the international/global health agenda. *Hypothesis*, *12*(1), 1–27. https://saludpublicayotrasdudas.files.wordpress.com/2015/04/birn_philantrocapitalism_2014.pdf

Bohrer, A. (2018). Intersectionality and Marxism: A critical historiography. *Historical Materialism*, *26*(2), 46–74. https://doi.org/10.1163/1569206X-00001617

Brah, A., & Phoenix, A. (2004). Ain't I a woman? Revisiting intersectionality. *Journal of International Women's Studies*, *5*(3), 75–86.

Foucault, M. (1990). *The history of sexuality: An introduction.* Vintage.

Freire, P. (1972). *Pedagogy of the oppressed.* Herder.

Ginwright, S. A. (2010a). *Radical healing with Dr. Shawn Ginwright.* [video file]. www.youtube.com/watch?v=TxbRQx_8TUA.

Ginwright, S. A. (2010b). Peace out to revolution! Activism among African American youth: An argument for radical healing. *Young*, *18*(1), 77–96. https://doi.org/10.1177/110330880901800106

Hennessy, R. (Ed.). (2012). *Materialist feminism and the politics of discourse (RLE feminist theory).* Routledge.

Kaba, M. (2020, September 25). *To stop police violence, we need better questions-and bigger demands.* https://gen.medium.com/to-stop-police-violence-we-need-better-questions-and-bigger-demands-23132fc38e8a

Marx, K., & Engels, F. (1967). *The communist manifesto (1848).* Samuel Moore (Trans.). Penguin.

Murphy, P. (2020). New video appears to show three police officers kneeling on George Floyd. *CNN.* www.cnn.com/2020/05/29/us/george-floyd-new-video-officers-kneel-trnd/index.html

Prilleltensky, I. (2008). The role of power in wellness, oppression, and liberation: The promise of psychopolitical validity. *Journal of Community Psychology*, *36*(2), 116–136.

Rodney, W. (2006). How Europe underdeveloped Africa. In P. Rothenberg (Ed.), *Beyond borders: Thinking critically about global issues* (pp. 107–126). Worth Publishers.

Tudge, J. R., Payir, A., Merçon-Vargas, E., Cao, H., Liang, Y., Li, J., & O'Brien, L. (2016). Still misused after all these years? A reevaluation of the uses of Bronfenbrenner's bioecological theory of human development. *Journal of Family Theory & Review*, *8*, 427–445. https://doi.org/10.1111/jftr.12165

Waxman, O. B. (2017, May 18). How the U.S. got its police force. *Time.* https://time.com/4779112/police-history-origins/.

## Resources and Suggested Readings

### Academics for Black Survival and Wellness (A4BL)

A4BL offers resources opportunities for non-Black academics working towards accountability and collective action, as well as space for healing and wellness for Black people. Launched in Summer of 2020, A4BL has provided training for over 10,000 participants from across the world. (academics4blacklives.com)

### #8toAbolition

#8toAbolition is an abolition resource based on a platform that recognizes the ways in which policing and prisons were designed to uphold oppression. Their website includes resources, readings, and demands. (8toabolition.com)

## *The New Jim Crow: Mass Incarceration in the Age of Colorblindness*

Written by Michelle Alexander, *The New Jim Crow* explores the ways in which mass incarceration perpetuates a system of racial control in the United States.

## Radical Healing With Dr. Shawn Ginwright

This five-minute YouTube video narrated by Dr. Shawn Ginwright explains equality, equity, and liberation, continuing on to explore what comes "next." (www.youtube.com/watch?v=TxbRQx_8TUA)

## Marxists Internet Archive

The Marxists Internet Archive includes a compilation of resources, readings, and references related to Marxism. Their "Beginners Guide to Marxism" offers an overview of Marxism with selected readings providing insight into Marx's philosophy and politics. (marxists.org)

# 5 Intervening to Support Empowerment

*Lynne-Marie Shea*

In this chapter, I use my own story to explore best-practice community interventions designed to prioritize the values and expertise of members of the communities the intervention intends to support. In working with a community partner, I had to confront my assumptions and oversights about what it means to include community voice in projects and what it means to be in true partnership with community members. We will end with some lessons learned around intervening to support empowerment.

In establishing any sort of new collaboration or project, agendas are often created, developed, and prioritized with the aim of ensuring that order is maintained, goals are established, and progress is made. In the case of community and social justice work, agendas are often used as a tool to ensure that all stakeholders have been given a voice and that their needs are being considered (Rubin et al., 2012). In this way, we often approach relationship building as we would any other sort of business project: as a list of tasks that, once accomplished, will have the cumulative impact of goal achievement. As an achievement-oriented society, agenda setting is often seen not only as practical but as ethical—a way of ensuring that we are not wasting the time and energy of our new collaborators in the building of our partnership. In the push to show respect for relationships by ensuring the production of some sort of product and the elimination of any sort of "wasted" time, though, we often overlook the fact that partnerships are made up of people and not of tasks.

**Before jumping in, let's take some time to think about your own experience with agenda setting. How do you normally enter into new partnerships? What sort of agendas do you bring with you to the table?**

_____

_____

_____

In the summer of 2019, my involvement in the establishment of a community partnership began with many of these same goals and assumptions. In collaboration with my research mentor and lab and with some of our key community

DOI: 10.4324/9781003055587-5

partners, I had committed to creating and supporting a new relationship between my university and a local alternative high school (AHS) designed to provide wrap-around support to students who, for various reasons, had not received the resources and scaffolding needed to succeed in traditional learning environments. Meetings were held throughout the semester with the purpose of establishing aims and goals for the students with whom we were to work. I was particularly excited by the idea of working with an alternative high school, not only because of my own research interests in resiliency, meaning making, and civic identity development, but because of the opportunities we saw for undergraduate service-learning students from our university to bring their own interests and skills into this unique learning environment. I knew that in order for service-learners to have authentic outcomes, **critical pedagogy** needed to be used. In this framework, I assured myself, students would have the room to begin applying knowledge to their lived experiences, instead of simply relying on their educators to deposit truth and knowledge (Freire, 1972).

**Critical Pedagogy**—The application of critical framework to the education sector. In his work with farmworkers in Brazil, Paulo Freire laid the foundations for this framework with his assertion that educational content is always context-dependent and, as such, is only meaningful when it can be applied to the lived experience of learners. Critical pedagogy asserts that an understanding of truth as subjective means that educators must relinquish their role as "truth providers" in order to make space for the voices and expertise of students in the consideration and solving of the problems that impact them.

**What motivates you to do your community work/research? What skills and interests do you bring?**

_____

_____

_____

The planning meetings that lasted throughout the summer often felt overwhelming and ill defined. While each of the **stakeholders** seemed to be coming to the room with shared intentions of supporting and empowering students and building community, we often seemed to be having parallel conversations about our aims, goals, and hopes that would end with an agreement that we were moving forward together without any real tangible sense of what that meant. Our shared goal and desire to work in collaboration, it seemed, lacked the kind of common language and understanding of what each of us was bringing into the room that was needed before building partnership could truly begin.

Nevertheless, I entered into this new collaboration with the staff and students at the AHS in the fall full of goals around empowerment and mutually beneficial relationships, many of which I had created on my own. I made some effort to include what I thought the others in the planning meetings had probably meant, in ways that supported my own needs and aims. Above all else, I wanted to work to establish the kind of partnership needed to support authentic service-learning experiences and opportunities for critical reflection for the undergraduate students at my university. I knew, from both research and experience, that effective service-learning partnerships are **mutually beneficial**—meeting the needs of both the students and the partner. The fact that this balance often proves much more challenging to operationalize than to conceptualize drove me forward, as I believed I had found the sort of nontraditional space in which experiential pedagogy could really be implemented and supported (Butin, 2015; Harkins, 2017; Morton & Bergbauer, 2015). I walked into this new space armed with my understanding of critical frameworks (Kincheloe, 2008) and my commitment to redistributing power and prioritizing authentic relationship building (Mitchell, 2015), if not with an understanding of who was there and what this community meant to them and to their learning.

---

**Stakeholders**—Anyone who has an interest in something. Generally thought of in terms of someone with a business interest. In the nonprofit sector, though, this takes on a new significance as stakeholders include anyone who is interested in or impacted by the fulfillment of the organization's mission (rather than those who will benefit if the organization makes a profit). This includes people at every level of the work (beneficiaries, or those receiving the services, funders, employees and volunteers, and the overall community).

---

**If we consider stakeholders to be anyone who will care about a project or who is likely to be impacted by it (intentionally or unintentionally), how can we best identify all of the stakeholders in the planning phase of our projects? What will our relationship with these stakeholders look like if we are truly committed to mutually beneficial relationships (ones that meet the needs of all those involved)?**

_____

_____

_____

In order to ensure that this partnership was built for the promotion of my goals around authentic critical service-learning and to hold myself accountable to honoring the time of my collaborators, I prepared myself with a well-defined project, detailed in a carefully crafted agenda. I centered my project around **narrative inquiry**, in order to ensure that my agenda focused on the experience of the partner and was used to highlight their voice. This, I reasoned, would allow for me to be the kind of researcher who sought to understand and explore experience and who shared this tool with others seeking to do the same (Clandinin, 2006). The use of stories as research felt powerful, not only because of the respect it gave to individuals as the experts of their own experience, but because of the potential of storytelling to promote and inform both personal and societal change (Bamberg & Georgakopoulou, 2018). More importantly, though, stories seemed to be a kind of great equalizer, given the universal truth that each of us use our stories not only as points of reference and as means of reflection but as the contexts in which we live and through which we understand our world and those in it (King, 2003). What better way, I thought, to create an opportunity to empower students from both academic settings to teach and learn together than to ask that they share their stories with one another?

> **Narrative inquiry** is a type of qualitative research that considers lived experience by using stories, interviews, photos, journals, and conversations as data sources.

With the aim of lifting the voices of both the students at the AHS and the service-learners from my university, I created an agenda around establishing a skill-based mentoring program. This program, I argued, would provide the kind of structure needed for authentic service-learning as it would include the voices of both the partner and the service-learners throughout the entire process—from planning to implementation through assessment. This approach, as I understood it, showed faith not only in the research and the process, but in the people of which these things were composed (Cammarota & Fine, 2010). Moreover, the program would be sustainable, as it was set up in such a way as to allow the AHS students to work with their service-learning mentors to establish their own curriculum that would be used the following semester to mentor students at an elementary school.

**Community-based interventions that are designed to empower communities should, at some point, be able to function without our help. What does making a community program sustainable mean? What are some of the challenges to making this happen?**

_____

_____

_____

I felt somewhat hesitant to slow my ideas down in order to use the first semester as a piloting phase but became convinced that slowing down was necessary for the creation of a truly sustainable program. In the first phase of the pilot, AHS students would work with undergraduate service-learners to consider and learn curriculum designed to build and promote important life skills. During these ongoing lessons, the undergraduate students would invite their high school mentees to take on expert roles by applying the life skills to their own stories and identifying which of the skills felt most valuable and which they wish they could have learned earlier. This insight would then be used to create a curriculum that gave AHS students the opportunity to use both their learning and their expertise to teach the life skills that they identified as most applicable to elementary school students during the second phase of the pilot. When this curriculum was implemented the following semester, elementary school students would be invited to take on their own role as experts, using their own stories to consider and apply life skills. Once this implementation stage of the project had been reached, I was convinced, mutually beneficial support and mentoring would be happening at each stage of this scaffolded model with me working from outside of the network of relationships to provide neutral structural support, guidance, and resources.

> **Participatory action** is a research strategy that calls for the inclusion of community members at every stage of the process—from planning to implementation and through evaluation and next steps. When Kurt Lewin first considered what he called "action research" (1964), he suggested that the best way to understand lived experience is through participation in the space being considered. For community projects to be truly participatory, they must reflect the kind of community norms, customs, values, and belief systems that can only be understood by those who have spent time in the community.

My agenda became compromised from the very beginning. I was confronted right away with the reality that the alternative structure of the school was designed not to support creative projects imagined by well-intentioned community researchers, but to meet the complex needs of students who had been let down by and shut out of traditional systems. Most students were carrying the kind of pain that made it hard to make it through the door, much less to jump head-first into a series of modules that asked them to share this pain and its insights with people they did not even know, much less have any reason to trust. I was struck by the way that the teachers and support staff met these students where they were at, providing support and love that often fell squarely outside of even the most alternative conceptualizations of an academic framework. I was both intrigued and made uncomfortable by the ways in which these staff members seemed to blur boundaries and to share themselves with students in ways that did not seem to support the maintenance of the sort of professional distance I had always been taught to value and work toward.

The staff member with whom I was working most closely, Ms. M, had a special kind of bond with the students that felt hard for me to name, much less to understand. She taught a course for the young women at the AHS designed to support them in creating and achieving goals. The course in combination with my ideas and agenda felt like the perfect combination. Ms. M had the kind of rapport and insight needed to ensure student buy-in. As a committed community researcher, I believed in **participatory action research** that includes the voices of the community being researched from the project's inception through its implementation and assessment (Lewin, 1946; Harkins, 2017; Rink et al., 2016). Working with Ms. M, I thought, would mean that I could check off this box, since she could serve as the **community expert** through which I could operationalize my agenda (Dari, Laux, Liu, & Reynolds, 2019).

> A **community expert** is an individual who is trusted and respected by the stakeholder community. Experts are able to provide historical perspective and insight into community norms and practices. Most importantly, community experts understand the issues that are most important to community members—from their perspective and lived experience.

As I spent more time with Ms. M, her relationships with the students continued to both strike and confuse me. She seemed unphased when explaining that most of her students were unlikely to come to class on Wednesdays, the day that I was working with her, because it was the day of the week when the class started early. She welcomed these students into her classroom, whenever they got there, and seemed to know exactly what was going on with each of them no matter what time it was or what else she had been doing minutes before. She was always busy and always stopped to give any person her whole attention in ways that I could tell made them feel seen and understood. I found myself having a hard time appreciating these relationships in spite of myself because they fell so far outside of the framework I had in mind for the success of "our" project. The time and space that Ms. M gave to each person, to each crisis, to each event was far beyond what I had built into my agenda.

**Where do you imagine yourself in the implementation of community-based interventions? What roles are you most comfortable playing? If we are committed to participatory action, what does this look like?**

_____

_____

_____

As I spent more time with Ms. M in the classroom, where we were often without any of the students, I began to really listen to her voice instead of just trying to figure out how I could add what she was saying into the "community voice" aspect of my agenda. She pointed out that life skills looked different for people living different lives—that some people had to learn ways to take care of themselves and to keep themselves safe that others would never have to think about. She explained that skill sets for the youth with whom we were working are often matched not with their age but with their experience and circumstances. She explained, for instance, that at 8 she knew how to navigate the public transit system alone—something I still do not know how to do very effectively. Pairing volunteers with students could not be based in a one-size-fits-all program curriculum, because each semester would bring with it different students with their own sets of skills and experiences who would have different things to offer and different ways in which to relate to the high school students.

In sharing my insights and my feelings of being untethered from my agenda with my research mentor (DH), I was asked a question that I had never before given much thought: *why did I feel able to ask others to share their stories with me without first being willing to share my own?* The question was particularly poignant given the setting and scope of the project I was working to implement. Why would students share the kind of complex pain they were already receiving support around with someone who was not offering any sort of personal content through which connection and trust could be built? What, given my commitment to the building of these relationships, made me so unwilling to share? I was struck by the reality that I had just spent months constructing an agenda built around the power of stories to empower and to influence connection and change, without ever having considered what the role of my own story in this process might be.

The assumption at the core of my project, that stories are what unite us all, that they are inherent to the human experience, had not been extended to my own reality. I began answering the question with my knee-jerk response—that I simply did not have a lot to share given all of the support and privilege I had experienced in my life. How could I possibly ask students with experiences so full of intricate challenge and resilience to listen to my story? I was quick to have the lack of logic in my response pointed out. I was not being humble by leaving space for the stories of those with less power to be told; I was too afraid to accept any of the vulnerability that comes with filling some of that space with my own experience. I was asking those in the margins to move away from these margins and offer me the gift of their stories, without any sort of willingness to do the same.

I spent the next week reflecting on the question that remained: *why am I so afraid to share my story?* One morning, when my mind was occupied trying to convince myself not to abort a workout halfway through, an unconscious thought suddenly came to the surface of my thinking: "I don't trust people to take care of themselves." The thought truly struck me. Was I a community researcher who did not believe that people could care for themselves? The thought, while painful to sit with, made sense. If I did not trust people to manage their own realities, I certainly could not ask them to help me in holding my own.

**Which aspects of your identity and experience are you most comfortable talking about? Which do you avoid or not think much about?**

---

---

---

The first time that I pushed myself to share with the students at the AHS, it became even more apparent that I had been protecting myself with a shield of "humility" and my belief that I was holding back my own experience to make more room for the realities of those whose voices were so often silenced. Sharing hurt me in a physical way—a tightness in my chest, a knot in my stomach. I responded to a question from a student about the necklace I always wear by telling the real story—that it had been a gift from my dad at my brother's wedding, made from jewelry he had kept after my grandmother passed away and had made into matching tie pins for himself and my brothers and into matching necklaces for me, my mom, and my new sister. The story took only a few moments to tell, but it felt like ripping off a band-aid. Normally quite at ease in social interactions, I found that I had to mentally coax myself into continuing forward, much the same way I had been doing during the workout where this hurdle had first come into my mind. "Don't stop. You can do this. Just keep going." My story invited one of the students to tell us about her own necklace, and her connection to her Godmother by whom it had been gifted. My ability to appreciate this connection, though, was compromised by the self-doubt that began to flood my mind as soon as I finished talking. Had I shared too much? Made myself seem unrelatable? Flaunted my relationship with the kind of unwavering father figure I knew many students at the AHS were missing?

In processing this interaction with DH a few days later, another harsh reality became clear: I was expecting people who had lived about half as long as I had to share openly about their trauma and challenges while, at the same time, being afraid that I might be judged for talking about a necklace. DH pointed out that until I could share, I could not really listen. It was true, I realized, that I would not be genuinely able to take in people's stories if I did not trust them to hold my own. After all, how could their stories get in around the guards that I had worked so diligently to erect in order to keep my own from getting out?

**As helpers building new relationships, what do we ask community partners to do for us? In what ways do we show them that we trust them the way we are asking them to trust us?**

---

---

---

As discussions about how to best incorporate service-learners at AHS progressed, Ms. M shared with me her habit of paying close attention to the expressions on the faces of any volunteers that come into the school. The AHS students, she explained, are incredibly attentive to the ways in which people carry themselves when they enter the school community. They quickly intuit ways that volunteers are feeling about being at their school and draw conclusions about how college students feel about coming to work with them. College students, Ms. M went on to explain, often enter the school with a sense of fear that is quickly noticed by the youth. Growing up in urban areas, youth learn when to be afraid from an early age. If they sense fear in you, she explained, they know they need to mind themselves with you because there is something there that they cannot trust.

I knew Ms. M was not intentionally talking about me in this conversation. I was not an undergraduate student, and I had spent years working in the kind of urban settings she was describing. I was not afraid to enter these spaces or to spend time with the people in them. I was left, though, to consider my own sense of fear in my community work. While years of community work had helped me to unpack the kinds of stereotypes and misinformation that informed fear of physically being in the space, my challenges in sharing myself authentically with the students left me with no choice but to admit that I was afraid of bringing myself emotionally into the space. I knew the students were as intuitive as Ms. M was saying, and I wondered to myself if they could see the fear in me that I was so reluctant to notice in myself.

Watching Ms. M balance her work and her commitment to relationships highlighted for me the way that I was framing a lot of my fear for myself as a commitment to my work. The ability Ms. M had to transition seamlessly from a story about her worries for her daughter to an administrative meeting, to a conversation about a student's new tattoo highlighted for me that what I understood as my commitment to professional humility was really fear that sharing might leave me stuck in vulnerability. If I got stuck there, I worried it might take away my ability to provide the kind of support services that I saw not only as an integral part of my role but as inherent to my value. This willingness to be authentic and vulnerable seemed to be the very reason that students who had a hard time walking in the door would take the extra steps to Ms. M's classroom for a hug or a check-in before going on with the rest of their day. Not only did vulnerability not keep Ms. M from doing her job, it was at the very core of why she did so with such effectiveness. She shared so openly with me, with students, and with colleagues: from the way she had her desk decorated to share her personality, to the way that she would share what was on her mind any given morning, especially if it was a struggle that she was worried might keep her from giving you her full attention.

Before service-learning students could effectively contribute to community projects, Ms. M pointed out, they needed to first unpack their own biases. It would be great, she suggested, if the class before the service-learning course could focus on addressing identity and preparing students to acknowledge the influences that have shaped them and the prejudices they hold. This way, they could come into the work knowing the biases they hold and be prepared to do the work because they know what they're coming into it with. In thinking about my own work unpacking, I realized that I had focused so much on unpacking my bias that I had come to use it as a kind of shield. I had unpacked my knapsack of privilege (McIntosh, 1988) and begun using my empty knapsack as a placeholder, to ensure that there was enough space between me and the people with whom I was trying to operationalize projects. I had never taken the time to fill this knapsack back up with the aspects of myself that I wanted to bring into my work.

**What aspects of privilege and bias have you worked to unpack? In what ways have you filled back up with values, beliefs, and parts of yourself you are willing to bring into your community work?**

_____

_____

_____

The way Ms. M worked to give people her full attention, in spite of her overwhelmingly full schedule, brought rise to another question for me. What was it that was driving me toward a continuous need to have an agenda and a task list to ensure that I was bringing value to the relationships I was working to establish? Why, when I was able to appreciate the value of simply connecting with others, was it so hard for me to just be with my community partners? I had, I realized, been so focused on my shift from _doing for_ to _doing with_ that I had not even thought about the importance of _being with_ before _doing with_. I could never really ask the students to let me know them enough to do important work together if I was not willing to bring myself authentically into the space and take the time to let them know me.

As my plans to implement a curriculum quickly fell apart, I began to challenge myself to move toward a willingness to remain in rather than run past the first step of relationship building. I worked to resist my urges to complete tasks and create goals for the sake of simply being with the students I wanted to know. More importantly, I challenged myself to let these students know me. Being present could not be broken down into items to check off a list, and it was an ongoing challenge to not slip back into my habit of "getting things done." I still found myself checking emails when it seemed that students were engaged with one another in a way that did not need my support, or answering a text while listening to a story. After all, if I was not accomplishing tasks, I was risking the vulnerability of offering the students nothing more than myself. Showing up authentically was hard and needed to be an ongoing commitment. While I continued to struggle to resist task lists, I also found myself admitting that it was hard for me to watch Tyler

Perry's *For Colored Girls* with the students because it scared me to let myself get too sad because of a fear that I might get stuck there. I even found myself sharing with one of the community partners about my mom's willingness to fly for the first time after 30 years and, later, to tell Ms. M how hard it had been for me to celebrate this success with her because of some resentment I had not realized I was holding onto because I never talked about it out loud.

As the semester neared its end and I began thinking about the "product" I would have to put forward in order to justify the time I had spent at the school as a competent researcher and not simply as someone working on their own emotional growth, I wondered how I might best produce a product that authentically portrayed the lessons I had begun learning about how integral the latter was to becoming the former. The students, as Ms. M had put it, were "used to" me. I was not sure, though, how to best articulate the amount of energy I had expended coaxing myself into practicing the kind of vulnerability needed to sit in a place without offering anything in order to get to the point of being an expected presence.

As DH and I considered the curriculum, we realized that the answer to the question of what to produce could be found in the same question we had been struggling to prioritize all semester: everything needed to start with relationships. Looking back at the original curriculum I had created around life skills, I realized that it was not the content that needed to be changed as much as its framing. The kind of life skills that are identified in the literature and in research as being most impactful for youth and adolescents, as it turns out, are largely based in abilities to engage in and maintain relationships.

**In what ways do we show up for our community partners? How do we balance our desire to be valuable and produce important work with the need to build relationships? What does it look like to really be with someone?**

As I move forward in reconsidering my project and sharing it with the people who are already maintaining and engaging in powerful relationships, I am mindful of my urge to apply my same comfortable agenda framework to this process. I recognize that after many months spent at AHS I have quite a way to go in sharing enough of myself to begin asking the people there to do the same with me. Just like unforeseen circumstances and life hurdles resulted in spending several weeks (instead of the intended two sessions) watching the *For Colored Girls* film without yet having finished, relationship building has been slow, sometimes messy, and often uncomfortable. I still feel a strong pull to quantify my progress in order to qualify my value to the students and to the community, though I am more authentically committed to my belief in the power and value of stories. I still struggle not to prioritize my own thoughts about how the stakeholders in this new partnership might best benefit from their relationships with one another, though I now have a much clearer understanding of who those stakeholders are and what they bring with them. I am still angry at my mom in a way that remains hard for me to understand, though carrying this feels less heavy without the added burden of working to deny its existence. Stories, as it turns out, are even more powerful than my agenda ever could have articulated.

## References

Bamberg, M., & Georgakopoulou, A. (2008). Small stories as a new perspective in narrative and identity analysis. *Text & Talk, 28*, 377–396. https://doi.org/10.1515/TEXT.2008.018

Butin, D. (2015). Dreaming of justice: Critical service-learning and the need to wake up. *Theory into Practice, 54*, 5–10. https://doi.org/10.1080/00405841.2015.977646

Cammarota, J., & Fine, M. (Eds.). (2010). *Revolutionizing education: Youth participatory action research in motion.* Routledge.

Clandinin, D. J. (Ed.). (2006). *Handbook of narrative inquiry: Mapping a methodology.* Sage Publications.

Dari, T., Laux, J. M., Liu, Y., & Reynolds, J. (2019). Development of community-based participatory research competencies: A Delphi study identifying best practices in the collaborative process. *Professional Counselor, 9*(1), 1–19. https://doi.org/10.15241/td.9.1.1

Freire, P. (1968, 1972). *Pedagogy of the oppressed.* Myra Bergman Ramos (Trans.). Herder.

Harkins, D. A. (Ed.). (2017). *Alongside community: Learning in service.* Routledge Press.

Kincheloe, J. L. (2008). *Critical pedagogy primer* (Vol. 1). Peter Lang Publishing.

King, T. (2003). *The truth about stories: A native narrative.* House of Anansi.

Lewin, K. (1946). Action research and minority problems. *Journal of Social Issues, 2*(4), 34–46. https://doi.org/10.1111/j.1540-4560.1946.tb02295

McIntosh, P. (1988). Unpacking the invisible knapsack. *Gender through the Prism of Difference,* 235–238. https://psychology.umbc.edu/files/2016/10/White-Privilege_McIntosh-1989.pdf

Mitchell, T. D. (2015). Using a critical service-learning approach to facilitate civic identity development. *Theory into Practice, 54*(1), 20–28. https://doi.org/10.1080/00405841.2015.977657

Morton, K., & Bergbauer, S. (2015). A case for community: Starting with relationships and prioritizing community as method in service-learning. *Michigan Journal of Community Service Learning, 22*(1), 18–31.

Rink, E., Bird, E. A. R., Fourstar, K., Ricker, A., Runs-Above, M. W., & Hallum-Montes, R. (2016). Partnering with American Indian communities in strength-based collaborative health research: Guiding principles from the Fort Peck Ceremony of research project. *American Indian & Alaska Native Mental Health Research: The Journal of the National Center, 23*, 187–205. https://doi.org/10.5820/aian.2303.2016.187

Rubin, C. L., Martinez, L. S., Chu, J., Hacker, K., Brugge, D., Pirie, A., & Leslie, L. K. (2012). Community-engaged pedagogy: A strengths-based approach to involving diverse stakeholders in research partnerships. *Progress in Community Health Partnerships: Research, Education, and Action, 6*, 481–490. https://doi.org/10.1353/cpr.2012.0057

*Resources*

Participatory Action Planning Guide: www.ramsar.org/sites/default/files/documents/library/outreach_actionplanning_guide.pdf

Quotes from For Colored Girls by Ntozake Shange: www.goodreads.com/work/quotes/505856-for-colored-girls-who-have-considered-suicide-when-the-rainbow-is-enuf

Racial Equity Tools: www.racialequitytools.org/

Six Degrees of Lois Wiseberg: http://croker.harpethhall.org/Must%20Know/Psychology/WeisbergGladwell.pdf

# Part 2

# Helping Build Empowering Skills

# 6 Building a Team to Work for Social Justice

*Elizabeth Robinson and Debra A. Harkins*

## September 24, 2020 Meeting

ER: How are you? How are things?

DH: Okay. Um, my husband had to get tested for COVID because he's been sick for the past couple days. We thought maybe he got it, but he just got his test results back, and he's negative. So I don't know. Maybe it's just allergies or something that's bothering him, but he's got a slight fever. You know, he's exhausted. He's on his third day of just being in bed. So I don't know what's going on. But they tested him for strep, and he doesn't have strep.

ER: That's scary!

DH: That's what's gonna happen this whole winter, is people won't be able to tell what you have because the symptoms, you know, they look like the flu.

ER: How hard was it? Was it easy to get him tested?

DH: Yeah, he went to the urgent care clinic, and they ran the test. He got it done two days ago, and he just got the results this morning. I know they can do it quickly, but it took his results a long time to come back. And how are things going on your end?

ER: I'm fine. Sorry I was late. I was just saving fish! I took Henry and Anna fishing yesterday. We went and got some minnows at the bait store. We didn't use them all, so Henry last night was frantically trying to save the fish. I don't understand how he is fine putting a hook through their eye and throwing them out to be eaten, but then he wanted to save them? (laughing)

DH: You've done your good deed for the day.

ER: So, yeah. Where were we? So, we're going to start with being **open to learn** and draw on our experiences to explain what that looks like. I was originally writing about being **open to learning** in relation to my classes and my teaching, but I think we should instead be talking about our work together.

DH: Yeah, because the bigger frame is how we *became a team*.

When we (ER and DH) first began working together, it was under the auspices of a faculty professional learning community (FPLC) focused on

DOI: 10.4324/9781003055587-6

service-learning. I (DH) started the FPLC due to long-standing teaching and research interests in service-learning. Feeling like I was receiving little support from my department, the university's Center for Community Engagement or the university as a whole, this unique opportunity through a grant obtained from the Davis Foundation by the university's Center for Teaching and Scholarly Excellence seemed like an ideal chance to engage with my colleagues on the challenges and opportunities around service-learning.

While many changes happened during this five-year FPLC initiative, four constants remained and helped us continue to do this challenging social justice work: several faculty members, two graduate students, a cohort of undergraduate students every semester, and two community partners remained involved during our five-year funded FPLC project. What kept us involved and committed was our shared goal of building a community across higher education and our local community in the service of social justice.

This chapter is structured in the form of a dialogue to show our process of being a team focused on social justice. This structure resulted from our attempts to fit the seminal team building model proposed by Lencioni (2002) to our team-building work. We found that Lencioni's five behaviors of an effective team—trust, conflict resolution, commitment to purpose, accountability and a focus on results—did not align with the way we function as a team. Through dialogue, we have explored our process, which included critical, feminist and anti-racist theories as we processed our experiences as white female academics trying to engage in building teams to promote socially just helping. We critically reflected on the obstacles we faced within our academic institution and considered what is needed to build more supportive teams that can work towards social justice. Using a grounded approach, in this chapter we highlight the components that are important to our relational teamwork. Central to our teamwork are **openness to learn, commitment, empathy, flexibility** and **processing**. Challenges to building a team that can create sustainable social change include lack of commitment, lack of trust, lack of support, inflexibility and closed-mindedness. The following dialogue shows how we arrived at these components of teamwork and challenges to team building. We begin with openness to learn.

## Being Open to Learn

ER: Yeah, I'm just thinking of an example of being open to learn. I think I came to service-learning knowing that service-learning was about working with communities, but in my head I thought it was very similar to teacher preparation. I thought I was going to find a new way to do teacher preparation, by working in schools. And so I had to learn about service-learning from you. And it wasn't what I had assumed it was. So I think, for a lot of faculty, even though I shouldn't say for other people—but, I could imagine that if you join a group, and it's not what you were expecting, you might not stay with the group. But for me, all of the values of service-learning were so much in line with what I believe in and what I wanted to do anyway. So I could write about my being **open to learning**, even though service-learning was something new and different.

DH: Right. And I think we had a continuum in that some people felt like they already know what service-learning is. And they just went on their way. And, they did know it at some level, but it wasn't at the community level that you and I realized it needed to be. The community piece was missing within the university that we needed in order to move forward, to actually have a bigger impact on the community, outside of the university.

ER: I think in being **open to learn**, there's also something about using yourself and your experiences, right? That's what we're doing. As learning? But I think that that disposition, that's what we are talking about, that learning is not just acquiring new skills. I mean, it can be, but the kind of learning that we're thinking about, because our goal is social justice, is really thinking about how to do it better? And we are reflecting on our own actions and what we've done, and we are thinking about, you know, can we improve, can we learn? Can we do something different?

DH: Right. So, social justice is you're engaged in it, because you see some injustice. And that means that you're challenging the hegemony, challenging the current system you're in. And you have to be willing to see that the system is flawed and know that you've got to be open to new ways of seeing the system or the structure. So, yeah, I think being **open to learn** is really a key piece of social justice helping.

ER: So then, can we just talk through the obstacles to being **open to learn**?

DH: That's a good idea. I think you started to mention it earlier when you said the obstacle to being open is to be closed. Like, as you said, some already felt like they knew what service-learning was and how to do it. And they didn't try to engage more and really didn't engage with our group. Some were not willing to critically reflect with us about the process. And I think you have to **process** in order to be able to do this work because you have to be able to deconstruct what's happening. And that takes time because we're inside the system. It's like trying to "peel the onion." And so I think an obstacle to being **open to learn** is being closed to learning, which is kind of ironic, isn't it? For academics!

ER: Or just having a different sort of epistemology of learning. Right? And, believing that learning is being able to do something and then you've learned it.

DH: Freire's banking model, right?

ER: Right. Yeah, because I don't think anybody would say that they were closed to learning. I think some would say that "I've learned how to do service-learning, and I know how to do it."

DH: And I think that's what happened a lot. People joined our team, and some got defensive, because we started to try to talk about being **open to learn**. But some assumed that they already knew what service-learning was, and they wanted to just run with it.

ER: I think being **open to learn** is messy.

DH: Very messy. You have to be willing to *not know where you're going*. Right? And be okay with that.

ER: Right, because if you're really going to **critically reflect**, I think, that means questioning cultural standards and rejection of white power and the way things are. That's how you do **critical reflection** and critical anti-racist work, because the status quo supports our white power and dominance. And so to be able to reject the status quo we have to really **investigate** what's going on.

DH: We have to be able to change course, very rapidly, because you're talking about real time, real people. And things change. And, like, COVID is a perfect example, you know, preparing to teach in one way in a semester and then having to totally shift gears, which we were able to do. Yeah, not sure everybody else was able to do it, but you have to be able to **pivot,** be okay with the **pivot,** and not get too stressed about the need to **pivot.**

ER: Right. Right.

DH: You need to have a community partner that can **pivot** as well. Unfortunately, many community partners get overwhelmed, and shut everything down. Instead they would say, "Okay, so now we can't do X. How are we going to do Y? Let's do Y now."

ER: Right. And I think that **openness** and **pivoting** happen when **learning** is the goal. So, I think we understand that there are different ways to learn.

The previous dialogue reveals how important we believe being open to learn is to team building. We see openness to learn as a disposition that comes from a certain understanding or epistemology of learning itself. We understand learning from a sociocultural perspective (Vygotsky, 1978) as described in Chapter 4. Similar to Freire, as discussed in Chapter 1, we view language as the central tool of learning, which happens in interactions between people. Our dialogues demonstrate our learning process. Learning is shaped by people's social, political and cultural contexts, and in return what we learn shapes these contexts. There is a dialectical relationship between learning and sociopolitical and cultural contexts; they cannot be disconnected from each other. This understanding positions learning as a continual process that can never be completed.

It is important from the very beginning that we came together as a team with learning as a central priority, partly due to ER's education training and DH's strong psychology graduate training in Vygotsky. We believe there are several practices that support and maintain openness to learning: One important tool is critical reflection (Dewey, 1933; Mezirow, 1990), which is a valuable tool that requires team members to engage in the process of questioning their beliefs, values and behaviors (see Chapter 2). When we critically reflect, we ask why we do things and what other ways of believing, valuing and acting exist. If we are open to learn, then critical reflection forces us to de-center our own understandings and consider others' ways of thinking and being as possible.

Another practice that supports openness to learn is being flexible. As helpers, it is imperative to pay attention to and be responsive to the ever-changing sociopolitical context. When the needs of our community partners change, or policies are passed that impact the original plans we made, or a pandemic hits, the best way to move forward is through flexibility. Often this means pivoting or changing direction. Being open to learn about the new needs, new policies or new requirements helps inform the ways we are able to pivot.

Being part of a team or building a team that insists on an openness to learn can be challenging. Not everyone shares the same ideas or the same epistemology about what it means to learn. Many people view learning as an accumulation of knowledge. However, the learning we are talking about is messy and often uncomfortable. Interrogating oneself and challenging our assumptions and corresponding actions or inactions can be very unsettling. It generally does not feel good to realize how much more each of us has to learn. Therefore, for us in our teamwork focused on helping, it is important to value every interaction and experience as an opportunity to learn. In effective teams that are open to learn, every team member is valued and also open to learning about and from each other's experiences and beliefs. This disposition to learning in a team requires empathy and also commitment.

## Reflecting on Empathy and Commitment

DH: It's not just learning, though. It's **caring**. Because you don't give up on other people.

ER: Right, even though it's hard.

DH: To say, *Okay, well, we can't do that with each other. So I don't want to not help you, I want to help you. But we're going to have to figure out another way to work together. Because we care about each other.* So social justice is being **open to learn**, but also doing that because you care.

ER: Because you care, right? And that's where the **commitment** comes in. So what are the obstacles?

DH: Oh, I think you just gave an obstacle: **lack of commitment**. I think all of these interrelate with each other. So I think being **open to learn** relates to a lack of commitment, because if you're not committed to the cause, you're not going to invest in learning. And I think, like you were saying, most academics wouldn't say they're not open to learn. Most academics are academics, because they like to learn.

ER: Learning for many means acquiring knowledge, right? Like reading books. It doesn't necessarily mean exploring yourself and all the mess that's in there. But there is also being **committed to purpose**. So not being open to learn might be an obstacle for committing to purpose, right?

DH: Yes, it may not mean that you help a particular community, or you don't invest in a community as much as you invest in something else. So, you have to have made the **commitment** and say, *Okay, I really care about this community*. And some people will **pivot** (be flexible) because they **care** so much about the community. And then they will be **open to learn** because they care about the communities.

ER: Right. Right.

DH: So, sometimes **commitment** might supersede **open to learn**.

ER: Right, and they're all sort of interconnected.

In the previous dialogue, we struggled to understand how openness to learning, commitment and caring related to each other. We were still trying to fit our teamwork experience into Lenconi's model (2002) of team building, but every time we tried, we found ourselves going around in circles. Openness to learn often does not happen without commitment, and commitment does not happen without openness to learn or caring. We view commitment and caring as part of building relationships, the relational aspects of teamwork. Openness to learn can be blocked by a lack of commitment and/or care (empathy). Yes, our relationship allowed us to continually engage in dialogues to process and learn from the challenges that our team faced.

## Exploring Challenges

DH: Right, I think I would like to add one more thing to the obstacles to being **open to learn**. It is that whole piece about the institution. They think they're doing experiential learning and they just have to implement it. But they're not really **open to learn**, because they're not working with us, they're not reflecting with us, and they're not pivoting at all. I don't see pivoting.

ER: Right, I don't either. And I think power and structure are also obstacles to being **open to learn** because in order to maintain the power, you have to maintain the structure that keeps you in power, right? And then you're not really open. You can't afford to question yourself, and there's no **pivoting**. Those in power feel like, "We've got it. We know what we're doing, and we're in charge."

DH: I think the leaders are very much for service-learning in theory. They have experience with it and are open to it. But, because they're not engaging with faculty in the way that they should, by building a team of people that are on the same page with them, it's not working. They don't **trust** us. So they take what they already know, and keep trying to apply it and implement it. And so it doesn't work because there isn't a community of people that are working together and processing together and pivoting when needed.

We keep trying to work with them. We've tried and tried. We've presented white papers, you know, tried to have meetings with the administration. There has been no follow through. So there's a lack of **trust**. We can't build this further because we can't get the stakeholders that we need to come to the table.

ER: Right, absolutely. And I think lack of trust also manifests itself in lack of respect, like you were just saying; it's very clear that there's a lack of respect for faculty. How are you supposed to build a class that does really impactful work if you are perceived as the enemy? Right? The administration doesn't think faculty have the ability, because they don't trust faculty to actually do what is in the best interest of the university. Therefore, they tell faculty how to do it.

DH: So we have a whole system where people are disengaged and not communicating.

ER: I remember back to the conversations that you and I were having about how to get this FPLC group to come together. We continually asked about building community and how we could do it. "How do we do it? How do we do it?" Right? And we didn't have a model, but we knew that there had to be some **buy-in**. Everyone had to **have a valid purpose**.

DH: And we kept giving excuses, which were not really excuses. I mean, it's a reality. But it's also, you know, the obstacle, which is that everybody's trying to do 3,000 things. And I think it goes back to **commitment**, not everybody was as committed to service-learning, to doing this work. I don't know, maybe some of them came to the first couple meetings, but then they didn't come to more. So maybe it was that they didn't have time. Well, I know, part of it, too, was that they didn't feel supported by the university because the university kept decreasing the funding. You showed your **commitment**, E, because you stayed when there was the least amount of money.

ER: Right, I understand money is important. And that's how you support things, but the money has nothing to do with why I do it.

DH: And I think we have to partly acknowledge that that's because of our privilege, right? As white middle-class academics, we don't have to worry nearly as much about money.

ER: So maybe the money allowed us to have some lunches together or something. But yes, I agree we're privileged. So I don't worry where my lunch is coming from but the money really . . . demonstrates worth and what is valued.

DH: Yeah, I think there were different levels of commitment for all the reasons that we just mentioned. And those were all obstacles that prevented us from creating the kind of community that we knew we needed. We just couldn't make it happen. There were too many obstacles at so many levels. At every single level.

ER:  I think we can be pretty clear about what lack of support actually looked like.

DH:  Right. And **trust** is really about support, right? Because money is a reflection of **value**. And so if I reduce my funding to you, that is my message to you that I don't value you as much, which gets translated to I don't trust you. So I think we are fleshing out what trust means, and how trust presents itself in these kinds of situations. We experienced lack of trust in devaluing, and the devaluing came from reducing the money or not providing any money or not letting a program continue. And all that creates a lack of trust, which is a lack of support, and the lack of support comes from a lack of trust.

In our discussion of the challenges faced when building teams and engaging in teamwork, we focused on challenges within institutional settings. Several obstacles arose, including protection of institutional hegemony, which created an atmosphere filled with political factions, and resulted in a lack of trust and support. Our team experienced a lack of trust from administrators and university leaders who were not certain our work would align with their goals and objectives. It is important to understand how difficult it can be to operate as a collaborative or a community within traditional, hierarchically organized institutional structures.

We came up with a metaphor of navigating through the weeds to reflect the ways in which we continued our teamwork despite the challenges we faced. Our team sustained us and continues to be our source of power, inspiration and support. Working for change, working for social justice cannot be done alone. We recognize the importance of relationships, and our way of team building, and teamwork is dependent on supporting team members. Through our relational approach aligned with feminist models of knowing and being (Belenky, Clinchy, Goldberger, & Tarule, 1986), we used our own dialogue to reflect on our approach to team building. We recognized that Lencioni's (2002) five functions of a team that we mentioned earlier, did not fit all our ways of building and being in teams. As we tried to write about our teamwork using Lencioni's five skills as a framework—honesty leading to trust, the ability to constructively debate, commitment, accountability to the team and attention to results—we constantly changed or added new skills. While we agree that trust and commitment are foundational, the other functions Lencioni argues for did not fit our experiences. One example of how our relational team building differs from Lencioni's model can be seen in our approaches to conflict. We see differences in thinking as opportunities to engage in deeper dialogue, thereby creating a stronger team. We believe that you need to actually have conversations with people in order to build a community where all voices are heard. We could not come up with examples of debating between us. Instead, we engaged in a lot of dialoguing, critical reflection or processing.

**Reflection**: What challenges have existed or arisen in a professional setting that you have had to navigate?

How have you navigated these challenges?

_____

_____

_____

## Critically Reflecting

DH: Sadly, the administration is getting rid of the very people that are engaged in doing experiential learning. Given that social justice work is about challenging the current status quo, the way the current system is set up, you are going to be perceived as threatening, and you need to know what you're up against. So learn from our mistakes, social justice warriors. Even when an institution says it supports something doesn't necessarily mean it's going to be easy for you.

ER: Because, what we were asking was to disrupt the system that exists. For example, we wanted more faculty control and more faculty support. That was never going to be accepted by the administration because they are never going to hand over more control to the faculty.

DH: I think this is a lesson, for me at least. I didn't know that others perceived my social justice work as disrupting. I mean, we talked about it and we knew we had to go through the weeds but even in the weeds, we were still being perceived as disruptive.

ER: They move you to another department or give you another assignment where you have less power.

DH: And that's another part of the lessons. Even though you may be at the top, it doesn't mean you are safe!

ER: Right, if you are challenging the system you are never safe.

DH: That's why I think we need to write about it. So other people that care like we do, can figure out how to navigate the challenges better.

ER: But it's also evident how helpful **reflection** is as a tool. Because I obviously think about all of this a lot. But I think our collaborative reflection helps both of us to see the bigger picture and where we fit into the picture.

DH: And I think that's a good point too being able to **reflect** on it in this way allows us not to take it too personally. We can recognize we were challenging a system, and that's why we are in the situation we currently are because we tried to challenge the system. Not because of our own inadequacies.

ER: Right.

DH: And that's what the system tries to do to you. It tries to make you feel inadequate so that you stop challenging it. You are blocked. And that's what our whole society does right? It prevents people from making social change by focusing on the individual.

ER: Right, and I would also say that's what our society does to people of color. Just because of your skin color you are treated inadequately. So how does it make you feel? You just drop out of the system and stop playing the game because it's too hard to be stacked against an entire system that's working against you. However, we are privileged. We could drop out of academia.

But I also want to say I think we do have a valuable contribution to make. You and I are still here. We're still working together. We are still a team. We are still researching. We are still working with community partners. We are still doing our work. We just don't have support from a system. But that doesn't mean we can't continue as a team. I don't think I would be at this level of understanding without you to **process** this with.

DH: Aww, thank you and yes, the ability for us to **process** this with each other is allowing us to continue doing this work, and I think it has helped me recognize that I don't need the university to do this. I can do it without them. I will do it without them!

ER: We've been doing it without them forever! (laughing)

DH: And that's the lesson that we have to give to people who are reading this. Just keep talking. Just keep **processing** and **reflecting**, and don't let anyone shut your voice down.

ER: Right, but in order to do this and continue on . . . I wouldn't be doing it without you—

DH: Right same here.

ER: —so our team is important.

DH: Absolutely, I do think that more than ever, given what is happening in our society today, you need people that you can process with about everything that is happening because there are so many social injustices going on in the world right now. You can't do it alone. Trying to do it alone is what can destroy you.

We found strength by critically reflecting on our experiences. We had both experienced injustices within our university, and while we knew each other's stories, it wasn't until we processed our understandings with each other that we arrived at new levels of solidarity. This shared reflection further solidified us as a team. We want to point out that this processing of our grievances was possible because of our caring and empathy for each other, our openness to learning which required us to be honest and vulnerable, and our commitment to social justice. Through our critical reflection, we reached a new recognition of what we had accomplished as a team and what potential we still have.

## Team Building

### September 29, 2020 Meeting

ER: We ended our September 24th meeting talking about obstacles being synonymous with lack of support. We could even say lack of support instead of obstacles. We really have to define what lack of support looks like.

DH: Yes, I agree. And it's the language, you know. What I like is the feminist language, because lack of support is more relational. It feels closer to how we think and feel. So I like "lack of support" better than "obstacles." And so then we'd say lack of support is lack of trust, lack of commitment and not providing resources, not providing funding. These are all ways in which lack of support presents itself to us. Right? Except for the funding, these are all relational terms. Alignment, being on the same page, is a relational concept, right?

ER: Yes, and we generally talk about value instead of funding, and what does it mean, if you're not valued? You might not receive any funding? You might not get promotions, you might get moved to a different department, you might not get tenure.

DH: And because they don't value our pedagogy. I mean, they do, but they don't. It's very hard to tease it apart.

ER: I don't know why the word transactional is in my head right now. I wonder if it's because they're sort of running the institution as a corporation. They have a transactional understanding of learning, right? So, like, the teachers teach and the students learn. And, I don't think they understand that learning requires a lot more. It's messy.

DH: I think it's because they are trying . . . how do I even say this . . . higher ed is the hegemony, right? So the structure reflects the hegemony. If the leaders are, for whatever reason, not living the values, it reverberates through the entire system. So they're not walking their talk.

ER: Because I think, higher ed, back to the structure, is not structured as a team. It's not collaborative, right? It's a hierarchical structure.

DH: Yes, that's the word I was looking for, thank you. It's hierarchical.

ER: And you have to sort of go through the chain of command. And that means that one person makes the decisions and other people carry them out. And that again points to there being a lack of support for teams, because teams aren't operating from the same point of view. Right? When I think teams, we're saying everyone has to be onboard, you have to be committed, you have to all believe in what you're doing. But if you're operating within a hierarchical structure, the two views of the way you accomplish something and what you're trying to accomplish are almost opposed to each other.

DH: I think what we're saying is important because other people that are trying to do this, they need to understand that it's going to be hard to change a system.

ER: Right, but just for example, what would a leader have to do to change a system to a team? There would have to be open debate, right? There would have to be commitment to the same goals. You would have to trust each other.

DH: I think so. Because, you know, this reminds me of what we did in another setting. This worked because the executive director was open.

She said, *Okay, let's do it.* For two years, we did team building with them, and that's what shifted the organization. Now, I don't know if that would be the case all the time. But team building was definitely the leverage point. And the teachers were the ones that told us the leverage point.

ER: Leverage point meaning you focused on team building versus conflict resolution?

DH: In terms of systems thinking, there's always a leverage point, somewhere in the system, and if you tap that point in the system, you can make the whole system shift.

ER: Right. So what was the leverage point?

DH: **Team building**. Which is interesting! That's what this whole chapter is about! Isn't it? Yeah. It was **team building**. That's not what I was brought there for in my prior work. That's not what I thought I was doing. I didn't even think that was what we were going to do with the upper administration, but that's what the teachers identified. And in fact, they were right.

DH: So you have to get your team in alignment and be open.

ER: I think that's what we are talking about, being **open to learn**.

DH: Yes, exactly.

ER: Right. Going back to examples of that, its power, right? That would mean leaders would have to give up some of their power and trust other people with power as well.

DH: I think that hierarchical systems can actually function and have communities if the leader is **open to learn**. If the leader is open to giving some of the power away in order to create a socially just community. Leaders have to build their team and do team building and not just in a couple of sessions.

ER: But I'm wondering, does team building contrast with leadership? I mean, like in the business world, or if you're reading about educational leadership, are you reading about how to build teams or is leadership about maintaining the power and therefore with the power you can achieve your goals?

DH: When I was working with an executive director and trying to understand all that I learned from John Maxwell, who identified the qualities of a great leader—and Maxwell said a great leader leads from behind or beside, not in front. So leaders build good teams. They go in the muck. Leaders realize they're gonna get lots of "tomatoes" thrown at them. One team I worked with in a meeting, they had just had it with the executive director, and they started just metaphorically "throwing tomatoes" at her, basically throwing critique after critique after critique. And she sat there, and she listened to it, truly listened to it, and they felt heard by her.

That's a great leader, according to Maxwell. A leader says, "Okay, I'm going to pull all these people in, and then we're going to try to work together." And the leader has enough confidence in themselves that they can hear the critique and realize that it's done in the interest of meeting the goal, and that it's not personal. It's how things are achieved. We've all got to do our part. And a leader is one who can build a great team and recognizes that you've got to find people's strengths and get them to work together. That's mainly your job as a leader. It is really about *can you find good people that can make things happen?* And can you get people to work together to make it all happen?

ER: Your example resonates profoundly with me too, because that's the same thing with being a teacher. I don't believe that a teacher is in a hierarchical position and just talks at students, I think that a teacher needs to build a community and bring in the knowledge of the students to the classroom and build relationships and do all of the things we are talking about. So, for me, team building as leadership makes perfect sense.

Most people think that leadership and team building are two different things, when in fact we believe they cannot be separated. As the previous chapter on leadership discusses, a good leader is willing to accept criticism in the service of being open to learn. A leader is also willing to take risks because of their commitment to social justice (Friedman & Harkins, 2017).

**Reflection**: How do you feel leadership and team building are connected?

_____

_____

_____

Have you had experiences where a leader was or was not supportive of the social justice mission of the team?

_____

_____

_____

Have you had an experience where the team was not supportive of the social justice mission of the leader?

_____

_____

_____

## Meta Processing

ER: So I don't know. Thinking about the structure of this chapter. I have no idea how to do this.

DH: Yeah, I was just about to say the same thing. I feel like we should probably just transcribe everything we've said, and then see if we can cut and paste it. Because I feel like we've said a lot. And we know what we want to say in this. . . . Why do we keep getting stuck here?

ER: I'm wondering if we couldn't organize it as more of a conversation, instead of trying to split it up into these different components.

DH: That's a wonderful idea, E, I love that. Because then it shows our team-work; it shows how you and I function as a team, what about if we transcribe it?

ER: Right? So if we transcribe it, and then every time one of the components of team building comes up we could say, these are the components. And then we could highlight those things or those terms every time they come up in our transcription.

DH: I love it. And that's the thing about social justice work. Being a social justice warrior is partly starting out thinking you're gonna accomplish X, but you might end up accomplishing Y, and it might be more valuable than what X was.

ER: Right. Right. It requires you to be open to pivot, which is that openness to learn to change direction, if needed, based on your commitment to the work that you do.

DH: Yeah, So I love the idea of doing it as a dialogue. I think that's great. I think you've been saying it all along. We have to do this processing together. So, we've been heading this way the whole time. It's just our brains didn't catch up with what we knew had to happen. It's kind of funny, isn't it?

ER: Yeah. I think that was what was challenging because dividing the work of writing this chapter and just taking a section and writing it wasn't working. I kept saying, I can't write this because I have to do it with you.

DH: Right, right. So even this chapter could not be written in a traditional way because we're talking about team building, we have to show you what a team looks like. Because we just keep interrogating and processing. That's what our conversations are. Right?

ER: Right. Right. So amazing. I mean, we're researching ourselves just by thinking about it and talking about it.

DH: Right, right. And to me, that would be the most powerful thing to write. It's what we want our readers to do. So, we're modeling what we want readers to do, which is to interrogate themselves and process with each other.

## References

Belenky, M. F., Clinchy, B. M., Goldberger, N. R., & Tarule, J. M. (1986). *Women's ways of knowing*. Basic Books.

Dewey, J. (1933). *How we think: A restatement of the relation of reflective thinking to the educative process*. Heath.

Friedman, S., & Harkins, D. A. (2017). Researching to promote empowerment. In D. A. Harkins (Ed.), *Alongside community: Learning in service*. New York: Routledge Press.

Lencioni, P. (2002). *The five dysfunctions of a team*. Jossey-Bass.

Mezirow, J. (1990). *Fostering critical reflection in adulthood*. Jossey-Bass.

Vygotsky, L. S. (1978). *Mind in society*. Harvard University Press.

# 7 Leading With Heart, Hope, and Hustle in Educational Contexts

*Carmen N. Veloria with Amanda Bernasconi*

In hindsight, I should have known that it was just a matter of time before my actions bumped up against institutional structures that severely limited critical dialogue. In my heart I knew this, but in a new leadership role, I thought I could circumvent the limited structures and improve them in the process. I did sense the danger, and thus was rattled by an earthquake that left me flailing, questioning my actions, and balancing on a thin spider web like an enormous elephant. Anthony T. Hincks once said that "Elephants will never abandon their friends or family, but man does. I guess that's what makes us civilized." What I learned from this experience is that those who believed and trusted me as a leader remained steadfast and joined me on that spiderweb, like the infinite number of balancing elephants who hop one after the other in the traditional Spanish counting song: "un elefante se balanceaba" (a balancing elephant). Those were my fellow-travelers, who saw my vision and believed in my intent . . . not the civilized man who was willing to put students' success on the line due to arrogance, entitlement, and a bruised ego.

As a faculty member, I had grown accustomed to the institutional rhetoric on student success and the contrast in terms of how it played out in the lives of some of the most vulnerable students. For some time, students had been sharing stories of discontent and discouragement, and as the incoming director of a student success center, I thought I could make a difference. I first focused on rebuilding a sense of trust amongst students and staff members, by being more restorative, communicative, and collaborative. Given the constant leadership changes, and the fact that I had a history of working with the staff, in my new role I wanted to initially focus on restoring and building relationships in order to introduce practical supervision and management strategies, and more importantly in an attempt to repair trust, which was in short supply due to leadership shifts and feelings of isolation. The staff commented that the center was disconnected from the rest of the institution, and this fundamentally led to feelings of being unheard when it came to decisions that impacted the center, staff, and students directly. I knew that to effectively manage anticipated institutional changes, a focus on relationship building was needed as all human beings have a deep desire to be in good relationships (Boyes-Watson & Pranis, 2013).

DOI: 10.4324/9781003055587-7

> Student centric programming and service had always been at the forefront of how my program had run. From the onset it was clear that the institution felt my program was external to the goal of the university. The revolving door of leadership over the course of my tenure had routinely positioned me to spend more time insulating my staff and students from the toxicity of the institution rather than focus on how best to serve them. In this new wave of leadership there was a renewed sense of investment and legitimacy; a tenured professor, working in the field, who understood the gravity of our work firsthand. However, it quickly became clear that despite being legitimized by our direct leader our voices, and work, would continue to be silenced, invalidated, and ignored.
>
> —Amanda Bernasconi

Over time, this leadership stance led to improved communication and increased collaboration in co-crafting a new vision and mission for the center. Collectively the need for a carefully constructed space was understood. The new vision and mission guided the feel of the center to the point that students and staff alike began to feel like they belonged with a renewed sense of pride and connectivity. The creation of a co-constructed space was one of my primary goals given the extent to which feelings of rejection or not fitting in are closely related to student attrition (Heisserer & Parette, 2002). Tinto (1987, 1993), for example, has argued that students' levels of integration into the academic and social subsystems of campus are positively related to student persistence and degree completion (Museus, Zhang, & Kim, 2016). I understood this and assumed that those working on issues of student success did as well, especially given the population the center served: first-generation students and students of color.

Given demographic shifts and the emphasis placed on helping this population, I join the growing number of researchers and practitioners who have critically and conceptually diverged from Tinto's Model of Student Integration to challenge educators and educational leaders to think in more culturally conscious ways about student success. For example, the concept of cultural integrity suggests that institutions need to create programs and practices that reflect and engage the cultural identities of college students of color to foster their success (Tierney, 1999; Museus et al., 2016). For me, this meant fostering a sense of belonging replete with cultural familiarity, which refers to students' opportunity to physically connect with faculty and staff who have similar backgrounds, experiences, and culturally relevant knowledge, which affords the opportunity to learn and exchange knowledge that is relevant to their own cultural communities (Museus et al., 2016). In the confines of the center, all of this was possible.

Imagine my surprise when months into my new role, I was told that the center was being moved to a new open-space concept, alongside many other centers that did not work directly with this population of students. This open-space concept was completely devoid of any of the cultural aspects that staff and students had devoted time and energy to co-creating. For the first time in a long time, there was a collective sense of belonging that would be hard to reconstruct. Perhaps not surprising, not long after the announcement was made, issues of trust were reignited, and staff and students began to express their discontent once again.

This time, however, it was different. By then, most of them had a short-lived vision of what was possible, and they were no longer willing to merely complain. They organized, strategized, and informed me that they "were taking actions into their own hands." They realized that I was in a compromised position and informed me out of courtesy and respect. I did not encourage them, but I also did not dissuade them. I knew that their actions would mean trouble ahead, especially for me, but I was willing to take that risk because fundamentally I believed their actions were in alignment with the values of the center. Their sense of agency was certainly rewarding to watch. Students who had previously felt voiceless were organizing and demanding that they be heard, especially as this move coincided with the ousting of a new university president who had been vocal about issues of diversity. Thus, the time was ripe for the students to demand that the center move be reconsidered. The move, the ousting of the president, and the students' new sense of social agency converged into the perfect storm.

At face value, the decision to move the center may not seem like a huge deal given that the move was framed as a relocation of sorts. But for first-generation, low-income students who already felt marginalized in their home institution, who were dealing with yet another major leadership change, and who by then had some language to name what they had been feeling, the move signaled an institutional assault. They already felt unaccounted for, unheard, and invisible at the institution-at-large, but the center was theirs, a space where many of them simply indicated that "they can let down their guard," "they were free to put down their masks," and "just be." Their comments were a rallying call for deeper understandings of the institutional conditions that contribute to students' persistent decisions. Educational leaders need to consider persistence in ways that are relevant to the experiences of students of color, those who are first in their family to attend college, and students from low-income families and other historically underrepresented groups (Hurtado & Carter, 1997; Tierney, 1999 in Johnson, Wasserman, Yildririm, & Yonai, 2014).

As the leader of a center, I understood where their concerns were coming from, as well as the need to attend to cultural dimensions of their background (Braxton, 2000). Working directly with them, I often heard exclusionary stories that were consistent with the literature on the experiences of first-generation students and students of color at predominantly white institutions (PWIs). I questioned whether the institution was serving them, but I felt completely conflicted. If I openly opposed the move, I would be perceived as insubordinate, out of step with my direct supervisor, who was overseeing the entire relocation plan aimed at combining several essential offices into a large open-floor concept. If I did not support the students, I risked not serving them, especially as the new mission was squarely focused on advocacy, community, and scholarship. Especially nagging at me was the recognition that the students simply needed to be affirmed, heard, and cared for, not just by me, but by the institution (Bray, 1985; Braxton, Vesper, & Hossler, 1995; Holmes, 2000; Tinto, 1993). I felt stuck between a rock and a hard place; I felt alone balancing on a thin spider web.

> Traditionally educational competencies include critical thinking, problem solving and communication, etc. While these educational competencies remain invaluable when ensuring students' development and success the role of empathy, life experience, and cultural competency is weighted highly when working with low income, first generation students.
>
> —Amanda Bernasconi

**Reflection:** *What would you have done? Would you have gone with the institutional plan to relocate the center, by telling the students that they had to accept the decision? Why or why not? Would you have wholeheartedly supported the students and by doing so risked getting written up or worse, fired? What action(s) would you have taken and why?*

_____

_____

_____

_____

_____

_____

_____

Like most leaders, I was facing a conundrum that required that I take some sort of action. Leaders are called upon to make all sorts of decisions with the understanding that for the most part, "the buck stops" with them. Irrespective of one's leadership style, leaders need to make decisions that require some type of action. Inaction, most times, is not an option. Certainly, not all decisions require such agony: decisions range from the mundane ordering of office supplies, to deciding on a venue for an event, or deciding on how to strategize with multiple stakeholders.

Leadership experts often recommend that leaders lead with their core values in mind, to reflect on these when facing the proverbial fork in the road (see Chapter 3 for more information about values). Those interested in leadership positions need to explore the core values that will guide their practice as these inform how one approaches an issue and the types of questions raised, and offer solace when a decision is made and a tsunami hits. In the following is a list of core values commonly used by leadership institutes and other related programs. While not meant to be an exhaustive list, it will provide you with examples to review, reflect upon, and consider adapting. The goal is to come up with your top three core values. Why three? This is based on the notion that "if everything is a core value, then nothing is really a priority." Think about your top three values as a guiding light of sorts. They will be able to guide you when you navigate institutional choppy waters (see Table 7.1).

*Which top three values do you want to lead with and why? Think back to Chapter 3 and consider that a rudimentary definition of a leader is a person who leads others. Which values will guide you in leading others?*

1. _____
2. _____
3. _____

*Rationale:* _____

_____

_____

_____

_____

_____

   To me, community, responsibility, and service matter greatly, and they are grounded in a social justice orientation to leading and programming in terms of "the conscious and reflexive blend of content and process, intended to enhance equity across multiple social identity groups (e.g. race, class, gender identity, sexual orientation, ability), foster critical perspectives, and promote social action" (Carlisle, Jackson, & George, 2006, p. 57). I believe that most solutions to issues that arise can be solved by being in community with others. Certainly, embedded in this are notions of respect, trust, and

*Table 7.1* Core Values List

| | | |
|---|---|---|
| Authenticity | Autonomy | Balance |
| Boldness | Compassion | Community |
| Determination | Equity | Friendships |
| Growth | Happiness | Honesty |
| Learning | Love | Openness |
| Optimism | Peace | Popularity |
| Recognition | Responsibility | Self-respect |
| Service | Trustworthiness | Wisdom |

wisdom, but the term "community" encapsulates all of this. As a member of communities, I have the responsibility to be in the service of others, particularly those who have been marginalized and silenced.

---

**The Democratic Leader:** Include others in the decision making; encourage feedback, innovation, and creativity.

**The Laissez Faire Leader:** Let others handle the day-to-day, and they mostly focus on the big picture.

**The Autocratic Leader:** Is involved with every aspect of the daily running of a program, center, school.

**The Bureaucratic Leader:** Lead "by the book." They are often versed on both policies and procedures as formally established by higher authority.

**The Tyrant Leader:** Often lead by fear, where staff and others often second guess their own decision-making.

**The Inspirational Leader:** They "work the room." They understand the value of inspiring others, build strong loyal followings, and can ask more of others. They understand educational issues that can hinder student success. (Simplicio, 2011).

---

It took time and maturing to arrive at this leadership orientation. Despite the prevalence of social justice language in educational settings, in practice, educational leaders desiring to create inclusive, socially just programming often find themselves constrained by rules, regulations, and other forms of institutional control measures (Foster, 2004). At the end of the day,

> leaders are not born but made. It is increasingly accepted, however, that in order to be a good leader, one must have the experience, knowledge, commitment, patience, and most importantly, the skills to negotiate and work with others to achieve goals.
>
> (Amanchukwu, Stanley, & Ololube, 2015)

While I agree with this definition, I also see the complexities that can arise in practice. It is not easy to negotiate and work with others within hierarchical structures, imbued with power dynamics that often do not permit or curtail critical dialogue. For example, how does one work with those who may have conflicting agendas or goals? As exemplified in my narrative, it was not just an issue of working with others, but ultimately attending to the needs of those I felt needed to be heard. Ultimately, how a leader wields power determines the fate of those under their authority. This power can be effectively utilized to the benefit of the educational project and its people or greatly abused for personal gain and even more power (Simplicio, 2011). Thus, values matter because fundamentally I had to make a value-laden judgement call: succumb to the request of the university and simply move the center or support students to contest the move, even if it meant that my role could potentially be on the line.

**Reflection:** *What type of leader am I if I opted to support the students? How does one's standpoints or sense of being in the world impact one's leadership styles? (See Chapter 2 for a discussion of how social identity influences one's perspective and experiences.) How does context influence one's leadership style and approaches?*

_____

_____

_____

_____

_____

_____

_____

## Leading in Context and Learning to See the Forest From the Trees

Leadership can be broadly defined in terms of traits, characteristics, and behaviors that focus on a clear vision, action, modelling the way, ethical relationships, congruence, trustworthiness, and collaboration (Avolio, Zhu, Koh, & Bhatia, 2004). A leader can be defined as a person who delegates or influences others to act to carry out specific objectives (Nanjundeswaraswamy & Swamy, 2014). There are countless definitions aimed at articulating leadership and detailing how leaders lead. Overtime, researchers have also proposed many different styles of leadership that can be considered universal (Amanchukwu et al., 2015). The ones listed earlier relate to leadership at university settings. At the end of the day, leadership styles are shaped by unique experiences, one's epistemology, personality, education and training, context, institutional culture, and staff dynamics. These styles are the way in which leaders influence staff and navigate institutional contexts. It is not uncommon for leaders to utilize multiple approaches rather than a one-size-fits-all method (Khan et al., 2015).

However, from a social justice framework, leading for me entails being critically educative, meaning that "it can not only look at the conditions in which we live, but it also must decide how to change them" (Foster, 1986, p. 185). A call to activism to challenge entrenched institutional structures reproduced by the dominant culture is what unites many of us who lead with a socially just orientation (Bogotch, 2002; Goldfarb & Grinberg, 2002; Grogan, 2004; Gruenewald, 2003; Marshall, 2004). This is because despite the prevalence of social justice language in educational settings, those on top often give only token consideration to social justice concerns

(Marshall, 2004). For example, while I focused on repairing relationships, building trust and collaborations broadly, in the case of my leadership dilemma, I did not delegate or instruct the staff or students to act or carry out specific objectives that were at odds with upper administration. I knew that I had to act and voice my concerns. This is where leadership and management can potentially collide. Individuals with management responsibilities focus on administrative rules, tasks, and functions to ensure the managerial goals of the organizations are met effectively (Ramsden, 1998). The fact of the matter is that the relocation of the center was being touted as an efficacious one—a one-stop shop for many services currently under different offices. However, this is not what was in the best interest of the students and would have ultimately led to additional discontent and silencing.

As a leader, I felt it necessary to openly share the concerns both staff and students shared about the relocation with the recognition that what was at stake was the loss of belonging, cultural space, and impact on student and staff morale. The staff did not want to relocate and openly expressed their feelings to me. I could sense that this move also brought back feelings of distrust. All this led me to focus on human outcomes, not efficient ones. However, these are harder to quantify as they do not always seem to count. Perhaps this is the pitfall of being a teacher-scholar-leader? Teacher leadership happens amid a complex context of policy, content, students, peers, and administrators, and its enactment in practice is far messier (Klein et al., 2018). Depending on context, all leaders are motivated by different outcomes, and my motivation was to prevent the undoing of the great strides collectively made in the backdrop of institutional distrust, lack of engagement, and uncertainty.

While some leaders in the business world may be motivated by meeting or exceeding quarterly goals and positively impacting the bottom line, leaders in the educational sectors may be motivated by students' well-being, the myriad of ways that they learn and grow, and programming that leads to successful educational outcomes. As a leader, who also happens to be a woman of color, leadership for me is not just about leading to meet objectives, but leading in a manner that signals to all, but especially to students, that leadership in higher education is in response to calls for more relevant democratic cultures and less hierarchical models of leadership. This approach emphasizes democratizing spaces in a distributive leadership style that focuses on "collective collaboration rather than individual power and control" to build leadership capacity in learning, teaching, and empowerment of students (Jones, Harvey, Lefoe, & Ryland, 2012, p. 67). I understood the power dynamics at play and the potential price I would have to pay, not only as a leader of color, but also as a woman in a leadership role (see Chapter 2). Audre Lorde eloquently comments on the devastating effects of silencing on the silenced. In her essay, *The Transformation of Silence into Language and*

*Action*, she captures the impact of silencing as spirit-murdering. Through a dream, she tells her daughter,

> Tell them about how you're never really a whole person if you remain silent because there's always that one little piece inside you that wants to be spoken out, and if you keep ignoring it, it gets madder and madder and hotter and hotter, and if you don't speak it out one day it will just up and punch you in the mouth from the inside.

I did not want to aid in silencing my students. I was not willing to assist in their oppression. I also wanted to remain whole, even if that meant having to ultimately submit my resignation. As a professor, I had taught courses on student activism and focused on students' agency and their authority to be authors of their future. How could I not support their activism? Why would I aid in muffling their voices and mine? In the end, I made the decision to support the students by stepping out of their way and opting to see the forest from the trees. The student demands to keep the center were not an unreasonable request. They were acting on what they had learned, that affirming identities matter, that issues of belonging are important, and that building relationships and social networks is imperative for first-generation, marginalized students. Like me, they knew the struggle to keep the center from relocating was beyond any one person; it was about acknowledgement, respect, and fighting so that future generations of students would not have the need to do so. As I was an educator, the students' personal growth and well-being mattered more to me. As I was a transformational leader, it was about influencing the change process with compassion, empathy, and dignity while managing the emotionally charged environment and helping to craft a wider vision of what it meant to work with first-generation and low-income college students.

A transformational leadership approach is known for its change-oriented leadership style at the organizational, group, and individual level of analysis with positive outcomes (Judge & Piccolo, 2004). At the organizational level, others at other centers and in other offices understood why the students did not want to relocate. They understood that symbolically, the center was more than just a physical space. The more and more that I shared about my dilemma, the clearer it became that supporting the students was the way to proceed. In discussions with colleagues and like-minded fellow-travelers, they believed in my mission and began advocating for me and the students, albeit in quieter ways. They began to leave all sorts of elephants in my office—ceramic, glass, wooden ones. Fearing retaliation from upper administration, this is the way they made their feelings known. Others started catching on, and soon staff members and students were adding to the collection. Collectively, this is how resistance was understood. It was no longer just me balancing on the spiderweb.

**Reflection:** *What was the significance of the elephants? Aside from resistance and resilience, what else could the elephants symbolize?*

_____

_____

_____

_____

_____

_____

_____

## Transformational Educational Leadership

In educational contexts, leadership not only matters, but is second only to teaching among other school factors that impact student learning. High-quality leaders impact teaching and learning by charting a clear course, helping to develop people, and making the organization work by making sure that a range of conditions fully support rather than inhibit teaching and learning.

What is known from the literature on student outcomes is that effective education leaders make a difference in promoting community, a sense of belonging, and impacting student learning by intentionally focusing on high-leverage practices that promote student success. For example, in terms of cultural responsiveness practices, Museus et al. (2016) highlight the following four indicators that focus on the extent to which campus environments are responsive to the cultural norms and needs of diverse populations:

1. Collectivist Cultural Orientation: this is based on the assumption that many students, especially students of color, originate from communities with more collectivist cultural orientation and might encounter increased challenges adjusting to and navigating colleges and university with more individualistic orientations (Dennis, Phinney, & Chuateco, 2005; Thompson & Fretz, 1991).

2. Humanized Educational Environments: this refers to the extent to which students can connect with faculty and staff with whom they can develop meaningful relationships and how they care about their success.

3. Proactive Philosophies: this refers to faculty and staff going beyond making information and support available to students and making extra efforts to bring that information and support to students whom they serve.

4. Holistic Support: this refers to the extent to which students have access to sources of support that they are confident will provide the information and support that they need or will serve as a conduit for students to access that necessary information and support.

By intentionally centering students and co-crafting spaces that attend to their needs, educational leaders can have a significant impact on the teaching and learning cultures of an institution by way of their approaches to sharing knowledge, forming positive social support networks, engaging in mentoring relationships, and facilitating change (Bolden, Petrov, & Gosling, 2008). From my perspective, all of this was taking place during my tenure at the center. For the community of students that I served, the educational stakes were and still are high. Fostering a sense of belonging is important to the success of all students, but especially for the retention of students who may be at risk of not completing their academic degree. Student support programs need to co-create culturally sustaining programming (Paris, 2016) that emphasizes teamwork, collaboration, developing meaningful relationships, supporting students to take advantage of opportunities that are available to them (e.g., waivers, scholarships, internships, professional development opportunities), and underscoring the importance of practitioners proactively serving as useful conduits for students to access larger support networks both on and off campus (Museus et al., 2016).

Jones and York (2016) make an especially important distinction between a leader and an effective leader. They entertain the question: what makes an effective leader? They posit that effective leaders focus on the following two key themes:

1. Relationships between people
2. Relationships between people who are working toward a common goal

They cite Warren Bennis, who expounds, "Leadership is grounded in a relationship. In its simplest form, it is a tripod—a leader or leaders, followers, and the common goal that they want to achieve. None of these elements can survive without the other" (Bennis, 2007). In their view, "Effective leadership, then, is grounded in an US mentality where the leader is in the role to aid the group in achieving its goal. The leader is neither a glory-seeker nor a self-aggrandizer" (p. 2). However, at the core, effective leaders must have a foundation grounded in the traditional skills like vision for success, field-specific knowledge and competencies, and related sector skills, in addition to essential skills like humility, empathy, and ability to communicate effectively across differences and with multiple stakeholders.

All this matters in the education sectors where deep structural inequities persist that prevent some students from progressing academically. In 2013, the Wallace Foundation conducted a review and synthesis of over 70 reports and significant publications on the effectiveness of school leadership. The report identified five primary functions of effective administrators as indicators of effective leadership:

1. Shaping a vision of academic success for all students
2. Creating a climate hospitable to education

3.  Cultivating leadership in others
4.  Improving educational outcomes
5.  Effectively managing people, data, and processes to foster improvement

From working in various educational programs and sectors, I am aware that all of this greatly matters. While effectiveness is a lofty goal, an even greater one is aiming for transformation, not only of the student being served, but of the staff that will more than likely go on to continue serving cadres of other students. According to educational blogger Judi Steele (2018), transformative leaders share the following eight attributes:

1.  **Disruptive Thinking.** Transformative leaders do not accept the status quo. They demonstrate the courage to bust out of the cage and openly acknowledge current structures that do not best serve students. They share their vision for new horizons and inspire others to do the same.
2.  **Active Listening.** Transformative leaders are open to listening. They acknowledge that others share similar interests and are critical thought partners. They seek continuous feedback and improvement for themselves, their team, their students, their school, and their system.
3.  **Cognitive Diversity.** Transformative leaders embrace big, bold ideas to better serve students. They acknowledge that as opposed to one panacea, transforming systems requires multiple ideas for programs, policies, data, and feedback. They identify other burgeoning leaders in their space and recruit them as partners for ideas and action.
4.  **Collaborative Problem-Solving.** Transformative leaders inspire colleagues and others in the community to mobilize around a common goal, and then lead these teams to develop and execute effective solutions to better serve students.
5.  **Finding Common Ground.** Transformative leaders acknowledge that different people can and will disagree on ideas and their execution. These leaders facilitate open, critical dialogue to reaffirm common goals, inspire open minds, and rally around shared ideas and ideals for change.
6.  **Cross-Sector Collaboration.** Transformative leaders understand the power of collaboration with various sectors—private and public, government and nonprofit, within and outside of education. They form meaningful bonds with key stakeholders from various sectors and assemble them around common goals to better serve students.
7.  **Leveraging Resources.** Transformative leaders understand the sources of financial and other forms of capital. They develop their human talent to maximize different resources efficiently and effectively, all to support their students.
8.  **Cultivating Higher Levels of Engagement.** Transformative leaders, through all these attributes, inspire others to view an expansive horizon about the role of education in a rapidly evolving world. These leaders inspire others to think deeply, improve purposely, and act boldly.

The staff was watching, and some may have even been influenced by my leadership style and approach to programming. For example, I have now formally and informally mentored the second author, AH, who has gone on to lead educational programs. Additionally, many of the students served at the center have gone on to graduate school—to someday become educational leaders. I may or may never know who else may have been influenced, or even transformed. For now, I take comfort in emails, notes, and tokens of appreciation received from time to time, like the beautifully crafted elephant coasters I received from a former graduate student who worked at the center during my tenure. I smiled when I received this gift. I took it as a sign that she had quietly been on that spiderweb with me, sharing in that complex hope that draws attention to the need to overcome historical and structural difficulties (Grace, 1994). Their support gives me hope as there is still work to be done, now more than ever.

# References

Amanchukwu, R., Stanley, G., & Ololube, N. (2015). A review of leadership theories, principles and styles and their relevance to educational management. *Management Science, 5*(1), 6–14.

Avolio, B. J., Zhu, W., Koh, W., & Bhatia, P. (2004). Transformational leadership and organizational commitment: Mediating role of psychological empowerment and moderating role of structure distance. *Journal of Organizational Behavior, 25*(8), 951–968.

Bennis, W. (2007). The challenges of leadership in the modern world: Introduction to the special issue. *American Psychologist, 62*(1), 2–5. https://doi.org/10.1037/0003-066X.62.1.2

Bogotch, I. E. (2002). Educational leadership and social justice: Practice into theory. *Journal of School Leadership, 12*(2), 138–156. https://doi.org/10.1177/105268460201200203

Bolden, R., Petrov, G., & Gosling, J. (2008). Tensions in higher education leadership: Toward a multi-level model of leadership practice. *Higher Educational Quarterly, 62*, 358–376.

Boyes-Watson, C., & Pranis, K. (2013). *Circle forward: Building a restorative school community.* Living Justice Press.

Braxton, J. M. (Ed.). (2000). *Reworking the departure puzzle: New theory and research on college student retention.* Vanderbilt University Press.

Braxton, J. M., Vesper, N., & Hossler, D. (1995). Expectations for college and student persistence. *Research in Higher Education, 36*, 595–611. https://doi.org/10.1007/BF02208833

Bray, C. (1985). Early identification of dropout prone students and early intervention strategies to improve student retention at a private university (Doctoral dissertation). Retrieved from *Dissertation Abstracts International, 47*(1). University of Texas.

Carlisle, L. R., Jackson, B. W., & George, A. (2006). Principles of social justice education: The social justice education in schools project. *Equity & Excellence in Education, 39*(1), 55–64. https://doi.org/10.1080/10665680500478809

Dennis, J. M., Phinney, J. S., & Chuateco, L. I. (2005). The role of motivation, parental support, and peer support in the academic success of ethnic minority first-generation college students. *Journal of College Student Development, 46*, 223–236. https://doi.org/10.1353/csd.2005.0023

Foster, W. (1986). The decline of the local: A challenge to educational leadership. *Educational Administration Quarterly, 40*(2), 176–191. https://doi.org/10.1177/0013161 X03260360

Goldfarb, K. P., & Grinberg, J. (2002). Leadership for social justice. *Journal of School Leadership, 12*(2), 157–173. https://doi.org/10.1177/105268460201200204

Grace, G. (1994). Urban education and the culture of contentment: The politics, culture, and economics of inner-city schooling. In N. Stromquist (Ed.), *Education in urban areas: Cross-national dimensions.* Praeger.

Grogan, M. (2004). Keeping a critical, postmodern eye on educational leadership in the United States: In appreciation of Bill Foster. *Educational Administration Quarterly, 40,* 222–239. https://doi.org/10.1177/0013161X03261237

Gruenewald, D. (2003). Foundations of place: A multidisciplinary framework for place-conscious education. *American Educational Research Journal, 40,* 619–654. https://doi. org/10.3102/00028312040003619

Heisserer, D., & Parette, P. (2002). Advising at-risk students in college and university settings. *College Student Journal, 36*(1), 1–12.

Holmes, S. (2000). *Student recruitment, retention, and monitoring.* www.diversityweb.org/ Leadershipguide/RRAA/Student_Retention/intrusive.html

Hurtado, S., & Carter, D. F. (1997). Effects of college transition and perceptions of the campus racial climate on Latino college students' sense of belonging. *Sociology of Education, 70,* 324–345. https://doi.org/10.2307/2673270

Johnson, D., Wasserman, T., Yildirim, N., & Yonai, B. (2014). Examining the effects of stress and campus climate on the persistence of students of color and white students: An application of Bean and Eaton's psychological model of retention. *Research in Higher Education, 55,* 75–100. https://doi.org/10.1007/s11162-013-9304-9

Jones, A. M., & York, S. L. (2016). The fragile balance of power and leadership. *The Journal of Values-Based Leadership, 9*(2), 1–14. https://doi.org/10.1177/1741143213510506

Jones, S., Harvey, M., Lefoe, G., & Ryland, K. (2012). Synthesizing theory and practice: Distributed leadership in higher education. *Education Management Administration & Leadership, 42,* 603–619.

Judge, T. A., & Piccolo, R. F. (2004). Transformational and transactional leadership: A meta-analytic test of their relative validity. *Journal of Applied Psychology, 89,* 755–768. https://doi.org/10.1037/0021-9010.89.5.755

Khan, M. S., Khan, I., Qureshi, Q. A., Ismail, H. M., Rauf, H., Latif, A., & Tahir, M. (2015). The styles of leadership: A critical review. *Public Policy and Administration Research, 5*(3), 87–92.

Klein, E., Taylor, M., Munakata, M., Trabona, K., Rahman, Z., & McManus, J. (2018). Navigating teacher leaders' complex relationships using a distributed leadership framework. *Teacher Education Quarterly, 45*(2), 89–112. http://doi:10.2307/90020316

Marshall, C. (2004). Social justice challenges to educational administration: Introduction to a special issue. *Educational Administration Quarterly, 40*(1), 5–15. https://doi. org/10.1177/0013161X03258139

Museus, S., Zhang, D., & Kim, M. (2016). Developing and evaluating the culturally engaging campus environments (CECE) scale: An examination of content and construct validity. *Research in Higher Education, 57,* 768–793. https://doi.org/10.1007/ s11162-015-9405-8

Nanjundeswaraswamy, T. S., & Swamy, D. R. (2014). Leadership styles. *Advances in Management, 7,* 57–62.

Paris, D. (2016). *On educating culturally sustaining teachers.* Teaching Works.

Ramsden, P. (1998). *Learning to lead in higher education.* Routledge Press.

Simplicio, J. (2011). It all starts at the top: Divergent leadership styles and their impact upon a university. *Education, 132,* 110–114.

Steele, J. (2018). 8 attributes of transformative educational leaders. *Education Week.* https://blogs.edweek.org/edweek/rick_hess_straight_up/2018/03/8_attributes_of_transformative_educational_leaders.html

Thompson, C. E., & Fretz, B. R. (1991). Predicting the adjustment of Black students at predominantly white institutions. *Journal of Higher Education, 62,* 437–450. https://doi.org/10.2307/1982004

Tierney, W. G. (1999). An anthropological analysis of student participation in college. *Journal of College Student Personnel, 28,* 485–495. https://doi.org/10.2307/1982046

Tinto, V. (1987, 1993). *Leaving college: Rethinking the causes and cures of student attrition* (2nd ed.). University of Chicago Press.

## Resources

Core Values List: https://jamesclear.com/core-values

School Principal as Leader: www.wallacefoundation.org/knowledge-center/pages/the-school-principal-as-leader-guiding-schools-to-better-teaching-and-learning.aspx

Un Elefante Se Balanceaba Lyrics and Activities: www.spanishplayground.net/un-elefante-se-balanceaba-lyrics-activities/

# 8 Mentoring to Promote Social Justice

*Lauren I. Grenier, Elizabeth Robinson,
and Debra A. Harkins*

We begin this chapter by exploring what it means to promote social justice as we consider how critical, multicultural feminist mentoring can be used as a tool to shape and promote social justice. To demonstrate how this model can be implemented, we present a framework of a tiered service-learning mentoring program. Unfortunately, COVID-19 happened in the midst of this pilot service-learning multi-tiered mentoring program and provided unforeseen lessons to us and all involved, which we explore in this chapter. While our framework is specific to the context of higher education and community collaboration, the perspectives from our mentors and mentees have powerful lessons that can be applied across mentoring relationships. From reflection on this mentoring program, we hold onto the lessons we have learned as we look forward and imagine mentoring as a tool we can use in our work of creating a society that champions peace, love, equity, liberation, and freedom.

## Promoting Social Justice

Social justice requires changing what is unjust in our society. We want to be clear that the term "social justice" itself can perpetuate injustices. As Tuck and Yang (2012) argue, the recognition and celebration of diversity or the language of inclusion within racist and colonial structures does nothing to change the harmful structures themselves. Instead, what is needed is a "change in the order of the world" (p. 35). This type of change cannot be created on an individual level. Critiquing and redistributing power requires collectivity, reciprocity, and mutuality (Grande, 2019), with a focus on collaboration in pursuit of the collective good over individualistic desires. However, for many living and working in the systems and structures produced by capitalism and the neoliberal belief in meritocracy, collaboration is not promoted or rewarded.

> **Colonialism** is the process of one country or nation seeking to extend or retain its authority by dominating and exploiting other peoples and territories. Colonizers or settlers view the people and the land they

DOI: 10.4324/9781003055587-8

colonize as commodities to be leveraged for capital gain (money). Colonizers impose organization, governance, and policies necessary to rationalize their power through maintaining unfair, inequitable social structures. White, European settlers have colonized all of the Americas.

As critical educators, we draw on Paulo Freire's theory of "conscientization" to think about moving individuals toward the collective action necessary to bring about change. *Conscientização*, or consciousness-raising, refers to the processes in which an individual moves from magical to naive to critical social consciousness (Freire, 1973). According to Freire, the "magical stage of awareness" refers to people's assumptions that problems or inequalities in life are beyond human control, and therefore people accept life as it is. Naive consciousness is a state in which people are aware of problems but see problems as attributed to individuals. In the naive stage, addressing problems becomes an individual's responsibility. Many helpers are at this stage and assume they are saving others, in what is often referred to as a savior complex—an attitude that may promote more harm than good. It is not until reaching critical consciousness that people understand systemic issues and the ways that systems and structures create problems (Lake & Kress, 2013). In order to reach critical consciousness, people need space to reflect, ask questions, and recognize the inconsistencies in their social and political context, in order to acknowledge that change must occur on the collective level. The outcome of the process of consciousness-raising results in working together in the creation of new societal norms, rules, procedures, and policies.

Neoliberalism is a political ideology that was embraced by Margaret Thatcher, Ronald Reagan, and Deng Xiaoping in the very early 1980s. This ideology now defines the way most people view the world. Competition is the defining characteristic of human relations. Meritocracy, the belief that everyone must make their own way, promotes individualism and consumerism. The markets and corporations have unregulated and indisputable power. Neoliberalism promotes privatization, deregulation, tax cuts, and free trade deals all for the purpose of accumulating wealth. Protections for people and our planet have been sacrificed in order to maximize profits.

## Critical Multicultural Feminist Mentoring

We use mentoring as a tool to engage others in this process of consciousness-raising, in an effort to reach critical social consciousness. We adopt a critical multicultural feminist model of mentoring (Arczynski, 2017; Benishek, 2004; Fassinger, 1997) that demands attention to context, practices of relationality, collaboration, and reflexivity in a mentoring relationship. Contextual consciousness examines "the influencing function of governing ideologies, like neoliberalism, on systems and individuals" (Arczynski et al., 2018, p. 956). Relationality is a focus on the relational aspects of the mentoring relationships, moving beyond a transactional relationship to one grounded in mutual respect and trust. Collaboration focuses on the mentor and mentee working together to identify and work towards the mentee's goals. **Reflexivity** is the practice of engaging in critical reflection about one's mentoring practice (see Chapters 4 and 6).

Within a mentoring relationship, both the mentee and mentor engage in a process of growth. In a relationship grounded in mutual respect and trust, the mentee learns from the mentor and feels relational support as they engage in their own journey of conscientization. The mentor provides guidance, validation, and follows through on their commitment to the mentee, while reflecting more deeply on their own learning. Additionally, the mentor and the mentee both collaborate together to act towards social justice and create change. Through this action and in combination with reflexivity, both the mentor and the mentee engage in their own learning process.

Mentoring has an undeniable power dynamic between mentor and mentee. While traditional mentoring relationships are often viewed as hierarchical with an emphasis on what the mentee gains from the mentor, a critical multicultural feminist model recognizes power differentials within a mentoring relationship, understands these limitations, and makes a concerted effort to redistribute power. Critical feminist mentoring highlights:

1. power dynamics exist through both status positions (mentor or mentee),
2. power dynamics can be exacerbated through intersecting identity differences between the mentor and mentee.

Critical feminist mentoring states that while power differentials are unavoidable in mentoring relationships, we can work to manage and minimize these power differentials through collaboration and transparency. Where power differentials cannot be eliminated, the mentor and mentees should turn towards conversations about power and critically reflect on how it impacts the dynamic of their relationship, and how power influences social structures and relationships in society more broadly.

Another way to manage power dynamics within a mentoring relationship is to put an emphasis on the relationship itself. Feminist mentoring advocates for shared power within the relationship with an emphasis on the reciprocal and relational component of mentoring, where all are benefiting from the relationship. Multicultural feminist mentoring also recognizes and incorporates the identities of those in the relationships (e.g., race, ethnicity, gender identity, sexual orientation, socioeconomic status, ability, and more) in an attempt to build a deeper connection. With this structure in place, multicultural feminist mentoring allows not only for transformation of the mentee, but also for personal transformation for the mentor. Both the mentor and mentee engage in a mutual process of consciousness-raising, where they both learn from each other and shift their understanding through critical reflection and engage in action oriented towards a more equitable society.

**Reflection:** Reflect back on an experience when you were either a mentor or a mentee. How did power impact this mentoring relationship? Were there efforts made to acknowledge and address this power?

_____

_____

_____

## Our Context: Service-Learning Mentoring

Feminist mentoring values attention to context—personal, relational, community, historical, and sociopolitical (Arczynski, Christensen, & Hoover, 2018). In pursuit of these aims, we present our context as an applied example of feminist mentoring: a service-learning mentoring program that bridges a mid-sized urban university with urban community partners. This model represents a mentoring practice with the aim of promoting critical service-learning pedagogy. This unique pedagogy aims to promote justice through working with communities and engaging learners in raising critical consciousness around their own identities and positionality, and the ways in which these factors influence the sociopolitical landscape. **Critical service-learning** pedagogy combines experiential service, academic content, and critical reflection in a course-based, credit-bearing educational experience (see Chapters 2 and 4 for additional information about service-learning approaches). This pedagogy is opposed to more traditional models of service-learning, which often reify and deepen existing power differentials. Critical service-learning pedagogy aligns with feminist mentoring in three ways:

1. valuing authentic relationships,
2. recognizing power differentials with a commitment to redistribute power,
3. employing a social change orientation targeted towards recognizing inequalities and engaging in asset-based strategies for meaningful change.
   (Mitchell, 2008)

Our service-learning mentoring program was born out of the need to provide more support for service-learning students and for faculty teaching service-learning courses in an attempt to reach more critical service-learning outcomes. Our team of faculty and graduate students, led by DH, developed a multi-tiered service-learning mentoring program at an urban, private university in the northeast (Harkins et al., 2020). Faculty from various disciplines in a FPLC—faculty and professional learning community— (including DH and ER) joined with a graduate psychology student (LG) to develop a mentoring program. Lessons learned from this faculty service-learning mentoring is described in an earlier publication (Robinson & Harkins, 2018) and in Chapter 6, where we describe one faculty mentoring relationship that arose from this initiative. The initial goal of the FPLC program was to mentor faculty who were new to service-learning pedagogy as they learned this new approach to teaching and learning through the provision of support for the more challenging task of teaching critical pedagogy.

---

In an effort to reach more justice-oriented outcomes, **service-learning mentoring** is a relationally focused process that supports students' professional, social, and civic development through reflection on what it means to help, the role of power in helping, and how personal values impact helping (Harkins, 2017).

---

I was interested in service-learning because I had previously supervised student teaching practica. I thought it would be similar, but I still had many questions. When I found out that Debra was willing to mentor me as I explored and developed a service-learning course, I felt like I had hit the jackpot! I had never had someone offer to mentor me and help me.

—Elizabeth Robinson, Ed.D, Service-Learning
Educator (second author)

As the program grew, it encompassed multiple levels of mentoring including faculty-faculty, faculty–graduate student, graduate student–undergraduate student, and undergraduate student–undergraduate students (see Figure 8.1). In structuring our service-learning mentoring model, we were attuned to power dynamics and context within the relationships depicted. With an awareness of power dynamics inherent in mentoring relationships, we represent our model in a cyclical shape, rather than a hierarchical pyramid. Furthermore, the dotted circles within each position represent the fluidity among positions as time progresses: a service-learning student may become a service-learning assistant mentor, or a new service-learning faculty may transition into a senior-SL faculty as they build their skill sets within mentoring and service-learning.

Attending to context, our mentoring program encompasses both the context of higher education and community partners, and where these contexts merge—with a recognition of the challenges that may arise as the individualistic and meritocratic values of higher education meet the values of local communities. These contexts are situated within the larger sociopolitical sphere. Social and political events will directly or indirectly influence the relationships within the model.

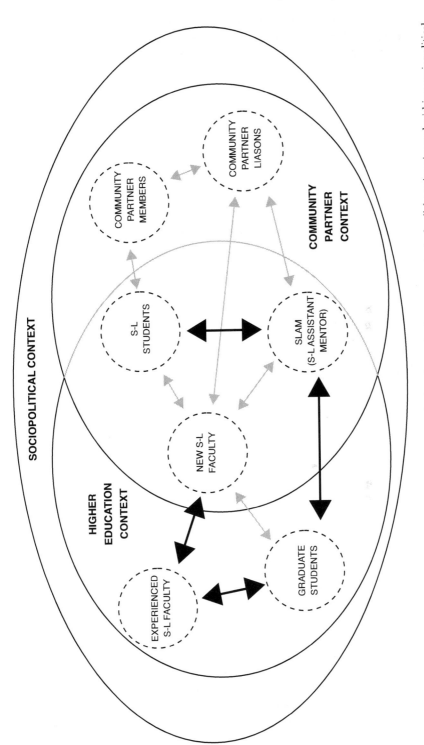

*Figure 8.1* Our service-learning mentoring model highlights the complexity of engaging in a cross-contextual collaboration situated within a sociopolitical context. We value creating strong relationships among different represented parties. We recognize the importance of power, and work collaboratively to redistribute power.

### Service-Learning Assistant Mentor (SLAM) Model

A unique component of this scaffolded mentoring program is peer mentoring, which serves in part to address some of the power differentials inherent in mentoring relationships. While faculty engage in a peer mentoring model, there is also a student peer mentoring component. Undergraduates with experience in service-learning, **service-learning assistant mentors (SLAM)s**, are placed in service-learning classes to mentor other undergraduates engaging in service-learning. The major role of the student mentor or SLAM is to mentor service-learners as they work with the community. This mentoring relationship opens a new space for critical reflection and increases the service-learners' civic engagement attitudes, serving as a bridge to authentic critical service-learning outcomes. Students working as SLAMs take a leadership position in service-learning classrooms and partner with faculty members teaching service-learning courses. To demonstrate the feminist mentoring values of relationality, collaboration, and reflexivity, SLAMs share their experiences serving as mentors during the unique semester transitioning to remote learning amidst the COVID-19 pandemic later in this section.

*Relationality*

The ability to stay connected in these mentoring relationships and with the community proved critically important during the COVID-19 pandemic and the resulting shift to remote learning. For many, separation from classmates, teachers, and friends resulted in an increased sense of isolation. The importance of relationality was highlighted by SLAMs during this experience of adjusting to remote learning that was shared across the mentoring relationships. SLAMs engaged in a relational approach with their mentees by validating student struggles and following through on their commitments to serve as their mentor (Arczynski & Morrow, 2017; Benishek, Bieschke, Park, & Slattery, 2004). One SLAM, Dhoma Gurung, who managed her role while in a different time zone from others in the course, highlights her shared experience with students during the difficult transition to remote learning, and how she utilized her role as a mentor to support her students:

> This experience has taught me how to be a better listener and a speaker in some ways. I have learned to understand the struggles and challenges that teachers go through when unexpected things happen, and we are forced to close down all the schools. One of the difficulties I had was to get everyone to share issues with their partners and even when they did, I struggled to respond to their challenges. Since I felt the need to help them with problem-solving, but I myself was not sure about how to overcome those issues that they were having. I also struggled with the difference in time zone. . . . I had to lead by example so the students

in Dr. Robinson's class would take it seriously as well. This experience definitely made me a better leader and allowed me to know where my flaws are.

—Dhoma Gurung, SLAM Spring 2020

Here, Dhoma exemplifies qualities of relationality through her commitment to her students. Dhoma related to the struggle of her mentees, as she had a shared experience of engaging in remote learning during this public health emergency. While validating her mentee's responses, she also led by example and continued her commitment to be a mentor during these challenging times. Through this process, and by remaining connected to her faculty member and fellow SLAM, she learned more about herself.

In addition to relating with student mentees, SLAMs also shared a sense of community among their SLAM peers and under the guidance and mentorship of a graduate student (LG). In this way, students are supporting students in this new type of classroom work, while under the guidance of graduate students and faculty. SLAM Donyka Dumornay highlights the impact of this community:

I think the SLAM program is so important, because its format is so unique and powerful. Usually when someone takes a leadership role there is a generic training that covers all of the basics, but as a SLAM you are weekly gaining tips and tools to use for leadership. More importantly, the reflections that we have with each other are important because we can bounce ideas off of each other. There's no better feeling than when someone can relate to what you are going through. I definitely felt like I related to my fellow mentors and it was nice to know we had that network.

—Donyka Dumornay, SLAM Spring 2020

Donyka appreciated the relatedness and sense of community among her SLAM peers and understood the importance of feeling validated by others. Donyka embodied this relationality and translated it to her work with her mentees.

### Collaboration

We want to highlight the importance of collaborative learning between those who serve as mentors and mentees. Feminist mentoring values the dynamic of collaborative learning, where each party learns from the other; as opposed to a top-down model where the mentor is the sole teacher, or provider of knowledge, and the mentee is the student, or recipient of knowledge. The double-sided arrows of the service-learning mentoring model (see Figure 8.1) represent the bidirectionality of learning between both parties in the mentoring relationship.

We also incorporated two different types of relationships: formal mentoring relationships, and informal learning relationships. Within a complex system such as service-learning mentoring, we are constantly impacted by and learning from those surrounding us, regardless of whether we enter into a formal mentoring relationship with them. The relationship built between SLAMs and faculty proved to be an important relationship in this service-learning mentoring program:

> I am grateful for my partnership with [S-L professor], who valued my input and made sure to check in with me on a personal level before we discussed the course. She gave me the opportunity to be a leader and make decisions for the class, such as how we should design the honors project and what each team should be working on at the service site. I think that I have grown through this mentor role as I became more comfortable talking in front of the class and leading group discussions.
> —Olivia Marotta, SLAM Spring 2020

Olivia identifies the importance of collaborating with her faculty, and how shared power between the SLAM and professor helped Olivia increase her sense of competence and her efficacy as a peer mentor.

### *Reflexivity*

In many ways, the service-learning classroom, and those who are engaged in the work—SL students, SLAMs, and faculty—represent a bridge between the context of the community partners and that of higher education institutions. SLAMs serve as a bridge between the service-learning students and community partners. One of the responsibilities of the SLAMs was to engage students in reflexivity. Through leading group critical reflection, SLAMs helped students start to recognize sociopolitical power structures, and how they shape society. SLAM Madison Mignola comments here:

> This experience not only shed light on how important connection is for a community to truly flourish. I sensed that many of the students' perspectives had changed from what they were in the beginning of the semester. Over time, it was more apparent to me that the students "got it," in terms of understanding not only their influence, but the overall influences of the power structures that exist within society and how they adversely affect certain groups. I became more cognizant of that, too.
> —Madison Mignola, SLAM Spring 2020

Madison identifies the experience of consciousness-raising for her student mentees, through the process of service-learning and critical reflexivity. Madison, through her role as mentor, also engaged in her own learning process throughout her semester's work, and increasingly recognized power structures in our unjust society.

**Reflection:** Think back to a time where you grappled with sociopolitical issues and inequities. How did the values of collaboration, relationality, and reflexivity play a role?

_____

_____

_____

These words from the SLAMs involved in this mentoring process highlight the importance of critical multicultural feminist mentoring for consciousness-raising and working towards creating a more equitable and just society. Reflecting back on this service-learning mentoring program during the COVID-19 pandemic, we share our reflections and plans for moving forward.

## Lessons Learned and Future Plans

Authoring this chapter has given us the space and time to critically reflect on our roles and our experiences as faculty and a graduate student who developed the program. Critical multicultural feminist mentoring theories have given us a lens through which to conduct our reflection.

Our first lesson is that building relationships is at the heart of mentoring and social justice. The successes of our mentoring model were largely due to strong and mutually beneficial and respectful relationships. This lesson is supported by critical multicultural feminist mentoring's insistence on attention to relationality.

Our second lesson is related to critical multicultural feminist mentoring's call for collaboration and attention to context. We recognized that our critical work of challenging traditional hierarchical structures and working to share power more equitably was not promoted or even recognized within our context of higher education. We saw this as we faced various hurdles in the development and implementation of the program. Our goals of promoting social justice require addressing injustices and working to change them. Many of these injustices are upheld, promoted, and maintained through institutional systems of dominance. Maintaining the dominance of mentor over mentee, professor over student, administrators over faculty, and higher education over community partners are all relationships within the context of higher education that need to be challenged. We believe that social justice work within the sociopolitical context of higher education is a challenge and most likely a threat to the operations of institutions of higher education. Therefore, collaboration and critical reflection is a necessary component of engaging in critical work. It is necessary to have people with shared values of social justice to lead critical programming within institutional structures in an effort to break down these existing barriers and power structures.

Finally, we recognize that change is constant. In our ongoing attention to our context and reflection on our program and ourselves, we have all discussed at various times how challenging it is to build a program, or maintain participation in our mentoring program, when guidelines, funding, departments, regulations, and more are constantly shifting and changing. We have found ways to adapt critical service-learning to a remote learning environment through the shifting needs brought on by the COVID-19 pandemic. Through our collaboration, we have learned to be flexible and adaptable. We value our ability to pivot, to react, to change.

As we balance looking backwards through reflection on our service-learning mentoring program, we value this flexibility and willingness to pivot as we embrace the change to come in higher education. We recognize the need for higher education to adapt as our society reckons with the ever-growing inequalities and inequitable distribution of resources. As we grapple with the necessary change of higher education that will come in a post COVID-19 world, we leverage critical multicultural feminist mentoring as a tool to promote social justice outcomes. We have collectively learned to plan for change, we have adapted with this change, and we work together to embrace the change that will come.

## References

Arczynski, A. V. (2017). Multicultural social justice group psychotherapy training: Curriculum development and pilot. *Training and Education in Professional Psychology, 11*, 227–234. https://doi.org/10.1037/tep0000161

Arczynski, A. V., Christensen, C., & Hoover, S. M. (2018). Fostering critical feminist multicultural qualitative research mentoring. *The Counseling Psychologist, 46*(8).

Arczynski, A. V., & Morrow, S. L. (2017). The complexities of power in feminist multicultural psychotherapy supervision. *Journal of Counseling Psychology, 64*(2), 192–205. https://doi.org/10.1037/cou0000179

Benishek, L., Bieschke, K., Park, J., & Slattery, S. (2004). A multicultural feminist model of mentoring. *Journal of Multicultural Counseling and Development, 32*, 428–442.

Fassinger, R. E. (1997, August). Dangerous liaisons: Reflections on feminist mentoring. *Invited "Women of the Year" Award address presented at the Annual Meeting of American Psychology Association*, Chicago, IL.

Freire, P. (1973). *Education for critical consciousness* (1st American ed.). New York: Seabury Press.

Grande, S. (2019). Refusing the university. In E. Tuck & K. W. Yang (Eds.), *Toward what justice? Describing diverse dreams of justice in education* (pp. 47–65). Routledge.

Harkins, D. A. (Ed.). (2017). *Alongside community: Learning in service.* Routledge Press.

Harkins, D. A., Grenier, L. I., Irizarry, C., Robinson, E., Ray, S., & Shea, L. M. (2020). Building relationships for critical service-learning. *Michigan Journal of Community Service Learning, 26*(2), 1–17. https://doi.org/10.3998/mjcsloa.3239521.0026.202

Lake, R., & Kress, T. (2013). *Paulo Freire's intellectual roots: Toward historicity in Praxis.* Bloomsbury Publishing.

Mitchell, T. D. (2008). Using a critical service-learning approach to facilitate civic identity development. *Theory into Practice, 54*(1), 20–28. https://doi.org/10.1080/004058 41.2015.977657

Robinson, E., & Harkins, D. A. (2018). Lessons learned from faculty service-learning mentoring. *Journal of Community Engagement and Higher Education, 10*(9).

Tuck, E., & Yang, K. W. (2012). Decolonization is not a metaphor. *Decolonization: Indigeneity, Education & Society, 1*(1), 1–40.

## Resources

Establishing Mutually Beneficial Partnerships: https://rampages.us/ceinstitute/wp-content/uploads/sites/15845/2016/05/Brown2015_StrategiesforEstablishingMutuallyBeneficial Service-LearningPartnerships.pdf

Mentoring Training Manual: https://studylib.net/doc/7717112/mentor-training-manual-washington-campus-compact

Reflection Toolkit: https://forumea.org/wp-content/uploads/2018/04/ST-Reflection-Toolkit.pdf

# 9 Teaching for Social Justice

*Mary Beth Medvide*

As I prepared to write this chapter, I reflected on my own training as a graduate student at Boston College, where I had the privilege to learn from professors whose commitment to social justice was evident in their teaching pedagogy and research endeavors. These professors believed in the things they were teaching and lived these principles in their actions outside the classroom. This authenticity provided the foundation of meaningful teaching interactions with students and an atmosphere where social justice issues are at the forefront of course design. Ultimately this authenticity challenged me to be a critical thinker personally and professionally. These were lessons that I carried with me through my professional training and into my academic career. In many ways, these lessons and the reflections they fostered form the basis for this chapter and what I hope to offer the reader.

This chapter will focus primarily on teaching for social justice in counseling psychology graduate courses and psychology undergraduate courses. However, the themes that weave the chapter together are relevant across the social sciences, the humanities, and STEM coursework and for those who hope to supervise, mentor, or coach others. Throughout the chapter, reflection questions are placed to foster self-exploration among instructors who are already infusing social justice concepts and values into the planning and execution of their courses, and instructors who want to revitalize their pedagogy with a more explicit focus on social justice.

*Reflection Question: What has your education or training experience been like, and how has it influenced your understanding of best practices when it comes to teaching?*

---

## Teaching for Social Justice

Teaching for social justice in this chapter is situated in formal and informal aspects of teaching in ways that have long been planned out and in the spontaneous moments that arise in class discussion. This can be realized through

DOI: 10.4324/9781003055587-9

the work of individual instructors as well as the collective efforts of entire programs and departments (Goodman et al., 2014). Scholars such as Sue and Sue (2016) and Ratts (2009) provide examples of the formal integration of social justice issues into coursework and syllabus design where the topics are explicitly identified prior to the semester and are integral to graduation requirements and competence-building. Neville (2015) discussed how her values and commitment to social justice inform her formal decision-making when designing a course and more informal interactions with students as a semester unfolds.

These informal interactions are particularly relevant in our current historical moment in the context of movements such as Black Lives Matter (BLM) that challenge racism in the United States and galvanized activism in communities and on campuses across the country (Castillo-Montoya, Abreu, & Abad, 2019). The actions and ideologies of BLM provide opportunities for spontaneous discussion of specific events, such as the death of George Floyd, and bridge the current political climate with the larger sociopolitical history of a specific discipline, such as psychology, and society in general (c.f., Hargons et al., 2017). While students may be drawn to reacting to specific events that have garnered media attention, it is an opportunity to discuss the activism as a personal and professional obligation beyond the initial outrage of current news reports. Class discussions can connect contemporary forms of activism, such as BLM, to broader dialogues on long-standing systemic racism, white privilege, and white supremacy within higher education and society in general (Castillo-Montoya et al., 2019). This can become a catalyst to introduce students to ideologies, scholars, and activists that fall outside of the assigned readings for any particular course or the standardized curriculum for a program.

*Reflection Question: In what ways can you integrate contemporary political movements, such as BLM, and current events into class discussions and conceptual frameworks in your courses?*

## Benefits to Students' Personal and Professional Development

Within psychology coursework, social justice concepts carry the risk of running into what I call the "intellectual wasteland of one PowerPoint slide" that is already the landing spot for multiculturalism in some classes. By this I mean professors who treat social justice topics as "add-ons" to the core content in the course and give it thirty seconds of reverence before unceremoniously moving on to other topics (c.f., Sue & Sue, 2016). The "add-on" effect most likely has the intention of acknowledging experiences with oppression, which on the surface is a reasonable goal. However, my concern is how it is acknowledged and the unintended effects on students. For students who are genuinely curious about these topics or are already engaging in social justice–oriented work, it sends a message that these ideas are not important (or at minimum do not rise to the level of importance of other topics in the course). For students who have not thought critically about these ideas, it sends a message that self-reflection and action are not needed because the concepts do not necessitate any "heavy lifting" intellectually or experientially.

This is problematic beyond the curriculum of any individual class. Primarily, it limits the professional development of students, particularly those who will be entering fields like counseling, where a commitment to social justice is viewed as an ethical obligation (Ratts, 2009). Consequently, blunted development of the intellectual knowledge, awareness, and skills to address issues of social justice ultimately lands at the feet of clients and communities who are affected by the topics that were given "thirty seconds of reverence" in coursework. Learning social justice concepts thirty seconds at a time not only lacks meaning but ultimately threatens the health and wellbeing of those who stand to benefit most from social change. This disjointed view of power, privilege, and oppression at best superficially introduces students to topics they are free to explore elsewhere and at worst leaves them unprepared to address challenges facing marginalized clients and communities.

Sue and Sue (2016) argued the consequences of such incomplete training are the lack of readiness to work with diverse and marginalized populations and to effectively implement interventions. These consequences include victim-blaming and ignorance to the impact of environmental conditions on wellbeing (Ratts, 2009). Furthermore, Prilleltensky (1989) suggested the collective consequence is psychology's reinforcement of the status quo in a society built upon legacies of oppression. Therefore, the decisions of individual instructors to illuminate or obscure social justice issues have implications long after class discussions have concluded and coursework has been completed.

*Reflection Question: How do the courses you teach or those you supervise and/or coach contribute to your students' professional development and (later) career identity?*

_____

_____

_____

## Orientation of the Professor

Teaching from a social justice perspective is personal, meaning professors are real people in the room with real social identities. Moreover, students are real people in the room too. Neville (2015) discussed this in describing herself as a mentor and professor dedicated to social justice. There are many valuable lessons from Neville's speech at the Teachers College Winter Roundtable, which was later published in *The Counseling Psychologist*. At the forefront of these lessons is Neville's transparency in her interactions with her students about her intentions and her values. This is a stance that should be emulated by others, whether working with doctoral students as Neville often does, or work in other educational contexts. Students deserve to know the values of their instructors and how social justice issues will be incorporated into the coursework. This does not mean students are obligated to agree, but such transparency can take steps to establish an atmosphere of respect, humility, and intellectual curiosity.

*Reflection Question: How apparent is your commitment to social justice in your course description, syllabus, and reading assignments? If you have not infused social justice concepts into a course before, how can you modify the description, planning, and execution of an existing course?*

---

Goodman and colleagues (2014) provided a case example in masters-level training that also demonstrates the personal nature of teaching for social justice. It requires the instructors to be ever vigilant to their own biases and cognizant of their social identities because these will inevitably surface in frank discussion and in-depth exploration of power, privilege, and oppression. It also asks the instructor to listen humbly and with an open heart to students. Neville (2015) suggested this is not only the case when an instructor agrees with students or is hoping to support their critical consciousness. It is also the case when students are challenging the very values and beliefs that instructors view as fundamental to their professional identities. This is indeed a challenge to the instructors who are already weary from social justice work outside the classroom, but it is a challenge that must be embraced to prepare students for the work that invariably must be done in marginalized communities.

*Reflection Question: How have you responded to students who were struggling with social justice concepts or challenged the relevance of these topics for their training/professional development?*

---

## Example Activities in a Required Course for Counseling Students

As a professor in a mental health counseling master's program, I routinely teach a course on psychological testing, which is required by the ACA and the state licensing board. The topics in this course, such as reliability and validity, can routinely be found on licensure exams, and many students are best served by having basic knowledge of the scoring and interpretation of the psychological tests they will routinely encounter in their clinical work.

A standard structure for this course would be to review descriptive statistics, psychometric concepts, and selected psychological tests, such as the WAIS-IV or the MMPI-2-RF (e.g., Whiston, 2016). Indeed, this is a well-accepted and almost unquestioned blueprint for the course, and it is also one that can potentially miss opportunities to infuse social justice issues into readings, discussions, and assignments.

I have taught the course using the familiar blueprint of necessary topics, and I have also supplemented this with historical and current issues that reflect both the basics of testing and social justice issues. For example, when reviewing aptitude tests like the GRE and SAT, we discussed current controversies surrounding their use and the proposed alternatives, such as holistic review in college and graduate admissions and the ill-fated adversity index designed by the College Board (Bastedo, Bowman, Glasener, & Kelly, 2018; Jaschik, 2019). Similarly, our review of the WAIS-IV and WISC-V included a discussion of the historical context behind its use in the United States. For example, I have assigned an article by Helms (2012) that reviewed the dark history of intelligence testing and the support of eugenics by eminent psychologists, such as Galton and Cattell. This dual focus on conventional (and expected) topics and social justice issues provided a richer and more relevant way of reviewing the course materials and ultimately better prepared students to utilize psychological testing in their clinical work.

*Reflection Question: In what ways can you infuse social justice issues and current events into your courses?*

_____

_____

_____

## Challenges to Teaching for Social Justice

Despite revised ethical guidelines from professional organizations and the calls from scholars to integrate social justice ideals into multicultural theory and practice, substantial challenges remain (Ratts, 2009). Goodman and colleagues (2014) suggest that teaching from a social justice perspective is most effective when it is a core organizing feature of the curriculum across courses rather than the sole responsibility of individual instructors. This requires a collective vision among faculty to educate students with the shared goal of preparing them to incorporate social justice values into professional roles upon entering the field.

Even in cases where a shared vision does exist, there remains the tension between knowledge of fundamental theories and social justice work. In the case of counseling and psychology, this tension can be more pronounced because students are expected to take licensure exams early in their professional careers in order to become independently licensed. Sue and Sue (2016) and Ratts (2009) suggest that both can be achieved, namely, to think critically and to competently grasp the fundamental knowledge and skills of a profession. It does, however, require a vision for what instructors and programs hope to accomplish and what it means to be competent to practice.

Goodman and colleagues (2014) described the broad brushstrokes of this vision in their description of how programs can be formed around a commitment to social justice. Neville (2015) spoke of the intentionality of specific classrooms and the need for ever-present authenticity. Ultimately, both are true. The most intentional and authentic teaching cannot be fully effective if it is not supported by the mission and vision of a program and department, and the vision of the collective needs to be realized in everyday interactions with students. Thus, while this chapter aims itself primarily at the instructors focused on their social justice teaching, it also aims to shed light on the need for support and shared responsibility by colleagues.

The ideas of authors such as Goodman et al. (2014) are undoubtedly useful when there is a shared vision among like-minded colleagues, but this is not the reality in all departments where colleagues may not prioritize social justice in their coursework and may see it as a competing focus with other skills and knowledge they hope to infuse into their teaching. A commitment to social justice may be realized as the individual choice of specific instructors rather than a defining feature of a department or a degree program. In these cases, it is important to protect against feelings of social isolation and find opportunities for personal and professional growth outside the ivory tower of the academy. Neville (2015) describes her involvement in community efforts towards social justice and how this ultimately contributed to her vision for teaching and mentoring students.

*Reflection Question: What are the personal and professional challenges you may encounter as you infuse social justice concepts into your courses, and what sources of support can you utilize?*

## Recommendations for Social Justice Teaching

Incorporating social justice into coursework can be accomplished in how the core curriculum and training opportunities are structured (Goodman et al., 2014). This ensures that all students are introduced to social justice concepts and can develop critical consciousness. In the case of counseling and psychology, it also aligns with professional codes of ethics (Ratts, 2009; Sue & Sue, 2016). This provides the bedrock for training all students, but it does not fully capture the potential to incorporate social justice into coursework. Elective courses allow students to engage in deeper exploration of social justice frameworks and provide additional opportunities for self-reflection and consciousness-building.

In my own teaching, I designed an elective for graduate students that was designed as a follow-up course to their required research methods classes.

This course, which presumed students already knew the fundamentals of research design, allowed us to discuss the intersection of research and advocacy using examples by scholar-activists, such as Fine (2016) and Lykes (2010). It also allowed us to move beyond the most often discussed research designs taken from the experimental and correlational domains in order to study qualitative methods, ethnographies, action research, and PhotoVoice. This opened avenues for discussion about relational ethics and introduced concepts like catalytic validity, impact validity, and provocative generalizability (Greene, 1995; Lather, 1986; Massey & Barreras, 2013).

Elective courses, such as this one, provide an avenue for students interested in developing skill sets to be critical researchers and clinicians and advocates to find a place to do so while receiving the mentorship and guidance of faculty committed to social justice work. An elective in research methods is just one example. Mallinckrodt, Miles, and Levy (2014) provided other examples of courses that benefit students beyond the required curriculum mandated by professional organizations and state licensing boards. The potential to build upon core curriculum can be directed in numerous directions related to theory and practice to deepen an existing skill set or to introduce the framework for another. The First Year Experience in the counseling psychology doctoral program at Boston College is one such example where a community-based component is present (Goodman et al., 2014). This is an ideal scenario. However, the realities of restricted abilities to offer electives, particularly ones involving fieldwork components, can shortchange students and faculty hoping for supplemental coursework specifically geared towards social justice work. This is why recommendations to change the content and structure of required courses becomes that much more important (Pieterse, Evans, Risner-Butner, Collins, & Mason, 2009; Sue & Sue, 2016).

*Reflection Question: What are electives your program can offer to support consciousness-raising of students and supplement the focus on social justice in required courses?*

---

---

---

My course design was accompanied by an authenticity that strengthened the quality of teaching and what I could offer students as their instructor. This is relevant not only to elective course offerings but to the teaching of social justice issues across interactions with students. Issues of teaching pedagogy aside, students learn best from instructors who are active in social justice pursuits professionally and personally. Neville (2015) discussed this as her own professional stance towards teaching, which is undoubtedly commendable, and it also raises the question of how programs can demonstrate the same authenticity in their social justice commitments. This can be in the collective vision for education and training and in the faculty hired

(Mallinckrodt et al., 2014). This aligns with the point made earlier that social justice should not be an "add-on" to any one class. Moreover, it should not be the sole responsibility of any one faculty member charged with educating students. For programs looking to shift their teaching and course offerings, guidance is available (e.g., Pieterse et al., 2009), and exemplars are available to study (Goodman et al., 2014; Mallinckrodt et al., 2014).

*Reflection Question: In what ways can your program and department incorporate social justice into their vision and mission statement? What challenges do you anticipate, and how can your program or department respond effectively?*

_____

_____

_____

## Conclusion

Teaching from a social justice perspective is a demanding endeavor that challenges instructors to be authentic and transparent about their values and pedagogy. This can be reflected in how required courses are taught or the electives that are offered to students. Ultimately, instructors, regardless of their best intentions or qualifications, will find limited success in their consciousness-raising efforts if their goals are not shared by their programs and departments. A collective vision for how social justice can be infused into the education and training of students provides the bedrock for the actions of individual instructors across courses dedicated to the professional development of the next generation of researchers, clinicians, and activists.

## References

Bastedo, M. N., Bowman, N. A., Glasener, K. M., & Kelly, J. L. (2018). What are we talking about when we talk about holistic review? Selective college admissions and its effects on low-SES students. *Journal of Higher Education, 89*, 782–805. https://doi.org/10.1080/00221546.2018.1442633

Castillo-Montoya, M., Abreu, J., & Abad, A. (2019). Racially liberatory pedagogy: A Black Lives Matter approach to education. *International Journal of Qualitative Studies in Education, 32*, 1125–1145. https://doi.org/10.1080/09518398.2019.1645904

Fine, M. (2016). Just methods in revolting times. *Qualitative Research in Psychology, 13*, 347–365. https://doi.org/10.1080/14780887.2016.1219800

Goodman, L. A., Liang, B., Tummala-Narra, P., Borges, A. M., Claudius, M., & Woulfe, J. (2014). A model for integrating social justice roles in psychology doctoral training: The case of counseling psychology. In C. V. Johnson, H. L. Friedman, J. Diaz, Z. Franco, & B. K. Nastasi (Eds.), *The Praeger handbook of social justice and psychology: Well-being and professional issues* (Vol. 2, pp. 249–266). Praeger/ABC-CLIO.

Greene, M. (1995). *Releasing the imagination: Essays on education, the arts, and social change* (1st ed.). Jossey-Bass Inc.

Hargons, C., Mosley, D., Falconer, J., Faloughi, R., Singh, A., Stevens-Watkins, D., & Cokley, K. (2017). Black Lives Matter: A call to action for counseling psychology leaders. *The Counseling Psychologist, 45*, 873–901. https://doi.org/10.1177/0011000017733048

Helms, J. E. (2012). A legacy of eugenics underlies racial-group comparisons in intelligence testing. *Industrial and Organizational Psychology: Perspectives on Science and Practice,*
*5*(2), 176–179. https://doi.org/10.1111/j.1754-9434.2012.01426.x

Jaschik, S. (2019). New SAT score: Adversity. *Inside Higher Ed.* www.insidehighered.
com/admissions/article/2019/05/20/college-board-will-add-adversity-score-everyone-
taking-sat

Lather, P. (1986). Research as praxis. *Harvard Educational Review, 56,* 257–278. https://
doi.org/10.17763/haer.56.3.bj2h231877069482

Lykes, M. B. (2010). Silence(ing), voice(s) and gross violations of human rights: Constituting and performing subjectivities through PhotoPAR. *Visual Studies, 25*(3), 238–
254. https://doi.org/10.1080/1472586X.2010.523276

Mallinckrodt, B., Miles, J. R., & Levy, J. J. (2014). The scientist-practitioner-advocate
model: Addressing contemporary training needs for social justice advocacy. *Training and Education in Professional Psychology, 8*(4), 303–311. https://doi.org/10.1037/
tep0000045

Massey, S. G., & Barreras, R. E. (2013). Introducing 'impact validity'. *Journal of Social
Issues, 69,* 615–632. https://doi.org/10.1111/josi.12032

Neville, H. A. (2015). Social justice mentoring: Supporting the development of future
leaders for struggle, resistance, and transformation. *The Counseling Psychologist, 43,*
157–169. https://doi.org/10.1177/0011000014564252

Pieterse, A. L., Evans, S. A., Risner-Butner, A. R., Collins, N. M., & Mason, L. B. (2009).
Multicultural competence and social justice training in counseling psychology and
counselor education: A review and analysis of a sample of multicultural course syllabi.
*The Counseling Psychologist, 37,* 93–115. https://doi.org/10.1177/0011000008319986

Prilleltensky, I. (1989). Psychology and the status quo. *American Psychologist, 44,* 795–
802. https://doi.org/10.1037/0003-066X.44.5.795

Ratts, M. (2009). Social justice counseling: Toward the development of a fifth force
among counseling paradigms. *Journal of Humanistic Counseling, Education and Development, 48,* 160–172. https://doi.org/10.1002/j.2161-1939.2009.tb00076.x

Sue, D. W., & Sue, D. (2016). *Counseling the culturally diverse: Theory and practice* (7th ed.).
John Wiley & Sons, Inc.

Whiston, S. C. (2016). *Principles and applications of assessment in counseling* (5th ed.). Cengage Learning.

### Resources

Putting Social Justice into Practice in Psychology Courses: www.psychologicalscience.
org/observer/putting-social-justice-into-practice-in-psychology-courses

Social Justice Toolkit Resources: www.wwu.edu/teachinghandbook/course_design/
social_justice_toolkit.shtml

# 10 Training and Supervising Social Justice–Oriented Clinicians

*Julia Catlin and Lauren Mizock*

Oppression deleteriously impacts mental health, and mental health disparities occur across groups that experience bias with regard to race, ethnicity, gender, socioeconomic status, and other backgrounds. In addition, oppression and mental health disparities significantly impact wellbeing, including hypertension, high blood pressure, obesity, breast cancer, as well as distress, anxiety, depression, and posttraumatic stress disorder, respectively (Pascoe & Richman, 2009). Mental health providers sorely need training and practice in social justice–oriented care. Scholars-practitioners with a socially just approach to health care examine the impact of discrimination on mental health challenges, and target social inequity in mental health treatment. Recommendations based on this research and practice seek to reduce the mental health effects of prejudice for clients and communities. In this chapter, we review several of these social justice–oriented models in the fields of counseling and psychology and explore the associated recommendations for clinical training and supervision.

## Social Justice Practice in Counseling Psychology

Criticisms levied on contemporary practices in mental health include focusing too heavily on intrapsychic change without involving the social change needed to fully achieve mental wellness (Ibrahim, Dinsmore, Estrada, & D'Andrea, 2011). As a result, prevalent individual models of psychotherapy risk diminishing social action by positioning providers as professional experts in mental wellness, and emphasizing internal deficit models of mental health problems (Greenleaf & Bryant, 2012). As mentioned in Chapter 1, the traditional model of individual therapy often situates the provider in a peripheral stance as an ally as opposed to a central player in achieving social action. Furthermore, traditional mental health practice often posits mental illness as an individual issue rather than a symptom of structural oppression or inequality.

In general, the social justice model of counseling and mental health care posits that all people are deserving of human rights and equal opportunity (Ratts, DeKruyf, & Chen-Hayes, 2007). In these models, mental wellness is seen as dependent not only on individual change, but also upon change

DOI: 10.4324/9781003055587-10

in the social and economic contexts that impact daily life (Lee, Jorgensen Smith, & Henry, 2013; Prilleltensky, 2008). This social justice model draws from ecological theory by highlighting the impact of community and cultural context on mental health and the need to enact change in these areas (Greenleaf & Bryant, 2012). As mentioned in Chapter 3, the idea from this model is that social justice–oriented clinicians use their values, knowledge, and clinical skill sets to break down systemic barriers and empower clients and their communities (Griffin & Steen, 2011; Ratts et al., 2007) and are trained to dialogue with the communities to identify and address community needs and establish collaborations to best enact social advocacy (Griffin & Steen, 2011).

Similarly, the American Counseling Association (ACA) Advocacy Competencies were developed to identify activism and social justice as vital to counseling competence (Toporek & Daniels, 2018). In these guidelines, the authors present counselors as change agents in the systems that affect their clients and students. They place importance on identifying factors within the experiences of students and clients such as their strengths and resilience, sociocultural concerns, and sources of privilege and oppression. These competencies also encouraged counselor-educators to train students in developing advocacy plans and helping implement them with the clients and communities with which they work. Finally, in this framework, clinicians take on roles as social justice advocates who lobby policymakers for political change.

The Counselors for Social Justice (CSJ) Ethics Committee also advances a focus on social justice in counseling by creating a code of ethics, identifying social justice as the ethical responsibility of counselors (Ibrahim et al., 2011). For example, in the CSJ guidelines, counselors are urged to validate the oppression experienced by clients across various social identities. Collaboration with clients is encouraged to facilitate empowerment and enhance self-efficacy in facing the many systems that they confront. Counselors are advised to become aware of their privilege and the history of mistreatment of people from non-dominant groups in order to reduce injustice. The CSJ Code of Ethics also indicates that counselors must be more than just aware but also ethically responsible for using their power to reduce inequality in the lives and systems of clients.

Clearly, social justice is central to the training and practice models of the counseling field in particular. Although not always practiced, their founding documents and ethics are meant to guide counseling practitioners. The aforementioned counseling guidelines can serve as valuable templates for other psychological disciplines and training programs to promote social justice in the provision of mental health care.

## Social Justice Practice in Clinical Psychology

As practitioners in the field of psychology, we also feel it is important to note the recent work of the American Psychological Association to promote issues of social justice in the work of psychologists. Leong, Pickren, and Vasquez (2017) detailed this history, ranging from the Board for Social and Ethical Responsibility in Psychology to the Board of Ethnic Minority Affairs. These recent initiatives have also been carried out by a variety of task forces and policies, and in the development of psychological practice guidelines (e.g., multicultural; addressing racial/ethnic identity; LGBTQ+ people; and transgender and gender-nonconforming people in particular). The APA Divisions for Social Justice includes 10 social justice–oriented divisions that meet annually at APA and at the Multicultural Summit. There is also now a mandate in the APA training guidelines that psychologists become knowledgeable about theory, research, and practice with diverse groups from a social justice perspective throughout doctoral training and in continued education.

Some of these guidelines state that psychologists help their clients become aware of the injustices in their lives and take action in a manner that is empowering and enables clients' autonomy (Lemberger & Lemberger-Truelove, 2016).

These authors put forth several principles, including:

- Advocates must understand that all forms of injustice require action
- Advocates must work diligently to regulate what is unjust
- Advocates must recognize that oppression is real and that oppression and victimization do not define a person's entire existence
- Advocates must practice empathy and compassion for all individuals: the oppressed, the oppressors, including oneself and others
  (Lemberger & Lemberger-Truelove, 2016)

These considerations also demonstrate that while challenging, it is the goal of a social justice–oriented practitioner to address all injustices, not solely the kind of injustice that is most convenient or comfortable for the practitioner to tackle. Clearly, social justice is becoming more central to the visions of training and practice of the modern mental health provider. Social justice continues to be of focus in the training and practice policy developed in counseling and now in clinical psychology, as well as in neighboring mental health fields like social work and marriage and family therapy.

## Social Justice in Clinical Training

Acknowledging intersectional identities is essential to social justice work in clinical practice (Crenshaw, 1991; Hays, 2008). As described in Chapters 2–4, **intersectionality** is a term first coined by Kimberlé Crenshaw (1991) that was initially used to describe the unique experiences of Black feminists and what it means to have intersecting identities (and this book includes a brief history of intersectionality in Chapter 2). Historically, many have referred to race and gender as separate entities, isolated from one another; it is rare, however, for the mainstream to acknowledge the unique plight of an individual with multiple marginalized identities—for example, one who is female, Black, and gay (Crenshaw, 1991). Intersectionality is currently used to refer to the overlapping social identities within an individual that include but are not limited to race, ethnicity, class, gender, sexual orientation, ability. These identities can create unique experiences with regard to privilege and oppression within an individual, as in the case of a white, wealthy, lesbian, cisgender woman versus a Black middle-class, straight, transgender woman.

Hays (2008) created a framework for addressing intersectional identities, which is referred to as the ADDRESSING framework. This model includes several components that can assist clinicians in helping clients explore their own intersecting identities, as well as improve clinicians' understanding of these intersecting identities. Hays' framework for intersectionality high-lighted the following aspects unique to each individual's identity: *Age and generational influences*, **D***evelopmental disabilities*, **D***isabilities acquired later in life*, **R***eligion and spiritual orientation*, **E***thnic and racial identity*, **S***ocioeconomic status*, **S***exual orientation*, **I***ndigenous heritage*, **N***ational origin, and* **G***ender identity*.

Brinkman and Donohue (2020) also made three recommendations for integrating intersectionality into clinical training. First, training programs must recognize subjectivity as unfixed, meaning that perspectives are likely to change with evolving information. Second, training programs must emphasize critical self-reflection and demonstrate self-reflection as a means of facilitating the ways in which trainees relate to others, including clients. Third, training programs should focus on teaching centering and de-centering as essential practices in doing intersectional work.

Using these recommendations as a launching point, clinical trainees are more likely to view intersectionality as a "way of being" rather than a theory in which they "check off the boxes" of race, gender, and class (Brinkman & Donohue, 2020). According to Brinkman and Donohue, conceptualizing intersectionality as a "way of being" encompasses affect, thought, and action, and allows the trainee to reflect on the question, "Who am I as a clinician in relation to a particular client?" Intersectional training and practice can assist trainees in their growth into clinicians who are more self-aware, more conscientious of their worldviews and their clients' worldviews, and more willing to challenge policies, institutions, and systems that oppress histori-cally disadvantaged individuals.

## Questions for Reflection

1.   Develop a case study in which you *describe* a person's unique experiences using the ADDRESSING model proposed by Hays (2008). **Remember that this model is not to be used as a template to check off boxes, but to explore more deeply a person's intersecting identities.** Complete a full description of the client in the case study after you have explored the following basic elements outlined by Hays (2008).

*Table 10.1* Addressing Model Checklist

| | |
|---|---|
| *Age and generational influences* | |
| *Developmental disabilities* | |
| *Disabilities acquired later in life* | |
| *Religion and spiritual orientation* | |
| *Ethnic and racial identity* | |
| *Socioeconomic status* | |
| *Sexual orientation* | |
| *Indigenous heritage* | |
| *National origin* | |
| *Gender identity* | |

2. Using the same model, apply Hays' (2008) framework to your own identity, and explore what it might be like to work with the client in the case study that you developed.

   a. In what ways are you and your client similar? In what ways could these similarities be helpful, and in what ways could they present challenges? In what ways may it be comfortable to work with this client, and in what ways may it be uncomfortable?

   _____

   _____

   _____

   _____

   b. In what ways are you and your client different? In what ways could these differences be helpful, and in what ways could they present challenges? In what ways might it be comfortable to work with this client, and in what ways may it be uncomfortable?

   _____

   _____

   _____

   _____

   c. What therapeutic or advocacy interventions might be helpful for your client? Explain your rationale for considering the interventions you chose.

   _____

   _____

   _____

   _____

## Social Justice in Supervision

Social justice is becoming increasingly centralized in clinical training, and some researchers are applying the Multicultural and Social Justice Counseling Competencies (MSJCC) framework (Ratts et al., 2015) to supervision (Fickling, Tangen, Graden, & Grays, 2019). In their article on this topic, Fickling and colleagues claim that supervision must be seen as a process which facilitates the growth of both supervisee and supervisor as competent social justice practitioners. Because supervision is a specialty in counseling practice, they argued that there must be an integrated framework in order for multicultural and social justice practice to be successful.

Similarly, Bevly, Loseu, and Prosek (2017) encourage supervisors to model an advocacy perspective by interacting with systems that influence their clients and supervisees. They recommend that doctoral students in counseling education possess a level of mastery in social justice advocacy, and teach master's level students to become social justice advocates. Additionally, they advise that doctoral students assist master's level students in learning to diagnose and assess clients through a social justice lens, examining both social and systemic contributors to health rather than a strictly medical model view of psychopathology and internal deficits.

Fickling et al. (2019) also recommend that supervisors exhibit behaviors which would allow the supervisee to discuss diversity, including the supervisee's own cultural experiences, identities, and lifestyle. They see the supervisor as having the responsibility to both teach and practice broaching with the supervisee (Fickling et al., 2019). *Broaching* is the "consistent and ongoing attitudes of openness with a genuine commitment by the counselor to continually invite the client to explore issues of diversity" (p. 10). They discuss four developmental domains in the practice of broaching, including 1) supervisor self-awareness, 2) supervisee worldview, 3) supervisory relationship, and 4) supervision and advocacy interventions. Bevly and colleagues (2017) provide some specific strategies for each of the four developmental domains, which will be woven into the following sections.

### *Supervisor Self-Awareness*

Fickling rightly points out that it is essential that supervisors educate themselves about a supervisee's worldview, rather than expecting supervisees to educate them (Fickling et al., 2019). Discussions of parallel processes may take place even in the supervisory environment with the supervisee in discussing what kinds of feelings, thoughts, and experiences the supervisee is having during the supervision process. Doctoral students can keep student journals and process with peers in addition to having conversations about parallel processes (Bevly et al., 2017). These processes may cause feelings of tension, discomfort, and cognitive dissonance in both the supervisee and the supervisor, but should ultimately lead to growth for both parties (Fickling et al., 2019). Furthermore, supervisors are not always more advanced in their racial identity development than are supervisees (Helms, 2006; Jernigan, Green, Helms, Perez-Gualdron, & Henze, 2010). Supervisors need to be engaged in self-examination to promote their racial identity development as well as their awareness of issues of class, gender, and other sociocultural identity issues.

## Supervisee Worldview

As supervisors spend time getting to know supervisees and seek knowledge about privileged and marginalized groups to which their supervisees may belong, supervisors must be aware of what supervisees have faced regarding stereotyping or bias in supervision (Fickling et al., 2019). It is also important for supervisors to learn whether these experiences may cause supervisees to approach supervision with caution and present as guarded with their feelings. Doctoral students acting as supervisors in a counseling education program may participate in immersion projects and develop supervisee conceptualizations as part of understanding the worldviews and unique experiences of supervisees (Bevly et al., 2017). Supervisor awareness of past supervisee experiences such as bias, discrimination, and stereotyping can help the supervisor to create an environment where the supervisee may feel safe, open, and willing to discuss matters of parallel process, transference, and countertransference, and be willing to be more transparent with the supervisor.

## Supervisory Relationship

Perceptions of multicultural competence in the supervisor by the supervisee have the benefit of creating a stronger supervisory working alliance and increased satisfaction with supervision, as well as greater self-efficacy in counseling practice (Fickling et al., 2019). *Supervisory humility* is a critical component of the supervisory relationship, as well. Fickling et al. (2019) recommend that supervisors refrain from taking an elevated stance related to their beliefs and worldview while recognizing their limitations and striving toward greater learning of others' cultures. Doctoral students might practice role-plays with supervisees in order to practice broaching multicultural issues (Bevly et al., 2017). Doctoral students could also be assigned to write a paper on their chosen supervision model and philosophy of supervision, identifying their beliefs and values with regard to culturally competent and social justice–oriented care.

## Supervision and Advocacy Interventions

Lastly, Fickling et al. (2019) recommend approaching advocacy interventions via a socioecological model, working from micro to macro levels of change. A socioecological approach suggests working to create change at multiple levels, including the intrapersonal, interpersonal, institutional, community, public policy, and international and global. Supervisors can work with supervisees to determine the extent to which services are focused on the individual or systemic level, and what interventions may be needed. In addition to evaluating recorded client and supervision sessions, doctoral students might choose client scenarios to discuss with peers and educators about advocacy interventions and the development of treatment plans for marginalized and oppressed clients (Bevly et al., 2017). Glosoff and Durham (2010) suggest that supervisors allow their supervisees to examine intake forms, treatment procedures, and interventions for indications of bias, such as heterosexism and classism.

Complex cognitive and critical thinking skills as well as a **critical consciousness** are required for one to be able to analyze social injustices and oppression in the world (Glosoff & Durham, 2010). Supervisors can aid trainees in developing critical thinking skills and cognitive complexity. Using **intentionality**, supervisors must preface discussions of power and privilege with empowerment of supervisees, encouraging supervisees to voice their opinions, share feedback, and discuss their learning style (Glosoff & Durham, 2010). More importantly, supervisors can encourage supervisees to advocate in a way that works for them and emphasize the multitude of ways that supervisees might fight for social justice in their work (Glosoff & Durham, 2010). Hence, we see the value of the concept of broaching and the importance of doing this in supervisory work here. Broaching can enhance awareness of both the supervisor and supervisee, fomenting a supervisory relationship that is sensitive to cultural issues.

## Conclusion

We clearly need more research to continue to develop social justice–oriented strategies for clinical practice, training, and supervision. We also know from our own clinical work and training that culture is a moving target in a constantly shifting landscape. Unfortunately, our global legacy of oppression has no clear end in sight. Cultural awareness is a lifelong journey, with culturally responsive clinical practices representing a complex skill set that perhaps can never be fully achieved. Hence, the goal of social justice–oriented clinicians is to engage in the dance of attunement to our clients' cultures and our own. We must regularly commit to self-reflection and self-education in these areas. And we should remember that while social- and self-transformation is long and arduous work, no other work could be more purposeful.

## Questions for Reflection

1. What is *broaching* in your own words? How is broaching important to your counseling and supervisory relationships?

_____

_____

_____

_____

2. Share your own ideas for creative interventions and advocacy interventions for your clients and supervisees. What makes these ideas helpful to the client(s) and the supervisee(s) you would be working with?

_____

_____

_____

_____

3. How might you work to develop *cognitive complexity*? What would you do to facilitate the development of the cognitive complexity in supervisees with regard to multicultural issues and social justice?

_____

_____

_____

_____

4. Describe what it means to be intentional about social justice. How do you use intentionality in your work as a clinician, advocate, supervisor, educator, or in another role?

_____

_____

_____

_____

# References

Bevly, C., Loseu, S., & Prosek, E. A. (2017). Infusing social justice advocacy in supervision coursework. *Journal of Counselor Leadership and Advocacy*, 4, 28–38. https://doi.org/10.1080/2326716X.2017.1282330

Brinkman, B. G., & Donohue, P. (2020). Doing intersectionality in social justice oriented clinical training. *Training and Education in Professional Psychology*, 14, 109–115. http://dx.doi.org.fgul.idm.oclc.org/10.1037/tep0000274

Crenshaw, K. (1991). Mapping the margins: Intersectionality, identity politics, and violence against women of color. *Stanford Law Review*, 43(2–3), 7–20. https://doi.org/10.7146/KKF.V0I2-3.28090

Fickling, M. J., Tangen, J. L., Graden, M. W., & Grays, D. (2019). Multicultural and social justice competence in clinical supervision. *Counselor Education and Supervision*, 58, 309–316. https://doi.org/10.1002/ceas.12159

Glosoff, H. L., & Durham, J. C. (2010). Using supervision to prepare social justice counseling advocates. *Counselor Education and Supervision*, 50, 116–129. https://doi.org/10.1002/j.1556-6978.2010.tb00113.x

Greenleaf, A. T., & Bryant, R. M. (2012). Perpetuating oppression: Does the current counseling discourse neutralize social action? *Journal for Social Action in Counseling and Psychology*, 4, 18–29. https://doi.org/10.33043/JSACP.4.1.18-29

Griffin, D., & Steen, S. (2011). A social justice approach to school counseling. *Journal for Social Action in Counseling and Psychology*, 3, 74–85. https://doi.org/10.33043/JSACP.3.1.74-85

Hays, P. A. (2008). *Addressing cultural complexities in practice: Assessment, diagnosis, and therapy* (2nd ed.). American Psychological Association. https://doi.org/10.1037/11650-000

Helms, J.E. (2006). Fairness is not validity or cultural bias in racial-group assessment: A quantitative perspective. *American Psychologist, 61*, 845–859. https://doi.org/10.1037/0003-066X.61.8.845

Ibrahim, F. A., Dinsmore, J. A., Estrada, D., & D'Andrea, M. (2011). The Counselor for Social Justice (CSJ) code of ethics. *Journal for Social Action in Counseling and Psychology, 3*(2), 1–21. https://doi.org/10.33043/JSACP.3.2.1-21

Jernigan, M. M., Green, C. E., Helms, J. E., Perez-Gualdron, L., & Henze, K. (2010). An examination of people of color supervision dyads: Racial identity matters as much as race. *Training and Education in Professional Psychology, 4*, 62–73. https://doi.org/10.1037/a0018110

Lee, M. A., Jorgensen Smith, T., & Henry, R. G. (2013). Power politics: Advocacy to activism in social justice counseling. *Journal for Social Action in Counseling and Psychology, 5*, 70–94. https://doi.org/10.33043/JSACP.5.3.70-94

Lemberger, M. E., & Lemberger-Truelove, T. L. (2016). Bases for a more socially just humanistic praxis. *Journal of Humanistic Psychology, 56*, 571–580. https://doi.org/10.1177/0022167816652750

Leong, F., Pickren, W. E., & Vasquez, M. (2017). APA efforts in promoting human rights and social justice. *The American Psychologist, 72*, 778–790. https://doi.org/10.1037/amp0000220

Pascoe, E. A., & Richman, L. (2009). Perceived discrimination and health: A meta-analytic review. *Psychological Bulletin, 135*, 531–554. https://doi.org/10.1037/a0016059

Prilleltensky, I. (2008). The role of power in wellness, oppression, and liberation: The promise of psychopolitical validity. *Journal of Community Psychology, 3*, 116–138. https://doi.org/10.1002/jcop.20225

Ratts, M. J., DeKruyf, L., & Chen-Hayes, S. (2007). The ACA advocacy competencies: A social justice advocacy framework for professional school counselors. *Professional School Counseling, 11*, 90–97. https://doi.org/10.5330/PSC.n.2010-11.90

Ratts, M. J., Singh, A. A., Nassar-McMillan, S., Butler, S. K., McCullough, J. R., & Hipolito-Delgado, C. (2015). *Multicultural and social justice counseling competencies.* www.counseling.org/docs/default-source/competencies/multicultural-and-social-justice-counseling-competencies.pdf

Toporek, R. L., & Daniels, J. (2018). *2018 update and expansion of the 2003 ACA advocacy competencies: Honoring the work of the past and contextualizing the present.* www.counseling.org

### Resources

https://iamaneducator.com/category/social-justice-pedagogy/

Journal of Social Action in Counseling and Psychology https://openjournals.bsu.edu/jsacp

www.tolerance.org/classroom-resources

# Part 3
# Helping Expand Social Justice

# 11 Researching for Social Justice

*Mary Beth Medvide*

Research as it is conventionally defined, conducted, and disseminated often falls into the trap highlighted by Fine (2006) of assuming that research endeavors are situated outside of societal systems and structures. Moreover, knowledge is disseminated to an audience that is likely viewed as equally indifferent (or oblivious) to societal injustices and feels little if any obligation to champion social changes. This "as if" contract is devoid of emotional discomfort or cognitive dissonance for all parties involved. Couched in the privilege to ignore, minimize, and distort, research that hinges upon a misguided allegiance of objectivity cannot be used to articulate a vision for social change or to contribute to social justice aims. In this chapter, I present a series of things for researchers to "know" as they explore questions about themselves, their work, and their visions for a just society.

## Know Your Methods and Methodologies

There is an unfortunate attitude that social justice methods are inherently qualitative or participatory in design, and quantitative methods cannot serve the purpose of addressing the needs of marginalized communities and redressing the wrongs of an oppressive society (Fine, 2006; Lykes, 2017). The idea that quantitative methods do not align with social justice commitments is not entirely untrue given that the post-positivist framework used to support them espouses neutrality and objectivity as the preferred research stance (Ponterotto, 2005). Quantitative methods are also intertwined with a societal legacy of perpetuating oppression in society and using scientific findings to support racist beliefs (Cushman, 2012; Prilleltensky, 2008). The testing movement in the United States, which was rooted in eugenic beliefs about the superiority of white segments of the population, is one such example that continues to affect educational policies and employment practices (Helms, 2006).

Qualitative methods have been promised as the solution to the problem of how research maintains the status quo, either by actively contributing to societal oppression or by failing to critically challenge oppressive conditions in society (Gergen, 2014). It is not to say that qualitative methods cannot

DOI: 10.4324/9781003055587-11

be such a solution, but capturing participants' lived experience does not necessarily illuminate social injustices, nor does it inevitably contribute to social change. These methods provide the framework for such possibility (Ponterotto, 2005), but they do not absolve the researcher from the need for self-reflection and critical engagement with the research questions to be explored. Gergen (2014) provided criteria to enhance the potential of qualitative research to accomplish social justice goals. This is captured in the move beyond the traditional aims of prediction and control in the service of replication and theory-building and into the realm of pragmatic outcomes as the hallmark of good science. Fine (2016) suggests such shifts are necessary but not sufficient for the promise of qualitative methods to achieve social justice ends. This work also compels the researcher to use methods in conjunction with a well-articulated vision for social change, a point I return to later.

Participatory action research, typically shortened to PAR (described with a case example in Chapter 5), shares with qualitative methods the potential to contribute to social change, although PAR is more integrally tied to such promises (Lykes, 2017). In the case of PAR (more so than qualitative methods), the lineage of current research can be traced across social science disciplines, continents, and time periods where scholars and activists fought for reform and revolution (Zeller-Berkman, 2014). Despite the clear social justice underpinnings of the perspectives informing PAR, Tuck and Guishard (2014) warned that PAR is not inherently empowering to communities if researchers have not considered the ethics of their actions or truly committed to relinquishing the role of hallowed expert. Fine (2019) suggests that any commitments to social justice must be accompanied by humility and patience while cultivating collective knowledge and action. As with qualitative methods, it is the case that a PAR framework provides a structure to do social justice work, and it compels the researcher to critically reflect on issues of power, privilege, and oppression.

A study by Smith and Romero (2010) showcased the strength of PAR as a catalyst for personal and community change. As is the case of many PAR studies, the authors reflected on their experience as co-researchers and equal partners with community members in New York City and demonstrated humility in their understanding of community needs and appropriate steps towards social change. Similarly, Fox and Fine's (2013) PAR study with New York adolescents suggested that participants are capable of not only insights on what social changes are needed but also on how to utilize data to accomplish these goals. Moreover, this strips statistics and data analysis of its rarefied position as being solely under the purview of the formally educated academic and makes data analysis a democratic process (Fine, 2019).

Quantitative methods when couched in a commitment to social justice can answer questions that can change social policies for the better and empower communities (Possamai-Inesedy, 2014). For example, Fox and Fine (2013) utilized quantitative methods with participants as co-researchers to unearth and unmask the critical social problems plaguing their communities. This example highlights another misperception that participatory action research must be qualitative (Zeller-Berkman, 2014). This is simply not the case, as Fox and Fine's (2013) documentation of work with New York City youth demonstrates. What this does reveal, however, is that a commitment to social justice requires more than competence in specific methods, whether those be quantitative or qualitative (Possamai-Inesedy, 2014). Similarly, Helms' (2006) model of test fairness blends traditional statistical methods that are historically linked to the eugenics movement with a critical lens to analyze test score differences among majority and minority groups. The conclusions drawn from the statistics of the model were meant to alleviate the threat of adverse impact. Fox and Fine (2013) and Helms (2006) demonstrate that research endeavors require knowledge of the underlying context (whether historical or philosophical) that informs specific methods and a vision of how research will contribute to social action (Ponterotto, 2005; Fine, 2006). This vision is something I will return to later.

*Reflection Question: What are the methods and methodologies that you use most frequently in your research? Why?*

---

---

---

## Know Where You Stand

Lykes (2017) debated the importance of knowledge (epistemology) and raised questions of who has the power to recreate knowledge and which knowledge is deemed legitimate within the larger political context. These questions are fundamental to participatory action research, which is often the focus of Lykes' work (see also Lykes, 2010). Fine (2006) argues that these questions are fundamental to research in general and wrote how the knowledge generated from research endeavors can transform participants, fellow researchers, and social policy (see also Lather, 1986; Massey & Barreras, 2013). The synergy of these positions is one that challenges researchers to uncover power arrangements in their work that can subjugate knowledge on the margins while elevating (and even naturalizing) forms of knowledge that maintain an oppressive status quo (Prilleltensky, 1989).

This challenge to the status quo is at the core of Prilleltensky's (1989, 2008) contributions to psychology and his calls for values-based praxis. Ponterotto (2005) discussed this as axiology, or the role of values in the actions of researchers. At a minimum, researchers committed to social justice articulate their values and acknowledge as part of the research process revealing the ways in which those values informed their decisions (Possamai-Insedy, 2014). However, this is the ethical floor, meaning that it is not enough to simply verbalize what you believe in reflecting back upon a completed research endeavor or to "set aside" biases before engaging in a study (Fine,

2006). These values should inform all aspects of research, never to be resolved in advance or to be exchanged for the false promise of objectivity (Prilleltensky, 2008). Ultimately, this contributes to the social impact of research and its potential to align with efforts elsewhere to fight injustice (Fine, 2006; Massey & Barreras, 2013). See Chapter 3 for more on biases in research with a relevant example.

*Reflection Question: What are the values, beliefs, and assumptions that inform your research?*

_____

_____

_____

## Know Your History and Your Lineage

Research, particularly research that claims to be objective and neutral, tends to treat the goals of a study and the participants as ahistorical entities that exist outside of multilayered contexts across time and place (Cushman, 2012; Gergen, 2014). The consequence is a study that appeals to (supposed) universals rather than the particulars of a given context and historical time period (Fine, 2006). However, qualitative methods are not absolved from such limitations despite their claims to be context-dependent and experience-oriented (Ponterotto, 2005). Possamai-Inesedy (2014) discussed the progression of qualitative methods from the shadows of post-positivist thought to the contemporary constructionist and post-modern forms. What can be gleaned from these points is that methods and methodologies by extension are historical artifacts. Therefore, researchers must fulfill two obligations, namely to know the history of research methods and the theories that support them and to recognize the self as a historical entity. In short, social justice researchers must be students of science first and foremost to recognize the legacies of previous eras and the battles yet to be fought.

Among the approaches to research discussed in this chapter, PAR has the historical legacy that is most clearly aligned with activism and social change. Zeller-Berkman (2014) traced the lineage of PAR across continents and eras and included in her discussion exemplar studies to further introduce readers to the cycles of action and reflection that constitute PAR. Qualitative research methods also have a rich history across the social science and humanities, and Lincoln and Denzin (2003) traced the progression of commonly used approaches from the mid-20th century into the modern era. Fine (2006) bridged PAR and qualitative methods in her "textbook" of research methods to fight oppression. She also highlighted key examples of social justice research within the quantitative tradition, including Civil Rights–era studies and the AIDS epidemic (see also, Barreras & Torruella, 2013). This documentation is a counter-narrative to the often told (and often true) story that quantitative methods reinforce the status quo, contribute to societal injustices, and create a false perception that neutrality should be the preferred stance of researchers (Cushman, 2012; Prilleltensky, 2008). The weaving together of the history of various research methods is also the weaving together of the history of injustices across societies and eras. This point cannot be stressed enough. Researchers committed to social justice readily acknowledge their own studies as nested within a larger sociopolitical context (e.g., Lykes, 2017). Fine (2006) argued it is also necessary to root methods themselves in such contexts, which lays the foundations for questions such as, "For whom, with whom, and for what purpose?" The question of purpose is one we will return to later.

*Reflection Question: Who are the researchers and scholars who have influenced your research and view of social justice?*

_____

_____

_____

Being a student of the history of a discipline is only part of the responsibility and the journey of the researcher. It is also necessary to trace one's own lineage and to reflect critically on the theories, frameworks, and people who inform a vision for social change. Fine (2019), for example, called herself the "academic grandchild of Kurt Lewin and Morten Deutsch," (p. 85) and has documented throughout her career the influence of other scholars, such as Maxine Greene, Carolyn Payton, and Marie Jahoda (Fine, 2006). While other researchers/activists, such as Lykes (2017), may not publicly trace their lineage with such detail, it is likely they have thought deeply and intensely about their academic forebearers and colleagues in solidarity (see Lykes, 2012). This should not be the work of a notable few but rather the task of any researchers aspiring that their work will contribute to social change. What is clear as well is that such linkages to the academic past move beyond well-cited articles, seminal works, and the prominent scholars whose ideas fill psychology textbooks. Fine (2006), for example, created a "textbook" built upon the pillars of critical scholarship within psychology, across the social sciences, and in the humanities. On one hand, this is a "how-to" manual for social justice work and on the other a tribute to past generations of scholars/activists. It acts as a model of how researchers can name and honor those whose work has created a pathway for reflection and action.

*Reflection Question: What are the lessons you would want to teach to future generations of researchers who are committed to social justice?*

_____

_____

_____

## Know Your Goals

The commonly accepted end point in the research process is a published article in a scholarly journal or perhaps a conference proceeding. For research aimed at social change, the professional audience of colleagues is one focal point, but it is certainly not the only place where findings can be disseminated (Massey & Barreras, 2013). Fine (2019) advised that all dissemination efforts must be strategic and reach the stakeholders and communities where research can do the most good. Smith and Romero (2010) documented their dissemination efforts through collaboration with agencies, local governments, and community activists, especially those most personally and deeply affected by injustice. Fine (2019) also pointed to efforts in two of her community-based projects to influence social policy in New York City and beyond. Although work by Fine (2019) and Smith and Romero (2010) was published in scholarly journals, their audience extended well beyond the professional circles of academia. Lykes (2017) considered this a necessary condition for PAR, and Massey and Barreras (2013) viewed it as a worthwhile goal for any socially minded research efforts.

Lykes (2017) warned this is not always a feasible outcome in participatory action research, and Gergen (2014) stated likewise for qualitative methods. However, the value-based praxis that Prilleltensky (2003) suggested should be at the heart of research aimed at social change. These values inevitably require a researcher to reflect on the goals of a project and how such efforts fit into larger social justice movements and advocacy efforts (Fine, 2006, 2019). Massey and Barreras (2013) discussed this as impact validity and the potential for research to contribute to social change and activism efforts, most often by other scholars and professionals. However, the reach and influence of research can extend to non-traditional audiences well outside of academia. Lather (1986) highlighted the reach of research on the participants themselves, something she termed catalytic validity. Smith and Romero (2010) gravitated towards this concept in their discussion of the impact on participants in their study, which they believe empowered women to verbalize the effects of oppression in their lives and to act in their communities. The concepts of impact validity and catalytic validity respectively reflect the need for foresight on the part of researchers to maximize the reach and power of their work and to put their findings into the hands of key stakeholders.

*Reflection Question: What are your hopes for the participants in your research, and how will you know if your research has a meaningful impact on their lives?*

---

---

---

## Conclusion

Researchers who view their work as a form of activism and use their power to advocate for social change face critical questions at all stages of the research process. These questions transcend conventional questions of design and method that form best-practice guidelines in the social sciences. Researchers committed to social justice carry the weight (and at times the burden) of knowing the history behind their methodologies and the lineage of their values, beliefs, and knowledge. However, it is a weight that is aptly placed if the goal of social change can be achieved through research that contributes to community empowerment and a vision of a better, more democratic society.

## References

Barreras, R. E., & Torruella, R. A. (2013). New York city's struggle over syringe exchange: A case study of the intersection of science, activism, and political change. *Journal of Social Issues, 69*, 694–712. https://doi.org/10.1111/josi.12037

Cushman, P. (2012). Defenseless in the face of the status quo: Psychology without a critical humanities. *The Humanistic Psychologist, 40*, 262–269. https://doi.org/10.108 0/08873267.2012.696411

Fine, M. (2006). Bearing witness: Methods for researching oppression and resistance: A textbook for critical research. *Social Justice Research, 19*, 83–108.

Fine, M. (2016). Just methods in revolting times. *Qualitative Research in Psychology, 13*, 347–365. https://doi.org/10.1080/14780887.2016.1219800

Fine, M. (2019). Science and justice: A fragile, fraught, and essential relationship. *Perspectives on Psychological Science, 14*, 85–90. https://doi.org/10.1177/1745691618794922

Fox, M., & Fine, M. (2013). Accountable to whom? A critical science counter-story about a city that stopped caring for its young. *Children and Society, 27*, 321–335. https://doi.org/10.1111/chso.12031

Gergen, K. J. (2014). Pursuing excellence in qualitative inquiry. *Qualitative Psychology, 1*, 49–60. https://doi.org/10.1037/qup0000002

Helms, J. E. (2006). Fairness is not validity or cultural bias in racial-group assessment: A quantitative perspective. *American Psychologist, 61*, 845–859. https://doi.org/10.1037/ 0003-066X.61.8.845

Lather, P. (1986). Research as praxis. *Harvard Educational Review, 56*, 257–278. https:// doi.org/10.17763/haer.56.3.bj2h231877069482

Lincoln, Y. A., & Denzin, N. K. (2003). Introduction: Revolutions, ruptures, and rifts in interpretive inquiry. In Y. A. Lincoln & N. K. Denzin (Eds.), *Turning points in qualitative research: Knots in the handkerchief* (pp. 1–20). Altamira Press.

Lykes, M. B. (2010). Silence(ing), voice(s) and gross violations of human rights: Constituting and performing subjectivities through PhotoPAR. *Visual Studies, 25*(3), 238–254. https://doi.org/10.1080/1472586X.2010.523276

Lykes, M. B. (2012). One legacy among many: The Ignacio Martín-Baró fund for mental health and human rights at 21. *Peace and Conflict: Journal of Peace Psychology, 18*, 88–95. https://doi.org/10.1037/a0026982

Lykes, M. B. (2017). Community-based and participatory action research: Community psychology collaborations within and across borders. In M. A. Bond, I. Serrano-García, C. B. Keys, & M. Shinn (Eds.), *APA handbook of community psychology: Methods for community research and action for diverse groups and issues* (Vol. 2, pp. 43–58). American Psychological Association.

Massey, S. G., & Barreras, R. E. (2013). Introducing 'impact validity'. *Journal of Social Issues, 69*, 615–632. https://doi.org/10.1111/josi.12032

Ponterotto, J. G. (2005). Qualitative research in counseling psychology: A primer on research paradigms and philosophy of science. *Journal of Counseling Psychology, 52*, 126–136. https://doi.org/10.1037/0022-0167.52.2.126

Possamai-Insedy, A. (2014). Social justice research methods: The problems of abstracted empiricism and the politics of evidence. In C. V. Johnson, H. L. Friedman, J. Diaz, Z. Franco, & B. K. Nastasi (Eds.), *The Praeger handbook of social justice and psychology: Fundamental issues and special populations: Well-being and professional issues psychology* (2nd ed., pp. 267–281). Praeger/ABC-CLIO.

Prilleltensky, I. (1989). Psychology and the status quo. *American Psychologist, 44*(5), 795–802.

Prilleltensky, I. (2003). Understanding, resisting, and overcoming oppression: Toward psychopolitical validity. *American Journal of Community Psychology, 31*(1–2), 195–201. https://doi.org/10.1023/A:1023043108210

Prilleltensky, I. (2008). The role of power in wellness, oppression, and liberation: The promise of psychopolitical validity. *Journal of Community Psychology, 36*(2), 116–136. https://doi.org/10.1002/jcop.20225

Smith, L., & Romero, L. (2010). Psychological interventions in the context of poverty: Participatory action research as practice. *American Journal of Orthopsychiatry, 80,* 12–25. doi: 10.1111/j.1939-0025.2010.01003.x

Tuck, E., & Guishard, M. (2014). Uncollapsing ethics: Racialized sciencism, settler coloniality, and an ethical framework of decolonial participatory action research. In T. M. Kress, C. Malott, & B. Porfilio (Eds.), *Challenging status quo retrenchment: New directions in critical research* (pp. 3–27). Information Age Publishing.

Zeller-Berkman, S. (2014). Lineages: A past, present, and future of participatory action research. In P. Leavy (Ed.), *The Oxford handbook of qualitative research* (pp. 518–532). Oxford University Press.

## Resources

The Martín-Baró Initiative: Resources: http://martinbarofund.org/

Participatory Action Research Map: www.publicscienceproject.org/files/2013/04/PAR-Map.pdf

# 12 Advocating for Public Policy

*Christina Athineos and Debra A. Harkins*

## Understanding Public Policy

Public policy entails all actions taken by the government to address a public problem. Although its impact is not always immediately recognizable, public policy plays a near-constant role in the lives of the American people. Consider the following example on policies related to housing:

> When buying a house, the Fair Housing Act ensures equal access to homeownership opportunities by prohibiting discrimination (U.S. Department of Housing and Urban Development [HUD], n.d.). Once you've identified a home you're interested in, the Real Estate Settlement Procedures Act and the National Affordable Housing Act help to ensure that you, as the future homeowner, are protected from lenders by requiring disclosures about relevant costs (HUD, n.d.). Similarly, the Dodd-Frank Act further protects homeowners from confusion by simplifying the language presented throughout the home-buying process (HUD, n.d.). After you've moved into your new house, the cost of gas, oil, and electricity to fuel your home are governed by national energy policies, which are in turn affected by national and state excise taxes (Environmental Protections Agency [EPA], 2007). The quality of your water and the safe removal and processing of your sewage are controlled by the Safe Drinking Water Act and the Clean Water Act (EPA, 2007). Likewise, the Resource Conservation and Recovery Act is responsible for the proper management of hazardous and non-hazardous solid waste, handling the proper removal and disposal of your garbage (EPA, 2007). Should you choose to add an extension to your home, you'll need to consult your town's local construction policies to ensure your plans fit within the current residential, building, zoning, electrical, land use, environmental, shoreline, and mechanical codes.

DOI: 10.4324/9781003055587-12

Policymaking has been described by many as a cycle of actions beginning first with problem identification. After a need has been identified, the cycle of policymaking continues with further evaluations, modifications, and, potentially, even terminations. As exhausting as it may sound, a good system of policymaking is never complete. In this way, policies are truly living documents that can and should be adjusted to fit the public's changing needs.

Although policymaking does not follow a simple path, it is typically thought to encompass the five steps listed in Table 12.1 (Anderson, 2014). Within this table, you will also find a number of questions to consider at each step of the policymaking process. These questions are meant to spark

*Table 12.1* The Policymaking Process

| Step | Process | Questions to Consider |
| --- | --- | --- |
| 1. Agenda setting | Problems are identified for consideration on the government agenda. | • What constitutes a public problem?<br>• What role do personal values of the policy-makers have on problem identification and prioritization?<br>• Who decides which problems will make it onto the agenda?<br>• Why might certain problems be identified over others for the government agenda? |
| 2. Formulation | After an issue has been placed on the agenda, multiple courses of action for addressing this problem are proposed. | • How are these proposals created?<br>• Where do these problem-solving ideas originate?<br>• What aspects of the issue might these proposals overlook? |
| 3. Adoption | Once solutions have been proposed, policy-makers decide which, if any, option will be implemented. | • How do policy-makers decide which proposal is the "best" option?<br>• How much negotiation and compromise goes into the adoption phase? |
| 4. Implementation | If a proposed policy is adopted, policy-makers then focus on how this policy will be put in place and enforced. | • How long does it take to roll out a policy?<br>• How are the consequences for disobeying a policy determined? |
| 5. Evaluation | Government officials assess the efficacy of the policy as well as other consequences of its implementation. | • Who determines if a policy is effective at addressing the initial problem?<br>• Upon what standards is efficacy judged?<br>• How are unintended outcomes addressed?<br>• When is a consequence considered serious enough to warrant changing or removing the policy? |

the type of careful reflection necessary in making the process of policy development more social justice–oriented. As you go through the steps, we recommend taking a few moments to pause and reflect on what you believe the answers to these questions might currently look like in our system of government. How does this image of government differ from one that is social justice–oriented? What do these differences reveal about our current system of policymaking?

To demonstrate the policy-related processes described throughout this chapter, we'll be referring to an example near and dear to our hearts, *Bill H.3933 An Act Rlative to Homelessness and Medicaid:*

> As part of a *Community Psychology* course, DH students engaged in community projects with Bostonians experiencing homelessness. Following these encounters, her students felt they needed to do more to address the problems faced by those who are unhoused. From here, Bill H.3933 An Act Relative to Homelessness and Medicaid was born and proposed in the Massachusetts Legislature. We'll use this example to explain the steps taken from identifying the problem, drafting the bill, collaborating with local representatives, and advocating for public support throughout this chapter.

## Determining Need for Public Policy

During the first stage of public policy, an agenda is set through a clear identification of needs. How are these needs identified and proposed for the agenda? To answer this question, we'll start by examining the path one undergraduate *Community Psychology* class took in becoming more aware of the problems facing their community.

> As part of this *Community Psychology* course, the students worked with several local nonprofit organizations (NFPs) with a mission to focus on reducing and eliminating homelessness and poverty in Boston. While working with these organizations, the students were exposed to areas of concern that they were unaware. In discussions with the leaders of these organizations, students learned of a Senator who was actively proposing a bill to address similar problems for Hawaii's homeless populations. Together, the students and the NFP leaders sought to do something similar in Massachusetts.

In this example, a piece of legislation originated from a group of concerned citizens (i.e., undergraduate college students); however, public opinion is only one of the many interacting factors that influence whether an issue becomes a major topic on the policy agenda. Physical conditions of the policy environment (such as the percentage of democrats vs. republicans, budget limitations/availability of funds, etc.) equally affect the capacity of the government to act effectively in response to requests for legislation. The process of recognizing and suggesting a problem for policy attention involves many different parties, from both within and outside the government.

Some policies happen without input from the general public, potentially by interest groups with direct access to government agencies (Kingdon, 1984). Interest groups are made up of people who seek to influence public policy towards achieving issue-specific goals. There are hundreds of interest groups at work in the United States, such as People for the Ethical Treatment of Animals (PETA) or the National Rifle Association (NRA). Each interest group is concerned with policies that specifically affect legislature related to their cause (e.g., PETA focuses on laws affecting the well-being of animals, whereas the NRA is a gun rights advocacy group). Interest groups pressure government officials to support relevant policies by lobbying for their cause. When lobbying, public interest groups may send representatives to testify in a congressional hearing, directly contact government officials, disseminate information and research, and/or talk with the media. One of the most substantive ways these interest groups influence public policies is through their Political Action Committees (PACs), which campaign for or against politicians depending on their positions. When campaign finance reform laws were passed in the 1970s to restrict individual contributions to campaigns, PACs remained a legal means for making large donations (Fortunato & Martin, 2016). For example, a corporation interested in financially supporting a candidate who opposes cosmetic testing on animals can contribute to PETA's PAC. Their PAC is then able to make direct contributions to this candidate's campaign; these contributions would otherwise be too large to come from a single individual. These types of financial incentives may sway a politician's leaning when it comes to supporting or blocking proposed policies. In this way, interest groups have been accused of corrupting public policies by "buying" government officials.

Similar to interest groups, media use has also grown more significant in influencing which issues are perceived as problems and, as such, defining agenda items. At a basic level, the news media plays an important role in informing the public about important issues. However, researchers widely accept that media goes beyond simply sharing the news to both filter and shape it (Kingdon, 2010). By offering greater coverage of a few key issues, the media shapes public perception to value these issues as more important than others. This increased awareness in turn leads to greater public demand for government action. In recent years, the power of those who control the media has transitioned somewhat with the rising prominence of social media. While traditional news outlets continue to be controlled by the powerful few or curated by professional journalists, social media has allowed politicians to communicate ideas directly with the public—and vice versa (Fortunato & Martin, 2016). This ability to circumvent the mass media creates opportunities for the spread of unfiltered ideas. While this process can lead to the spread of "fake news," the use of social media can also act as a powerful tool for citizens looking to advocate for important issues.

With such a large focus involving the shifting flow of ideologies, the agenda-setting process is inherently biased away from a purely rational selection of issues. Kingdon's Multiple Streams Framework of organizational choice provides a conceptual map of the parties involved in the agenda-setting process (Kingdon, 1984; see Figure 12.1). Within Kingdon's model, these parties are conceptualized as three distinct streams: problems, politics, and policies. When these streams come together (through advocacy efforts and the alignment of interests), this creates a window of opportunity from which policy change can occur. Essentially, problems become added to the agenda if they've been identified and recognized as having a viable solution. To better understand the viability of a solution, one must go beyond simply considering access to necessary resources. To be deemed viable, a policy solution also needs to be a supported political move at the time. This means also considering the intersection and alignment of the sociopolitical context and the administration in power.

From within this framework, it becomes easy to see how political issues may seem to follow a cyclical pattern, wherein they ebb and flow in popularity. When attempting to propose a problem for the policy agenda, it is important to consider the public and political sentiment towards your concern. If the issue is something relevant to the public and considered politically appropriate to address by your local politicians, the issue will have an easier time being picked up for consideration. This model also points out, however, that the solutions proposed alongside these issues must also be considered feasible and publicly acceptable. With this in mind, the most

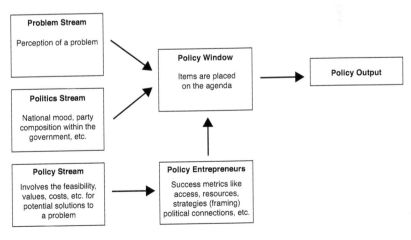

*Figure 12.1* Kingdon's Multiple Streams Framework

effective petitions need to be relevant to the public discourse and written in such a way that they highlight issues currently important to government officials.

## Writing Bills and Petitioning for Change

If you're reading this book, chances are your immediate role in affecting public policy will be through advocacy efforts. While some may argue that policy advocates have partisan or biased intentions, good advocacy efforts will be supported by data and written to appeal to a bipartisan audience. Advocacy and public policy work are by their very nature political—meaning they must satisfy the political (congressional and political constituents) stakeholders and must be crafted so each stakeholder sees value from their political position. In the next chapter, we provide additional details and examples on how framing and language usage play important roles in writing for legislative bodies. Here, we'll focus more so on drafting the *content* of a bill. Fair warning, this process can be lengthy, as much research is needed to prepare the bill for the inevitable scrutiny that will occur when it finally appears in front of congressional members.

When the *Community Psychology* students began the process of proposing a new bill, they didn't know how to write it. So, they started not by writing, but by researching the issue. Through these efforts, they learned that approximately 12,000 homeless people across Boston access health care through the Boston Health Care for the Homeless Program each year. For those with housing insecurity and complex health conditions, regular access to health care is often impossible. These compounding issues result in the excessive use of expensive emergency, inpatient, and crisis services. It seemed to the students that any proposed solution would need to not only better support homeless populations, but also reduce the costs on taxpayers. This information became the basis for their proposal and alerted them to work already being done in Hawaii to support homeless populations through Medicaid.

Much like in DH's class, the work in Hawaii began from the observation of a problem. Josh Green, an emergency room doctor and Hawaii state senator, noticed that many of the same people repeatedly coming through the emergency room were also dealing with homelessness, substance abuse, and mental illness (Friedman, 2017). He also recognized that it was these types of visits that were using most of the Hawaiian two billion dollars of Medicaid money (Barney, 2017). Green recognized that many of these people in the health care system cost the state on average $120,000 <u>per individual</u>

annually. Housing these individuals would result in an annual cost of $18,000 per person, thereby saving the state hundreds of millions of dollars a year. He knew something needed to be done and he formulated a bill to address this need.

Green wrote two pieces of legislation: one that would require health insurance to cover treatment for those experiencing homelessness (see references), and one written to require the creation of a Medicaid housing benefit plan for those experiencing homelessness (see references). Both of these bills went through significant amendments to make them more palatable for bipartisan support. Without agreement from those that will be voting on a bill, there is little chance that bill will receive the votes needed to pass. Often bills will go through amendments where one side receives less than what they wanted (i.e., exact funds requested or the ability to provide the service to all those requested in the original bill while accepting something that the other side wants (e.g., may include "add-ons" not directly tied to the original bill—like funds to small business)) in order to get the bill passed. This negotiation is often completed in small committees.

This legislation would essentially define homelessness as a medical condition and allow Medicaid to fund housing to the chronically homeless (defined as homeless for more than six months) as well as supportive services including living skills coaching. Green's legislation passed unanimously in the Hawaii senate in March 2017 and is still working its way through the House of Representatives. This bill passed unanimously due to Green's ability to frame the bill to appeal to both sides of the political aisle—conservatives (who value fiscal responsibility highly) were pleased that the bill would save the state money and liberals (who value care and concern for others highly) were glad that those experiencing homelessness would receive needed services.

Modeling the Massachusetts bill on the Hawaii bill allowed DH and her class to write their bill (Bill H.3933 An Act Relative to Homelessness and Medicaid, 2017) quickly. Also, being able to refer to a similar bill demonstrates precedent (a similar bill is happening or ideally was passed in another state, city or town, school, etc.) and provides a strong indicator to legislators that a bill has potential and helps to keep the legislation moving through the political process. They gathered data on the statistics regarding the numbers of people experiencing homelessness visiting the ER room, how many times per year, and their length of stay. They then determined the cost to the state to cover this program. They found that the state would actually save $2.5 million dollars annually. Similar to the Hawaii bill, they also suggested that the funds for the program be taken from the already-allocated federal money from Medicaid, so no additional funds were required.

When writing your own bill, you may not be so lucky as to have the same issue already proposed in previous legislation; however, chances are with a bit of research you will be able to find something similar enough to at least give you a jumping-off point. Reading previous bills on similar topics will provide insight into not only the formatting and wording of your bill, but into the legislative interest in your topic as well. By identifying government officials who have previously pledged their support to similar issues, you will have an idea of where you can begin to build support for your cause. Federal, state, and municipal entities provide open access to every bill and how each person voted. In addition, all legislators indicate how they have voted on previous bills. This information is invaluable to determining who to approach for building legislative support for your bill.

## Building Support

The first, and perhaps most important approach in building support, is to contact and meet with congressional senators and representatives. As we pointed out, selecting those with a history of supporting similar bills and issues is especially important when garnering support. The bill must be easily understood so that you can provide each political representative with a one-to-two-page summary of the bill's benefits for the public (e.g., social and economic benefits). The summary report should include not only the rationale but also statistics to back up major arguments in support of the bill (see Figure 12.2).

There are two major goals here: to get public support for the bill and to get one or more congressional members to file the bill on your behalf. Once a congressional member agrees to do so, the bill will then head to the relevant federal, state, city, or town subcommittee to determine if it should be sent further along.

---

The *Community Psychology* students took several approaches to bring attention to this issue including: a) researching which members of congress had demonstrated history of supporting similar bills and then calling and meeting with those congressional senators and representatives to achieve public support; b) reaching out to relevant stakeholders in the community to build alliances; c) writing and posting information on the issue in local newspapers and on NFP social media channels; and d) testifying to the public health committee that reviewed the bill.

From these advocacy efforts, five congresspeople agreed to support the bill if and when it came up for a vote in the state house. We were told by several congresspeople to get support before there is an actual vote. Several nonprofits with a mission to reduce homelessness publicly supported the bill. Students and two NFPs together testified in support of the bill to the Public Health Committee. A local street paper and several small-town newspapers wrote a story about the importance of the bill. Students created and posted weekly memes on a dedicated Facebook and Instagram page. These memes were shared with vested NFP stakeholders who also posted on their social media pages.

To: ████████████ and ████████████
From: Suffolk University Community Psychology Students, Spring 2017
RE:   Proposed homeless bill "An Act Relative to Medicaid"
Date: May 1, 2017

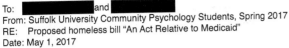

**Program that helps the homeless and reduces ER costs and visits by ER doctors writing 3-6 month Rx for housing using Medicaid funds.**

**Help the Homeless**

1. Housing
2. Health
3. Safety/employment

1. 19.5K are homeless
2. Health
   + 15/year visit
   + 4x longer stay
   + 150k/person/year
   **3 million cost to MA**
3. Shelters
   • Understaffed
   • Unsanitary
   • Dangerous
   • Turn people away

**Cost savings**

1. Medicaid
2. Reduced tax payer cost
3. Housing cost

1. Medicaid
2. 3 million → < 500k
   • 15 visits to 2 visits
3. Housing cost
   • $3-6k rent
   • $58.5 K – 117K for 19.5k Homeless

Notes:
• Average age and sex of a homeless person is a 9 year old girl
• 1/3 of homeless people are veterans
• 1/3 come from domestic violence situations
• 25% of teens in public high schools that are LGBTQ are homeless
• Save 2.5 million dollars **annually with housing**

*Figure 12.2* Program that helps the homeless and reduces ER costs and visits by ER doctors writing three-to-six-month Rx housing using Medicaid Funds

Of the state representatives who were reached out to by the *Community Psychology* students, one happened to be an alum of Suffolk University—State Rep. Brendan Crighton. Crighton recognized that many of Boston's citizens were being priced out of housing and ended up relying on large portions of the government's funds for health care. Crighton enthusiastically supported the bill and collaborated with Rep. Daniel Cahill, another Suffolk alum, to revise the bill to get it filed during the spring of 2017. Political officials understand the nuances of what will and will not be accepted by their respective committees, and we need to defer when possible to their willingness to revise the bill so that it is well received by a committee. That December, DH students, alongside members from the nonprofit organizations, spoke publicly on behalf of the bill for the Public Health Committee.

Testifying about the proposed bill to congressional members is a critical step in advocacy of public policy. When the congressional meeting to review this bill is held, you should work to have as many relevant stakeholders as possible in attendance to speak out about the bill's importance to their constituents. In our case, the Public Health Committee was shocked and pleasantly surprised to see college students not only attend a congressional meeting, but also testify on behalf of a public policy issue. Several committee members even contacted DH's students to indicate support of the bill should it come for a vote.

In conjunction with building support within the statehouse, equal effort should be put towards garnering as much *public* support for the bill as possible. This means contacting relevant stakeholders with the bill information (same white paper as earlier) and hopefully building alliances with a large group motivated to achieve the same goal. As described previously, public attention can drive government action by placing pressure on officials to respond to an issue of great public concern. Relevant nonprofits, universities, schools, community centers, and businesses can and should be approached. Researching who within each of these settings has previously demonstrated interest in this issue will provide insight into finding support. Reaching members of the general public can be done in a number of ways. The goal needs to be to get the story of the bill told to as many people as possible through traditional media channels (TV, radio, and newspapers) as well using social media (Facebook, Instagram, Twitter, etc.).

Do not underestimate the importance of people power in advocating for your bill. Unfortunately, this bill still languishes in this committee as more needs to be done to get it to a vote, including getting more public support, soliciting more committee members to publicly support the bill, and obtaining more traditional and social media coverage. The bill currently sits in the Public Health Committee and will need more advocacy to move from that committee to a full statewide vote. What is needed to reach this final stage is more support from stakeholders and people on the ground (e.g., students, volunteers, and nonprofits) to continue what was started across three sets of students. Unfortunately, for this Massachusetts bill, the political representatives that filed the original bill left their political office, so there is no political representative advocating for the bill within the legislature. To get this bill into law will require stakeholders to seek out more political representatives willing to advocate for the bill in committee while getting more public support for the bill.

## Steps From Bill to Law

- begins with an identified need
- a willingness for someone(s) to champion the cause

- research to determine what is needed by federal, state, or municipal government to address the need
- a clear and succinct document that clarifies the issue, need, and solution to be shared with stakeholders and the public (see document earlier as an example)
- someone(s) to research political representatives with a strong interest in the issue that would be willing to file the bill, advocate for it in committee, and vote for it
- political representative(s) to file the bill
- stakeholders willing to meet with representatives and advocate for the bill during public committee meetings and up until the final vote
- stakeholders to educate their constituents to obtain needed public support (e.g., through newspapers, social media, and radio/TV interviews)

Advocacy requires strong and passionate commitment to advocate for change. It is a lengthy process and requires research skills, motivation, determination, willingness to meet with people, and conviction that there is an issue that needs to be resolved and you have a strategy on how to do so at the political level. Finally, advocacy is not a one-person activity; it requires a group of dedicated people to make a difference.

## References

An Act Relative to Homelessness and Medicaid, H.3933, 190th Cong. (2017). https://malegislature.gov/Bills/190/H3933

Anderson, J. E. (2014). *Public policymaking* (8th ed.). Cengage Learning.

Barney, L. (2017, February 28). *Doctors could prescribe houses to the homeless under radical Hawaii bill.* www.theguardian.com/us-news/2017/feb/28/hawaii-homeless-housing-bill-healthcare-costs

Environmental Protections Agency (EPA). (2007, September 14). *Laws and executive orders.* www.epa.gov/laws-regulations/laws-and-executive-orders#majorlaws

Fortunato, J. A., & Martin, S. E. (2016). The intersection of agenda-setting, the media environment, and election campaign laws. *Journal of Information Policy*, *6*, 129–153. https://doi.org/10.5325/jinfopoli.6.2016.0129

Friedman, E. (2017, June 21). *Prescribing housing for the homeless in Hawaii.* https://oneill.law.georgetown.edu/prescribing-housing-for-the-homeless-in-hawaii/

Kingdon, J. W. (1984). *Agendas, alternatives, and public policies.* Little, Brown.

Kingdon, J. W. (2010). *Agendas, alternatives, and public policies* (updated 2nd ed.). Pearson.

U.S. Department of Housing and Urban Development (HUD). (n.d.). *Key HUD statutes.* www.hud.gov/hudprograms/keystatutes

## *Resources*

*Care2.* This website connects a network of millions of petitioners worldwide through the use of technology and experienced campaigners. They unite their members with nonprofits and mission-based brands currently working for causes of concern.

www.care2.com/

*Public Policy: Politics, Analysis, and Alternatives* by Michael E. Kraft & Scott R. Furlong
The *Student Resource Guide* is a free resource, including learning objectives, chapter summaries, and study tools to deepen your knowledge on a range of public policy issues covered in the book. Policy issues covered in this guide include economic, health care, welfare, education, environmental, and homeland security, among others.

https://edge.sagepub.com/kraft7e/student-resources-0

*Project Citizen.* Project Citizen is an interdisciplinary curricular program created by the Center for Civic Education. They aim to promote competent and responsible participation in local and state government by offering educational opportunities for individuals of all ages.

www.civiced.org/project-citizen

# 13 Writing Grants for Community Building

*Lynne-Marie Shea and Debra A. Harkins*

Grant funding requires that a partnership be built not just between an organization and the community it is seeking to serve, but between the organization and the agency it hopes will finance this service work. Organizations seeking grant funding are often advised to increase their likelihood of being funded by making sure that they understand the needs of funders and ensuring that their grant application tells a story of a project that meets those needs.

If projects are authentically aimed at promoting social justice, though, the ends cannot justify the means. If projects are to build community, the wants and needs of the community must be considered throughout the process. Applying a critical framework to traditional grant-writing considerations allows for the inclusion of community voice throughout the entire funding process—from the development of a project idea, to the identification of a funding source, to the creation of a narrative that brings the project to life, through the project's implementation and assessment.

> DH wrote a grant for her community partner, C4C, to a philanthropic organization (P1) that announced they would be providing emergency funding to organizations seeking to help feed families in need within Boston communities during the COVID-19 pandemic. Unfortunately, C4C did not receive this money as all funds were diverted to a large foundation in Boston who then distributed the money to more well-known nonprofit organizations in the Boston area. As C4C is only a few years old, this funder was worried about funding such a young organization in an emergency situation. Instead, the philanthropic organization directed their funds to more established nonprofits.

## Understanding the Values of Grantors

While grant writers are often encouraged to ask themselves why grantors are giving away funding and what they want from applicants in return, funding

DOI: 10.4324/9781003055587-13

for projects that prioritize community building must consider the values of funders and ask whether these values lend themselves to the proposed project.

## Questions to Consider

- What have these grantors funded before?
- In what ways have these previously funded initiatives impacted the communities they intend to serve?
- What will you be asked to do in order to receive funding? Are these "asks" in line with your mission and values? In what ways will they impact your community partner?

LS wrote a small grant for C4C from a small local funding organization to support the nonprofit's main mission of creating urban gardens in Boston's neediest schools. When LS wrote this small grant the first time, the agency was very receptive and supportive. The second grant proposal was for helping to feed children and families during the COVID-19 pandemic, and the agency reported that they were less interested as it was not directly connected to the agency's main mission of gardening. However, the agency did give 3/4 of the requested money with an explanation that they understood the situation was dire and that the NFP should seek additional funding from other organizations.

The response of the grantors that the work to provide emergency food to at-risk families was not directly connected to the main mission of creating gardens to address food insecurity demonstrated a mismatch between the values of the funder and the aims of the organization. The urgency of the project, though, led to a decision to accept partial funding without taking time to elaborate on and advocate for the connection between the organization's overall mission and its commitment to addressing acute needs in unprecedented circumstances.

## Matching Project Values With Grant Guidelines

**Coded Messages**—Coded language is defined by the National Education Association as "substituting terms describing racial identity with seemingly race-neutral terms that disguise explicit and/or implicit racial animus." This kind of language is often used by those in power or those with resources to use racial anxiety to garner support for regressive or harmful policies (or in the case of funders, to justify giving resources to some while keeping from others) while allowing the speaker plausible deniability that they are referring to or even thinking about race.

While traditional grant proposals may emphasize or build on specific aspects of their project in order to meet funding guidelines, projects aimed at community building are more than the sum of their parts. Projects that include community insight and voice cannot simply highlight the aspects that will most appeal to funders as this risks compromising the integrity of the project and devaluing the voices of those involved in its creation.

## Questions to Consider

- Can the project be fit into the guidelines of the funder without compromising its overall mission and aim? If not, is it possible to submit only parts of the project for funding while maintaining its overall aim?
- Are grantors unwilling to fund parts of the project that are inherent to its value?
- Are there any **coded messages** (Desmond-Harris, 2014; López, 2015) being sent in what is or is not deemed eligible for funding?
- Is anything being asked by funders that is in conflict with my values? Is this addressed in my application?

DH also sought funds for the C4C Coronavirus Response Resiliency Project through a dedicated fund source at her institution. While C4C primarily sought food, their secondary concern was providing educational resources for the children who could no longer attend school and had little access to the internet to do their schoolwork. Through this source, we were able to access needed funds while achieving the goal of the dedicated funds—to provide educational materials to those in need.

While the emergency funds available through the institution lay outside of the organization's primary aims, providing educational materials was in line with the overall mission of supporting wellness and increasing access to resources for **underserved individuals** (Bantham, Taverno Ross, Sebastião, & Hall, 2020). The grant that was written was unable to support the organization in supplying families with the food they need. It did, however, allow the organization to access emergency funds that had been made available in order to meet another one of their stakeholders' needs.

**Underserved Individuals**—An understanding of what it means to be "underserved" are varied and overlapping. The Department of Health and Human Services provides one definition for underserved and vulnerable populations as "communities that include members of minority populations or individuals who have experienced health disparities." Considered through a more critical lens, "underserved" populations might best be understood as those who are under-resourced—having limited access to crucial services like healthcare, education, healthy food, and safe spaces. These individuals are likely to face physical, mental, and economic vulnerability as long as systems are not set up to consider and address their needs (Bantham et al., 2020). Understanding what it means to be underserved through a critical lens can be particularly important when it comes to students. See the resource from the Learning Circle (2019) to consider student populations that are often at-risk and overlooked.

## Understanding Requirements and Commitments

**Assessment**—Assessment and evaluation of impact is often thought of as something that reduces important and complex work to a limited numbers/outcome framework. Using a critical framework and social justice lens, though, can allow assessment to be an important part of the planning and implementation process (see Center for International Media Action's booklet on considering evaluation). *Appreciative inquiry* (AI), for instance, can be used as a framework to highlight effective strategies for building on the strengths of a community to address its identified needs (Catsambas & Preskill, 2006). AI can also be used as a chance to recommit to participatory action and working with rather than for the community (Paige et al., 2015).

Effective grant writing includes consideration of how long an application will take to submit and how long review and decision-making processes will take. Consideration must be given to whether the amount of effort required for an application and subsequent reporting is justified by the potential impact of the project being funded and if the project being proposed will still be as relevant in the time it takes for funding to be approved and received. Projects that promote community building, though, require additional consideration around who will be charged with the added responsibilities around implementing a new project and the reporting and **assessment** required by the funder (Catsambas & Preskill, 2006; Paige et al., 2015).

### Questions to Consider

- Is the effort that will go into the application and reporting processes appropriate for its potential impact?
- Who will be charged with these efforts? Will they be compensated appropriately?
- Is the project time-bound or dependent on other factors? Will a lengthy application/decision process impact its potential?

DH helped C4C, which was seeking funding from a philanthropic foundation (P2) to address the urgent needs of Boston's neediest families during the COVID-19 pandemic. When the P2 foundation was initially approached, they verbally indicated they would match funds if another foundation (P1—described earlier) provided funds, or would provide funds if the P1 foundation did not fund the grant proposal. When funds were not received from the P1 foundation, P2 funders changed their minds and failed to provide any funding. However, through continued conversations with P2 funders who indicated desire to help during this crisis, a written proposal was sent to them. Unfortunately, their "funding committee" denied the request, arguing that they usually only provide funds directly to schools. They suggested that the NFP community partner should tell the schools to contact P2 directly. Frustrated and expecting little at this point, DH wrote an email explaining why that did not work as the schools were in dire straits and the bureaucracy of the public schools would lead to little to no funds to serve those in desperate immediate need. DH also explained that the schools trusted the NFP community partner, as its members had been serving Boston's needy for over 20 years. To our great surprise, P2 responded saying that they would make an exception and fund C4C.

The need for emergency funding calls for a unique and challenging balance between the effort put into applications and the likelihood that funds will be received in a timely manner. A difficult choice was made to continue pursuing a funding source that seemed unlikely to provide funds rather than to identify another funder. This choice was made because of already-established relationships and the potential for funds to be received right away if a case for urgency was made effectively. Using existing relationships allowed for quick trust building with the funder and made them more willing to consider the potential impact of putting the proposal through other channels, as would normally be recommended.

## Including Outside Perspective

While all grant proposals can certainly benefit from feedback from someone outside of the project, community-building projects must include community stakeholders throughout the entire process. Consideration must be given to everyone who might have a stake in the project—not only the first people who come to mind in the **project narrative**. Once these stakeholders have been identified, opportunities must be created to include their voice and insight in every aspect of the grant proposal.

**Project Narrative**—In grant writing, this is perhaps the most crucial aspect of the proposal. This is where the story of the project and its potential to make an impact is told. It is often suggested that this part of the proposal should "tug at the heartstrings" of the funders. Sticking to a social justice framework, though, means that a compelling story must be told without tokenizing community members or commodifying their rich and complex experiences.

## Questions to Consider

- Who is this project designed to impact? Who might be impacted apart from those who are thought of as central to the project's mission?
- How might project aims impact community members in ways other than those specified in the project narrative?
- How are insights from community members about the potential real-world consequences of the project being included in its proposal implementation and assessment?
- Are funders willing to provide the resources needed to minimize the risk of potentially negative impacts of the project or to address any unintended consequences as they arise?

When the dedicated funds were appropriated to provide books to C4C to distribute to children in Boston, many discussions took place to ensure that the books chosen met the needs of all stakeholders. The major stakeholders in this case included the Boston teachers who wanted to ensure the books would be useful towards school curriculum, multicultural Boston children who could identify with the stories and characters, and the education department's service-learning students who were learning about educational curriculum and providing educational resources.

Every aspect of a project design has the potential to impact stakeholders differently. In this case, choices behind books to distribute impact not only those by whom they will be read, but also the individuals charged with helping to read and those working to build on learning that is happening at home. While providing books to children in a time when they have been removed from their traditional learning spaces was an easy choice to make, this choice brings up many more complicated questions around different languages spoken in homes, varied grade levels of students, opportunity gaps, and the distance-learning content already being facilitated by educators and their partners.

## Bringing Community Resources to the Table

Funders often ask organizations to highlight the resources that they will bring to their proposed projects and that will support its maintenance outside of grant funding. Community-based projects must certainly highlight community strengths and resources in their proposal. Projects aimed at authentic community building, though, must also assess what it would mean to maintain projects outside of grant funding and consider whether this would risk draining **community resources**. Moreover, these projects must consider whether community members and resources are being included at every level, in ways that are meaningful and powerful, or simply as a means to fill any gaps.

> **Community Resources**—These are the strategies already being used by the community to meet its own needs. Asset mapping (see resource from Americorps VISTA Campus) allows for an identification of the tools communities are already using to care for themselves. In grant writing it is crucial to highlight these strengths while also shining a light on areas in which communities have not had access to resources that have been inequitably distributed.

### Questions to Consider

- Can resources identified to support the project outside of grant funding be allocated for a new project without being compromised or spread too thin?
- How committed are grantors to funding projects on an ongoing basis? How would the value and integrity of the project be impacted if it was only partially funded or funded only for a limited amount of time?
- Are those in the community being involved in the project at every level and included in positions of power and authority?

> In each of the cases described earlier, funders were informed about not only the strengths and resources of all the stakeholders involved in these projects but of other funding agencies that contributed funds to these projects. In this way, funders recognize that other funders and partners are committed to the project and of the many ways that the project is being supported and maintained beyond the individual funder's contribution.

Centralizing stakeholders in our community-building project narratives ensures that these projects maintain their integrity and remain based in community voice as we present them to funders. Funders who have agreed to support projects that are grounded in community voice and strengths can then be used to leverage funds from other organizations. In this way, we can invite new funders to buy into a community and its values rather than working to convince funders that communities can adapt or change to fit their funding vision.

## Bringing Your Project to Life

Having any project funded includes telling a good story. Funding a community-building project, though, means that the story being told must be not only good but also intentional and authentic. In order to promote social justice, the story that must be told about the project cannot simply be what funders want to hear. Community-building stories must be inclusive—highlighting the strengths of the community and all those of whom it is composed. In order to be authentic and meaningful, narratives cannot be polished for funder consumption; they must describe communities as they understand themselves and their experience.

### Questions to Consider

- Is the story that I'm telling inclusive? Has anyone or anything been left out of the narrative? Does including these things make the story harder to tell? Why?
- How are community strengths included in my project?
- Have I polished my story to make it easier to consume? Does it reflect the community as they want to be seen?
- Is my language accessible and empowering?

We have worked with C4C to help craft a story that is not only inclusive but highlights why they are uniquely positioned to meet the mission that others seek to obtain—feeding the hearts, minds, and bellies of Boston's neediest children and families. C4C has created a website with their story, a Facebook page, an Instagram account, and a GoFundMe charity page. In each of these spaces, C4C tells a similar story that is told when writing and talking to potential funders.

Prioritizing the voices of those in the community and those who have spent time building relationships and engaging in community work can be challenging, particularly when emergency needs arise and red tape needs to be navigated. When we justify our ends with our means by taking short cuts, allowing the community to tell only parts of their story, or trying to tell the story for them, our work becomes compromised.

Grant writing that prioritizes and promotes community building can achieve these aims only by centralizing them throughout the entire process. Grounding grant applications and funding requests in an authentic commitment to community is no small feat, particularly when needs are pressing and funding processes are complex and convoluted. No matter how complicated the system or pressing the need, though, community-building projects cannot justify or maintain the systems of oppression that have, in large part, caused the problems of the communities these projects are designed to serve. In this way, our means and our ends must be the same. Community building can only happen with and through the community.

## References

Bantham, A., Taverno Ross, S. E., Sebastião, E., & Hall, G. (2020). Overcoming barriers to physical activity in underserved populations. *Progress in Cardiovascular Diseases.* https://doi-org.ezproxysuf.flo.org/10.1016/j.pcad.2020.11.002

Catsambas, T. T., & Preskill, H. (2006). *Reframing evaluation through appreciative inquiry.* Sage Publications.

Desmond-Harris, J. (2014, March 15). 8 Sneaky racial code words and why politicians love them. *The Root.* wwwtheroot.com

López, I. H. (2015). *Dog whistle politics: How coded racial appeals have reinvented racism and wrecked the middle class.* Oxford University Press.

Paige, C., Peters, R., Parkhurst, M., Beck, L. L., Hui, B., May, V. T. O., & Tanjasiri, S. P. (2015). Enhancing community-based participatory research partnerships through appreciative inquiry. *Progress in Community Health Partnerships: Research, Education, and Action, 9,* 457–463. https://doi.org/10.1353/cpr.2015.0054

## *Resources*

Asset Mapping: www.vistacampus.gov/what-asset-mapping

Coded Language: https://neaedjustice.org/social-justice-issues/racial-justice/coded-language/

https://ctb.ku.edu/en/table-of-contents/assessment/assessing-community-needs-and-resources/identify-community-assets/main

Overlooked and Underserved Students: www.learningcirclesoftware.com/resources/equity-in-education/7-overlooked-underserved-student-populations/

www.theroot.com/8-sneaky-racial-code-words-and-why-politicians-love-the-1790874941

# 14 Sharing and Disseminating

*Christina Athineos*

## Why Publish?

As you'll soon become more aware, publishing your work takes a good deal of effort—so why do it? When you publish, you ensure that the lessons you've learned and knowledge you've gained does not end with you. Sharing and disseminating your work to a large audience can serve a great number of purposes, such as helping to inform the public about the work you're involved in; providing useful knowledge to others currently invested in and affected by similar social justice causes, who will benefit from your writings; and gaining additional support for the cause, be it monetary, person power, or media representation. Because the goals in social justice–related work may vary depending on the form and function of your service, this chapter will focus on how to publish and share your work as a broad concept, providing insights into a number of different publication arenas, from popular media to scientific journals.

## Deciding on Your Audience

Determining your audience is the first key step to effectively writing and sharing your work. To help understand the importance of this step, consider the differences in how you address your friends, boss, coworkers, and family. Depending on which audience you plan to address, you'll likely have to change your "voice" and adjust your tone. Now imagine if you spoke to your boss in the same way you speak to your friends. Chances are this wouldn't work out as well for you as if you had spoken in a more professional manner. This simple exercise offers a glimpse into the full value of knowing your audience and venue. If you address your audience inappropriately, you are likely to lose their attention before they make it to the end of your work.

Knowing your audience (and keeping their interests in mind) can help to inform your language use, framing, and publication space. However, with social justice work often being a collaborative and intersectional endeavor, it can sometimes make determining your target audience a bit trickier than

DOI: 10.4324/9781003055587-14

one might expect. To help answer this question of "who" you want reading your work, try first starting with "why?" Why are you writing about this topic?

While there could be endless reasons for writing something, an author's purpose can usually fit into at least one of three categories. The popular acronym "PIE" helps us recall these purposes as 1. Persuade; 2. Inform; 3. Entertain. Do you seek to convince somebody to think or do something? Are you hoping to provide information about a subject? Is your main goal to creatively express yourself for others' enjoyment? Remember, your goal may incorporate multiple purposes.

*When determining which purpose your piece may fit into, consider the following questions:*

What is your goal in publishing this piece?

_____

_____

_____

What do you want the readers to learn or do after having read your piece?

_____

_____

_____

Potential goals might include things like educating the general populace of an issue, accessing grant funding, or communicating knowledge to students, colleagues, and policy-makers. The benefit of knowing your goal is two-fold. Once you know your goal, you'll also know your audience and will thereby have a better idea as to the destination for your publication. For instance, if you decide that your goal is to increase your community's awareness about an issue, you know that your purpose is to inform. In this case, your audience is also identified as a large and varied group. You may therefore choose to publish your work in a blog as your best bet for broadcasting to a wide and diverse audience. On the other hand, if you determine that your goal is to gain grant funding for additional research endeavors, your purpose could be identified as persuasive. Rather than casting a wide net like the previous example, here your audience is much more targeted and likely consists of academics. For academic audiences, publishing in a peer-reviewed journal will better increase your chances of reaching the appropriate audience and accomplishing your goal.

After you've honed in on your purpose and the audience, there are a number of things you'll want to examine about your readers. First, it's important to consider what your readers may already know about your subject (Trimmer, 2004). Are they well informed on the issue or is this likely to be novel information? These types of questions can shine light on how much context or how many examples you need to provide before the reader understands. Secondly, you'll want to contemplate what your readers may be expecting from your writing (Trimmer, 2004). If you're writing to your own base, they may be expecting to confirm or expand upon their own ideas. However, if you're trying to reach new audiences, you might consider that their reaction could be more critical. In these cases, it's especially important to devote effort to piquing the reader's interest (Trimmer, 2004). Why should somebody who's apathetic—or potentially even opposed—to your ideas give your writing a fair chance? How might you gain and hold their attention? Regardless of who it is you are writing for, it is always recommended that you determine this audience before you get too deep into the writing process. For example, writing for a traditional academic audience is usually written in the third person, while blogs and popular magazine articles are in the first person. In addition, knowing how much knowledge your reader has of the topic will help determine how much background information needs to be included.

## Writing for Your Audience

Once you know *who* you're writing for, it's important to focus on *how* to write for them. Let me rephrase that: it's important to focus on how to write for *them*. If you have worked on an interdisciplinary team, you'll be familiar with the fact that your colleagues seem to express and comprehend ideas in ways that differ from your own. Engaging others in your writing can be especially challenging if your audience does not share your area of expertise and the linguistic knowledge that accompanies it (Carlile, 2004). In other words, if you don't use their terminology, they won't understand you. Even worse, if you use complex jargon that they aren't familiar with, you're likely to make them feel excluded.

Having a good understanding of the ways in which your audience communicates and why will help you to better reach them in an impactful and authentic way. Likewise, knowing their vernacular and using it correctly will help your audience to feel connected to the work. Research demonstrates that frequent interaction with members of your audience is an effective means of building linguistic knowledge in areas of expertise outside your own (Barley, Dinh, Workman, & Fang, 2020). Unfortunately, building relationships like these may not always be possible, as they require an extensive amount of time and energy to really engrain yourself in their culture. In that case, I recommend the next best thing to do would be to read things written by your audience. Pay attention to their language usage and how they structure their sentences. Take note of how many references they use (if any) and the perspective from which they're writing.

Just as important as the language you use is your framing of the issue. Framing influences the way information is perceived by providing a lens, or "frame," through which an issue is to be thought about (Goffman, 1974).

The way in which something is framed can have significant effects on how the audience processes this information (Goffman, 1974). Frames influence message meaning through multiple processes. One common framing technique, "spin," involves knowing the values of your audience and presenting your ideas in ways that draw on these principles (Fairhurst & Sarr, 1996). If you can align the issue with your audience's pre-existing values, you can make them care about the topic.

*Consider the following real-world example of framing at work:*

While working as an intern for the National Prevention Science Coalition's Research-to-Policy Collaboration (RPC), I (CA) learned a great deal about the ways in which the RPC remains non-partisan while still addressing politically charged, seemingly value-laden topics. Research demonstrates that Republicans and Democrats use different languages and even express different emotions when discussing the same current events (Demszky et al., 2019). Pushing through legislation that speaks to both parties seems like a sometimes impossible task considering how polarizing language can be. Yet it seems that the RPC has effectively found ways of maximizing these linguistic patterns, rather than shying away from them. The RPC is able to operate with the goal of gaining bi-partisan support on the same bill through their use of framing. Although the end goal is the same, and always evidence-based, I saw that the way an issue was "packaged" may differ from party to party, and how this packaging made a big difference in how it is perceived. For instance, my supervisor explained how knowledge of current Republican or Democratic values could be harnessed to inform the presentation of research related to issues of homelessness.

Evidence supports housing-first programs as being a worthwhile strategy for supporting homeless populations. This statement places value primarily on the importance of research as a worthwhile marker of efficacy. However, if one wanted to market housing-first programs to a specific party, it may be useful to draw on values they deem to be especially significant. For Republicans, it may be pertinent to focusing on the monetary benefits, wherein housing-first programs save government funding that would otherwise be spent on emergency care and aid programs for homeless populations. For Democrats, one might instead highlight how these programs improve the quality of life for homeless populations. In the end, both parties are made to feel that their values align with a housing-first initiative. This example again exemplifies that to be effective, you have to know your audience.

## Increase Readership

Believe it or not, the steps towards increasing your readership begin before you've even gotten published. Getting noticed amongst the endless content available online can seem like an insurmountable challenge, so it's important that you make yours stand out. While there are entire books devoted to this topic, I've also found that a simple Google search can effectively capture the same ideas everyone seems to be repeating. I've taken the legwork out for you by summarizing the most impactful recommendations I've come across.

### *Accessibility*

First, you'll want to consider ways to make your writing the most accessible. This involves keeping your writing short and simple whenever possible. Our attention spans aren't endless. When you're competing with all of the other content out there, you'll want to consider how long it may take your reader to reach the end. One way to calculate this is to go by word count. While it varies, the average adult reads about 250 words/minute (Brysbaert, 2019). If you simply divide your total word count by 250, you'll have a fair estimate of how many minutes it will take someone to read your piece. How much this reading time matters varies depending on your audience and publication space. For academic journals, you'll likely be given a maximum word count or page number to help determine the appropriate length for your work. In all cases, word selection and sentence structuring will be important components in making the most of the space you have. An easy way to do this is to simplify your word choice and remove extraneous words (Williams & Bizup, 2017).

### *Readability*

To truly analyze how simplified your writing is, it is recommended that authors consider using a readability test on their work. The most popular of these include the Flesch-Kinkaid readability tests, which determine the ease of comprehension based on word and sentence length (Kincaid, Fishburne, Rogers, & Chissom, 1975). After inputting your work, the readability test will analyze your writing and "score" it with a grade level. It is recommended to aim for between a sixth- and eighth-grade level when writing for the general public. This level allows for faster reads and is simple enough to allow your message to come across quickly to a wide audience with varied reading ability. Research demonstrates that anything above a ninth-grade reading level is considered difficult to read (Flesch, 1981).

### *Determine Appropriate Length*

After putting in the editorial efforts to shorten your writing, take a step back to make sure that your work actually appears short. Maximize the amount of white space between the lines of writing to visually break up the page. For example, if you have the option of writing three long paragraphs or six short ones, choose to write six. This spacing will give your readers' eyes a break and will make them feel as though they are progressing quickly through your work. These spaces also offer the opportunity to add images. A simple Google search will provide options for free or paid images, and some sites even have their own image banks built in. Use these images to your advantage! By chunking the information into smaller bites, it becomes more palatable and easier to keep going. This principle can also be implemented for more scientific writing. While an actual picture may not always be appropriate, consider the ways in which images like graphs, charts, and tables can help to display information and break up your writing.

### Powerful Titles

Another part of your writing that can increase readership is your title. Coming up with a title that represents your work and appears interesting enough to click is a lofty task. This is another area where framing comes in handy. Before your reader ever makes it to the first paragraph, the use of a catchphrase can influence the way they feel about your writing (Fairhurst & Sarr, 1996). More recently, these terms have been referred to by copywriters and marketers as "power words." By carefully using these power words, you can elicit emotional responses that prime your audience to expect certain things from your piece. For instance, the word "controversial" will tap into the reader's curiosity, whereas "accredited" elicits trust (Fernandez, 2020). One important thing to remember when considering these keywords is that the more popular the term, the more frequently it will have been used by other authors. While this may not seem like a big deal, I recommend you try googling the title you're considering. If there are hundreds of other articles with similar titles, your piece is likely to get bumped to a much later page.

### References Are Gold

Last, unless you're planning on making this piece a one-time thing in terms of publishing, I recommend capitalizing on the free advertisement space that is your references section. Whenever possible, reference and link to your other articles at the end of your work. If you're writing for a venue that allows you to add additional links, take this opportunity to connect readers back to your online profile (such as a personal website, LinkedIn page, ResearchGate listing, etc.), where they can find a listing of the other works you've written. Furthermore, whenever you publish something, go the extra step to share it on social media. If you can, get friends and family to interact with your post and share it again.

## Reflecting on the Importance

After reading through this chapter, you are hopefully more aware of the myriad of ways in which writing goes beyond the great task of actually typing up the content of your piece. To write a truly successful work, much effort must be placed into considering the audience, purpose, language, accessibility, and readability. In light of all this, you would be correct to think that writing takes a great deal of time and effort. However, it would be equally *wrong* to assume that the energy expended towards dissemination is better spent on more immediate acts of service.

So again, we return to the question, "Why publish?" The way I see it, social justice can be thought of as a communal quilt, with each individual contributing their own work to the final product. Each time we share our work with others, we add a square to the quilt, and it grows one step closer to completion. If we instead choose to continue placing all of our efforts into working on our one square rather than stitching it into the larger quilt, our work would never add to the greater project as a whole. In this way, sharing and disseminating one's work is a critically important step in creating long-term changes towards social justice. In publishing your work with others, you ensure that those outside your immediate circle can continue to learn about and carry on the work after you no longer can. Without this final step, our work becomes only a short-term solution that may not lead to lasting social change. So the next time you're struggling to find the energy to write, remember that your voice has the power to inspire policy change, galvanize direct action, and influence transformative thinking long after you're no longer around to do so yourself.

## References

Barley, W. C., Dinh, L., Workman, H., & Fang, C. (2020). Exploring the relationship between interdisciplinary ties and linguistic familiarity using multilevel network analysis. *Communication Research*, 1–28. https://doi.org/10.1177/0093650220926001

Brysbaert, M. (2019, April 12). How many words do we read per minute? *A Review and Meta-Analysis of Reading Rate.* https://doi.org/10.31234/osf.io/xynwg

Carlile, P. R. (2004). Transferring, translating, and transforming: An integrative framework for managing knowledge across boundaries. *Organization Science, 15*, 555–568. https://doi.org/10.1287/orsc.1040.0094

Demszky, D., Garg, N., Voigt, R., Zou, J., Gentzkow, M., Shapiro, J., & Jurafsky, D. (2019). Analyzing polarization in social media: Method and application to tweets on 21 mass shootings. *17th Annual Conference of the North American Chapter of the Association for Computational Linguistics (NAACL)*, Minneapolis, MN.

Fairhurst, G., & Sarr, R. (1996). *The art of framing.* Jossey-Bass.

Fernandez, M. (2020, July 31). *700 power words that will boost your conversions.* https://optinmonster.com/700-power-words-that-will-boost-your-conversions/

Flesch, R. (1981). *How to write plain English: A book for lawyers and consumers.* Barnes & Noble Books.

Goffman, E. (1974). *Frame analysis: An essay on the organization of experience.* Harper and Row.

Kincaid, J. P., Fishburne, R. P., Rogers, R. L., & Chissom, B. S. (1975). Derivation of new readability formulas (automated readability index, fog count, and flesch reading ease formula) for navy enlisted personnel. *Institute for Simulation and Training, 56.* https://doi.org/10.21236/ADA006655

Trimmer, J. F. (2004). *The new writing with a purpose* (14th ed.). Houghton Mifflin.

Williams, J. M., & Bizup, J. (2017). *Style: Lessons in clarity and grace* (12th ed.). Pearson.

## Resources

Freelance social justice writing opportunities:

Stanford Social Innovation Review (*SSIR*) produces authoritative, cutting-edge articles, podcasts, videos, webinars, and conferences on issues facing leaders of nonprofits, foundations, businesses, and government agencies. *SSIR* emphasizes cross-sector solutions to global problems and highlights individuals and organizations that have made significant contributions to the field.

Truthout is a nonprofit news organization dedicated to providing independent reporting and commentary on a diverse range of social justice issues. *Truthout* works to spark action by revealing systemic injustice and providing a platform for progressive and transformative ideas, through in-depth investigative reporting and critical analysis.

The Progressive is a magazine that aims to amplify voices of dissent and those under-represented in the mainstream, with a goal of championing grassroots progressive politics.

Unapologetic is a social justice magazine focused on societal issues that affect people of color. They accept submissions from BIPOC writers, artists, and photographers on a rolling basis and share their work across social media platforms.

Yes! Media is a nonprofit, independent publisher of solutions journalism that analyzes societal problems in terms of their root causes and explores opportunities for systemic, structural change. They aim to highlight the positive ways communities are responding to social problems.

# 15 Building Your Social Justice Toolkit

*Lauren I. Grenier and Debra A. Harkins*

Over the course of this book, you learned about the complexity of engaging in socially just–focused helping. You explored how your own social identity shapes your perceptions and beliefs, how theories for social justice interact with action to carry this work forward, and how to support working towards social justice in actionable ways. In an effort to balance theory, reflection, and action, we close this compendium of social justice helping with a toolkit on how to carry this work forward. What follows is a list of key takeaways and action steps with which you can engage to build your social justice toolkit.

Reading this book is not the end to this work, but a continuation: we encourage you to take the knowledge and resources you have learned here and incorporate it into your current roles to promote liberation and work for social justice. Our closing reflection tool is to develop an action and commitment statement to help you carry your work forward. As you reflect on what you have learned in this book, we encourage you to build action steps into your own commitment statement. Determine how these tools relate to your own profession, work, or life. Figure out your activist "lane." We reference the metaphor of picking a lane, highlighted by American activist and organizer Mariame Kaba, whose advice to young organizers is "to pick your lane and to focus on it" (Kaba cited in Novik, 2017). In the overwhelming work to be done for liberation, burnout is a consistent and real threat (Harkins, 2017). By focusing your energy in one lane, or area of liberation work that you are committed to, and engaging collaboratively in the fight for social justice, then collectively we can work towards change.

## Key Takeaways to Build Your Toolkit

### Tool 1: Know Yourself and Your Context

As mentioned early on, social justice–oriented work begins by getting to know thyself very well. This requires you to explore your own social identities and values. Review Chapters 2 and 3 and reflect deeply on your own social identity, family history, and values, which will lead you into a deep

DOI: 10.4324/9781003055587-15

dive into the role of intersectionality in your life and how helping others is impacted by your own and others' social identities. Exploring the roles of your values in social justice helping, and how you can educate other helpers on the sources of their values so that they, too, can examine their values, will move you and others to engage in positive liberatory helping. Having a deeper understanding of your social identity and values, and how these directly tie into your actions, is critical to engaging in liberatory practices. As discussed in the introduction, knowing yourself will help you engage in more liberatory practices when helping others to create a more socially just society.

In an effort to continue exploring these aspects of yourself, one action step we suggest is to continue this reflection by utilizing the tools of journaling, reading, and asking deeper questions. For example, learn where you come from, your family's origins, and your community's origins to develop a deeper understanding of your social, political, and historical self. A compilation of resources found at the end of the book can be utilized in your exploration.

**Reflection:** Throughout the course of this book, what have you come to know about yourself? How will this knowledge impact how you carry this work forward? What questions about your identity do you still have?

_____

_____

_____

In an effort to better understand yourself, you must build out this knowledge to recognize and understand how your context has shaped and continues to impact your own development—social, political, historical, and environmental. Understanding yourself and those with whom you work in context creates a critical, reflective foundation upon which your social justice work can be built. You need to develop an understanding of how institutional and cultural structures are built that maintain inequalities. You need to understand these structures in order to dismantle them. You can only do this by grappling with how these systems arose initially. As you may recall, Chapter 4 provides an overview of the theories of social justice that bring light some of these structural inequalities.

### Tool 2: Engage in Critical Reflection

An action step for building this deeper understanding of knowing your context involves reading critically, being in dialogue, and being willing to question hegemony. As we have discussed throughout this book, this is harder than it first appears, and you must be willing to handle the pushback that happens when you confront injustices. Knowing and understanding your context will allow for conscientization, or developing a deeper critical consciousness, that helps us better understand the state of affairs in this world, your role in these states of affairs, and how to work towards liberation (Freire, 1996). We hope our explanation in Chapter 5 provides this bridge for you from radical understanding of yourself, your social identity, values, and context to help begin the work of intervening to support a community through constant awareness of your own assumptions and agenda in an effort to check these impulses while you engage in this work.

**Reflection:** How do your social, political, and historical contexts impact your efforts for social justice helping?

_____

_____

_____

### Tool 3: Build a Team to Support Community

While it is important to continue an ongoing look at yourself and your context, we know this work cannot be done in silos or in isolation. In order to engage in transformative helping, you must work to develop a team that collaborates, supports each other, and lifts others up for liberation. As discussed in Chapter 1, traditional Euro-American helpers focus on the individual; but transformative helpers focus on how individuals are interconnected through a web of relationships. Individual liberation can be transformative only if it includes community liberation. Our liberation is interconnected; it cannot be achieved individually, but only through collaboration.

There are many ways to support community members and oppressed groups. Creating a team with which to surround yourself will help you better engage in this work. In the second section of this book, we focused on the ins and outs of how to bring others into social justice work with you to help build your team. Recall that in Chapter 6, we identified the complexities of building a team, and the importance of engaging in this work together.

**Reflection:** Who is on your team to work towards social justice? How do you support each other's work?

_____

_____

_____

### Tool 4: Lead for Social Justice

Equally important to consider is how you will lead for social justice, what risks you will take and what kind of power and privilege you will have to confront and work to dismantle during challenging times. Will you take the inevitable risks to stand up for the morally right thing? Most of us believe we will, but when faced with the choice may choose to act in ways that keep us comfortable or protect our own interests. In Chapter 7, you had a chance to reflect on how challenging authentic social justice work may be to your own personal and professional career. When the time comes to stand up, be sure to surround yourself with support from your community.

The action steps of building your community and leading for change are as varied as the types of teams that can be developed and maintained in support of this work. At the foundation of this work are the relationships that are built: being in the community, team building, and creating relationships that are grounded in mutuality, respect, and trust. You and your team must show up in allyship and solidarity for oppressed communities: calling out injustice and calling in people in your life who need to know better so they can do better. You must be skilled in conflict resolution or bridging across disagreement through dialogue. Having tough conversations and creating a space from the emotions in these conversations will help you create a more effective, stronger, and trusted team.

**Reflection:** What challenges do you anticipate, or have you experienced, when leading in social justice?

_____

_____

_____

## Tool 5: Spread the Word

Spreading the message of social justice and liberation for the oppressed is a critical and often forgotten aspect of social justice work. As Paul Kivel (2013) writes, the United States prides itself on prioritizing democracy, equality, and freedom, yet our country is wholly inadequate in ensuring that these values are practiced for all people. Practicing helping from a theoretical and practical frame of social justice ensures that we do not perpetuate inequality or decrease freedom and democracy for any citizen. Practicing from a position of social justice ensures that we are engaging in helping that works towards equality, freedom, and care for all.

There are various personal and professional avenues to promote social justice. In Part 3, we discussed a few of the ways that you can spread the word, including through research (Chapter 11), advocacy (Chapter 12), grant-writing (Chapter 13), and disseminating your work to reach the broadest audience (Chapter 14). In order to be effective, this work requires collective collaboration towards liberation; understanding where your skills and talents will best serve the work; and picking your lane so as to not become burned out, a critical step to activism work. Choose your "lane," and be willing to make this a lifelong effort.

**Reflection:** Which social justice lane do you occupy? What takeaways from this book will you build into your current work in this lane?

_____

_____

_____

## Commitment and Accountability: Carrying the Work Forward

As you review the previous action steps, know that this is just the beginning of a life-long commitment to social justice. In your own sphere of personal and professional work, there are limitless ways that you can engage in social justice helping and liberation of oppressed communities. We follow in the path set out by Layla F. Saad (2020) in her book *Me and White Supremacy* to write down your commitments to this work. These commitments are strong statements of action to engage in liberatory practices. We suggest you keep this statement in a visible place in order to use it to remain accountable. You may find that this statement is fluid and will evolve as your insights and commitments may grow as you continue this work.

In the space next, write down your commitment to social justice, how you will keep yourself accountable to this work, and how will you use your power and leverage your privilege to support the liberation of the oppressed. Keep this statement in a space close by as an accountability measure to stay focused on the work of fighting for liberation for all.

### Commitment and Accountability Statement

_____

## References

Freire, P. (1996). *Pedagogy of the Oppressed*. Penquin Press.
Harkins, D. A. (2017). *Alongside Community: Learning in service*. UK: Routledge Press.

Kivel, P. (2013). *Living in the shadow of the cross: Understanding and resisting the power and privilege of Christian hegemony.* New Society Publishers.

Novik, A. (2017). Overcome that burn-out: Reasons to keep protesting for discouraged activists. *Alternet.org.* www.alternet.org/2017/04/why-protest-answers-discouraged-activists/

Saad, L. (2020). *Me and white supremacy: How to recognise your privilege, combat racism and change the world.* Quercus.

## Further Reading

*A People's History of United States*, Howard Zinn
bell hooks, collected works
Dennis Fox, collected works
*Revolution in Psychology*, Ian Parker
*The Morals and Politics in Psychology*, Isaac Prilleltensky
*Toward Psychologies of Liberation*, Mary Watkins and Helene Shulman
*You Call This a Democracy? Who Benefits, Who Pays and Who Really Decides?*, Paul Kivel
*Writings for Liberation Psychology*, Ignacio Martin-Baro

## Resources

Color of Fear: https://stirfryseminars.com/products/the-color-of-fear-bundle-package/
Social Justice Action Toolkits: https://ctb.ku.edu/en/justice-action-toolkit

# Author and Subject Index